*Frank Lloyd Wright and
His Manner of Thought*

Frank Lloyd Wright and His Manner of Thought

JEROME KLINKOWITZ

THE UNIVERSITY OF WISCONSIN PRESS

The University of Wisconsin Press
1930 Monroe Street, 3rd Floor
Madison, Wisconsin 53711-2059
uwpress.wisc.edu

3 Henrietta Street, Covent Garden
London WC2E 8LU, United Kingdom
eurospanbookstore.com

Printed in the United States of America

Library of Congress Cataloging-in-Publication Data
Klinkowitz, Jerome, author.
Frank Lloyd Wright and his manner of thought / Jerome Klinkowitz.
pages   cm
Includes bibliographical references and index.
ISBN 978-0-299-30144-6 (pbk.: alk. paper)
ISBN 978-0-299-30143-9 (e-book)
1. Wright, Frank Lloyd, 1867-1959.
2. Wright, Frank Lloyd, 1867-1959—Criticism and interpretation.
3. Wright, Frank Lloyd, 1867-1959—Philosophy.
4. Architects—United States—Biography.
I. Title.
NA737.W7K55   2014
720.92—dc23
[B]
2014009150

Frank Lloyd Wright quotes are used with the permission of
the Frank Lloyd Wright Foundation, Scottsdale, Arizona.

FOR MY COLLEAGUES WITH THE FRIENDS OF CEDAR ROCK,
the home near Quasqueton, Iowa, designed in 1945 by
Frank Lloyd Wright for Lowell and Agnes Walter

Contents

Preface

Although Frank Lloyd Wright is a towering figure in American culture, nearly all discussion of him has concerned his innovative architectural designs. This is not a book about architecture. There is a widespread feeling that only architects, or at the very least architectural historians, can write about the subject and I do not wish to challenge that notion here. But given that it has been mostly specialists who have undertaken the existing commentaries on Wright, other aspects of his cultural importance have yet to be studied. The fact that Frank Lloyd Wright resisted the emerging and then dominant architecture of his time (first late Victorian, then modern), and that so many advocates of these architectures resisted his ideas, prompts an investigation of his manner of thought—especially because that manner has become characteristic of the era that succeeded him, and at odds with the modernism with which he was so uncomfortable.

This is a book about Frank Lloyd Wright, with an emphasis on how his manner of thought contributes to American culture. While several hundred books have been written about his architecture, no one has yet approached him in the way cultural critics have dealt with similar central figures. Wright distrusted the literary, complaining that in the four centuries preceding his work the book had replaced the cathedral (and other architectural masterpieces) as the key form of human value and expression. Yet he was very much a literary man, styling himself so for the popular media and contributing to his profession's journals, not to mention writing many books of his own. His collected works total more than one and a half million words, were widely read and commented upon, and remain in print today. Like the canon of any important writer, they are worthy of study. Like the works of any genius, they tell us much about the culture to which he was a major contributor.

Frank Lloyd Wright and His Manner of Thought tracks the development of Wright's thinking throughout his career, from his first addresses in 1894 to the last piece left on his desk in 1959. His work in architecture is notable for this same productive length, and in fact constitutes two careers, as after a difficult time in the 1920s he quite literally reinvented himself and was "rediscovered" by critics, clients, and the public alike, propelling him (with a newly founded Taliesin Fellowship) into another quarter century of bold innovation and enormous output. During especially lean years Wright had written in earnest—at the time because it and the sale of Japanese prints were his only sources of income. In retrospect those writings can be seen as examinations and endorsements of principles demonstrated in his first career and envisioned in his second. By 1932, with the Taliesin Fellowship operating and his ideas for the perfect community of Broadacre City committed to paper, the basis of his thinking was firmly established. Subsequently more of his time went into building than writing; and although he did write, often quite famously so, he could draw on previous material for refinement and popularization. Therefore the bulk of this study addresses the foundation and development of his thought, with a conclusion that relates it (as he did himself) to the great accomplishments of his later decades.

What are those foundational elements, and why are they important? American Transcendentalism, especially that of Ralph Waldo Emerson, has been long acknowledged as central to Wright's thought. Detractors have complained that it is the late Victorian Emerson, of the Gilded Age, front-parlor variety, that impressed the young architect. But Wright's use of Emerson is deeper than that, radicalized by notions from Walt Whitman and William Blake; Wright's sage of Concord is much like the Emerson scholars and readers know today. In a similar manner, Wright's Progressive Era enthusiasms are thought to originate with John Dewey, simply because the young man's aunts were progressive educators. In truth, the educationist influence on them was more direct and practical, coming from Francis Parker instead. And when Wright himself complained about the limitations of traditional schooling, it was the economist Henry George he would cite, in a metaphorical rather than theoretical manner. George's thought predates the Progressive Era by a generation. If one wants a more current model for Wright's intellection, it is found in the works of William James, especially his religious thought, the manner of which the young architect emulates through his revision of Emerson. Radical pluralism is what pleases Wright, not because it subverts the One but because it affirms the Many, so different from the nihilism of the impending modern age.

Frank Lloyd Wright had much trouble with modernism and modernists had even more problems with him. His notion of organic architecture never fit comfortably into theories and practices of the modern, and Wright's own distaste for (if not outright fury with) the International Style popularized as the essence of modernism is well known. That it was a European import bothered him; even worse were its antidemocratic aspects, as Wright perceived them. Architectural studies have noted this disconnect and found it bothersome; consequently the profession's history tends to acknowledge Wright's work as sui generis at best and idiosyncratic at worst. Yet after a brief period of fascination with architectural postmodernism (which is nothing at all like the postmodernism avowed by literary theorists and fiction writers), today's clients have expressed an emphatically environmental interest in what is called again "organic architecture," valuing the space as lived in far more than the structure as presented to view. This new organic architecture, anti-illusionistic and given to privileging experience over presentation, in fact shares its orientation with broader movements in thought that had emerged later in the twentieth century and which were exhibited in literature, art, and philosophy. Though no one would claim Frank Lloyd Wright foresaw the thinking behind this new era, the era has definitely embraced him, his work, and his ideas.

In completing this study, I am in debt to the work—a lifetime's achievement—of Bruce Brooks Pfeiffer. In addition to preserving and curating so much of Mr. Wright's documentation, Pfeiffer has edited *Frank Lloyd Wright: The Collected Writings*. Its five large double-columned volumes assemble the author's canon of written works from 1894 to 1959. Though the work has been available since the early 1990s, it is not surprising that it would take the better part of two decades for a scholar to approach it with an eye toward understanding the manner of thought behind it. Citations of these volumes are abbreviated as *CW*; a second abbreviation used, *WWBG*, is for Dustin Griffin's edition of *The Writings of Walter Burley Griffin* (2008), Wright's early associate; the third, *W*, refers to the 1925 *Wendingen* volume with essays by and about Frank Lloyd Wright. Frank Lloyd Wright quotes are used with the permission of The Frank Lloyd Wright Foundation, Scottsdale, Arizona; I wish to thank Margo Stipe, Curator and Registrar of Collections at The Frank Lloyd Wright Foundation, and Kristin Roeder of Rizzoli International Publications for their timely help. Other works are identified as they are quoted, with full references in my bibliography. While I have not named all of the many photographic volumes devoted to Wright's work, those that include especially insightful commentary are listed. I am grateful to the University of Wisconsin Press for its interest in my work and especially for obtaining two expert outside readings that helped me sharpen my focus on professional issues. As always, the University of Northern Iowa has been my sole source of support in this and all other projects.

*Frank Lloyd Wright and
His Manner of Thought*

Introduction

Truth against the World

"I WOULD MUCH RATHER BUILD than write about buildings, but when I am not building, I will write about buildings—or the significance of those buildings I have already built" (*CW* I: 315). Frank Lloyd Wright addressed these words to readers of *The Architectural Record* in December 1928, as part of his series "In the Cause of Architecture." Because of marital scandals, personal tragedy, and financial shortfalls, he did not have much architectural work at the time, and much of what he did have never got beyond the design project stage. Therefore he had to write to earn his living. The onset of the Great Depression following the financial crash in 1929 made chances for work in his proper profession even less likely, and so he had to write all the more, especially when Japanese prints from his collections no longer brought top dollar. Yet for all his emphasis on building, with no less than six varied repetitions of that term in his single sentence, these words follow over a quarter million that he had already written, nearly all of it published in important social and professional venues. Although passionate for building, he obviously cared for getting his thoughts on paper as well as erected in wood, brick, stone, and concrete.

The reason for this is simple. Introducing a new principle in architecture that he called "organic," Wright was arguing not just for a building method but for a supporting philosophy of how life should be lived. His principle ran counter to how western civilization had built since classical times, and even more so against social practices of the current era. But his family's motto, "Truth against the World," would inspire his

3

independence. The phrase had characterized the Lloyd Jones clan's proud affirmation of Unitarian beliefs that contradicted the Established Church's doctrines, just as their Welsh identity resisted assimilation into the British spirit of a United Kingdom and its establishment forces. Frank Lloyd Wright's organic principle for architecture challenged the establishment as well. Coincidentally, but no less frustrating to the architect, the popular colonial and Victorian housing styles of the day were English in origin and establishmentarian in their authority. If the family motto had not existed, its young member would have had to invent it to speak for his own manner of thought.

The brilliance of Frank Lloyd Wright's architecture has inspired the work of hundreds of scholars. Every aspect of his designs and buildings has been examined in great detail. But until now no one has studied the man's thinking as it was introduced to the public via a lecture in Evanston, Illinois, in 1894, and continued to be developed and expressed in books and essays throughout his lifetime, totaling by 1959 over one and a half million words. The canon of scholarship on Wright's work is helpful nonetheless for discovering aspects of that thought as manifested in his buildings. It allows today's reader of *The Collected Writings* to confirm how the architect's ideas worked out in practice. Indeed, the great public fascination with Wright's work is that his structures are such a delight to view, from the inside where possible but even from without. One does not need a Master of Fine Arts degree or a doctorate in art history to enjoy looking at a painting by Rembrandt or Jackson Pollock. But inevitably the enthusiast will wonder about the mind that created these works, whether on canvas or on a building lot.

What do visitors to a mature, fully realized Frank Lloyd Wright structure see? What do they inevitably feel? Before even looking into his published statements, what measure of the man is taken from the mere presence of his constructed work? The first quality one notes is its environment: the buildings often express a sense of belonging there, not just of fitting in but of enhancing the surroundings, making natural features all the more apparent because they are now integrated with a place of human habitation. This sensitivity to context is an element in Wright's thinking that begins with objections to ill-fitting structures, and then develops into a will to have all elements working toward a coherent purpose. Good landscaping can be a helpful supplement to a home's attraction, but for the Usonian Houses that characterized much of the second half of Wright's career he insisted that a site plan preexist any building design, and that the site be chosen with great care for its own beauty. The design that followed would integrate house and lot so that each improved the other, improvement being the factor of having human consciousness introduced. Of what use is beauty if it cannot be perceived?

The enhancement of nature by human consciousness is what visitors to Wright sites experience. What they so practically sense can be studied by experts, as Charles E. and Berdeana Aguar do in their *Wrightscapes: Frank Lloyd Wright's Landscape Designs* (2002). For them, Wright "effectively merged his skills as an architect, a planner, and an environmentalist with the skills he exhibited in so many other spheres of design. No one since Leonardo da Vinci has exhibited such brilliant versatility as a designer" (311). This quality of integration does not end when one steps inside the house. Instead, it is noticed all the more thanks to the architect's talent for connecting the inside with what lies beyond, and vice versa. An open plan does this, especially when augmented by walls dissolving into light screens and with thresholds replaced by continuous surfaces from terrace to floor. The beauty of nature outside seems part of the house itself, certainly in the way its presence is sensed. But one also feels safe inside. This is what Grant Hildebrand describes in *The Wright Space: Pattern and Meaning in Frank Lloyd Wright's Houses* (1991) as a balance of prospect and refuge, an almost primitive sense of enjoying a great range of vision from a comfortably sheltered point of view.

Although publicly accessible homes by Wright are visited today as virtual pavilions, the homeowners themselves would be spending immensely more time inside the house than outside. That they not only felt comfortable but noticed that their quality of life was improved is due to another of the architect's orientations, that of designing from the inside out. That too is evident to the visitor, as even a casual walk-through provides a natural and comfortable sense of movement, one room flowing into another, interrelated by use and welcoming perspectives. Stepping back outside, the viewer now sees that what at first may have appeared to be abstract is in fact a perfectly natural expression of internal function. That there is nothing ugly about that presumed abstraction is due to Wright's mastery of geometric form based on his childhood play with the Froebel blocks used as instructional devices in the most advanced nineteenth-century kindergartens, an influence noted as early as 1900 by Wright's friend and fellow architect Robert Spencer. In his eponymously titled study (1997) and biography (2006) of Frank Lloyd Wright, Robert McCarter credits this early schooling for fostering a capacity for visual and spatial memory far beyond common ability, which for most people is limited to music. Having learned how to see, Wright could perceive the shapes beneath appearances and thus manipulate them in a sensible way. The inhabitant of a Wright house may not know this theory, but the results of its practice are surely felt.

The Americans who had Frank Lloyd Wright houses built and the visitors who are drawn to them today did not themselves play with Froebel blocks, but are certainly familiar with their country's larger culture, and here they fall in step with the famous architect, who was influenced by the same literature that remains important today. It is the manner of Wright's thought that extends the pertinence of that culture from the nineteenth century to the twentieth, and even into the twenty-first. For someone born in 1867, an interest in the natural qualities of space would lead to the thinking of Ralph Waldo Emerson, especially as it was being popularized later in the century by the poet Walt Whitman. Transcendentalism, so revolutionary in the 1830s and politically charged during the next two decades, had by the time of Frank Lloyd Wright's youth and young manhood been resolved into a genteel rebuke of the country's burgeoning industrialism. Especially to popular readers and to intelligent but largely self-educated persons like Wright, the Emersonian tradition was something that related directly to the most practical aspects of life. A true philosophy of living is what Emerson offered, based on a reasoning from the seen to the unseen in a search for what McCarter in his biography calls "the underlying geometries of nature" (22). Although by the time Wright began working as an architect Emerson had died, the great man's thought was being kept alive by Walt Whitman. And Whitman was in personal touch with architect Louis Sullivan even as Sullivan was having long conversations, deep into the night, with his new employee Frank Lloyd Wright. These were dialogues that Wright would recall as beginning with matters in their profession and growing to include philosophies not just of design but of life.

Here are both the deepest sources for Frank Lloyd Wright's thought and the basis for his appeal to the Americans who had his structures built and to those who visit them today, not only Americans themselves but those who would understand this country. From Emerson's idea of nature comes Whitman's ideal of democracy—and from there the crowning notion of America itself as a promised land, even promised landscape, for humankind. This is how the great critical definers of American thought and literature see it, from F. O. Matthiessen in *American Renaissance* (1941) and Leo Marx in *The Machine in the Garden* (1964) to any number of more recent studies by critics such as Richard Slotkin and Sacvan Bercovitch. In "Buildings for Recreation," a contribution to editor David G. De Long's *Frank Lloyd Wright and the Living City* (1998), J. Michael Desmond sums up the importance of this connection between Americans and their country as it influences Wright's beliefs:

> In Emerson's work, the Romantic concept of nature lying between man and God was reworked to support a modern view of the self as the perceiver between nature and community. Building on the influence of Emerson (and especially on his legacy in the poetry and prose of Thoreau and Whitman), Wright's designs for communities redefined the tension between the individual and the democratic group in terms of a symbolic interaction of self and landscape that I believe lies at the heart of American myth and culture. (149)

Yet with Frank Lloyd Wright the cheerleading for democracy found in Whitman's poetry is no more a resolution of thoughts than were the blocks from Froebel or the similarly organic methods of Emerson. These ideas, even Whitman's, were for him not conclusions but beginnings. For his own gallery of inspiring figures Wright would add a third poet, William Blake, whose exuberance for nature would propel anything transcendental into new heights of rapture. Toward the end of his life, the architect would cite his example more frequently. And in a conversation with his wife Olgivanna just a few weeks before he died, Wright shared a confidence reported by Bruce Brooks Pfeiffer in a book edited with Gerald Nordland, *Frank Lloyd Wright: In the Realm of Ideas* (1988). Blake would be a perfect guest for tea, Wright remarked, confessing that "I would sit at his feet to worship him. Such a wonderful man! He would understand us, Olgivanna. There would be a remarkable bond between the three of us just as there has been between you and me. And it occurred to me recently that in the distant future when they think of us, they will think of us as one. We blend, Olgivanna. We *are* one" (175).

Less mystical but inspiring in its own way was the example of Wright's uncle, the Reverend Jenkin Lloyd Jones. Based in Chicago, he would host each summer a Unitarian Chautauqua at his religious camp-grounds at Tower Hill, Wisconsin, nestled among the Lloyd Jones family farms. Speakers included not just other leading preachers, such as William C. Gannett (famous for his "House Beautiful" sermon), but figures from progressive social and political movements of the day, including Jane Addams of Chicago's Hull House settlement organization, women's suffrage leader Susan B. Anthony, and senator Robert La Follette. Theirs were ideas young Frank would grow up among. And once he moved to Chicago, his uncle's church, almost a settlement house itself, would provide a virtual salon of influences and inspirations. As a practicing architect, Wright began the design of his uncle's last and largest religious structure, the Abraham Lincoln Center (1903). He did not continue with it, but in undertaking the commission for Unity Temple the next year allied his plan with Unitarian progressive thought even beyond the style favored by Uncle Jenk. The motto Wright chose to adorn the structure's entrance, "For the Worship of God and the Service of Man," is reflected in his binuclear design: a cube to the left for the auditorium, and a smaller rectangle to the right for a social center. The four-square space of the building for worship, as tall as it is wide to accommodate balconies on three sides, is itself presented in a manner of the meeting house, with the congregation gathered around the minister with equal access to oratory and participation. Members make nine right-angled turns to enter, moving through low and dark spaces to seek the high, bright triumph of the temple itself, there to find unity in shared belief. Following the service, a pair of doors flanking the pulpit open for exit. In *Unity Temple: Frank Lloyd Wright and the Architecture of Liberal Religion* (1996), Joseph M. Siry relates the patterns of thought. "If Wright, after Emerson, saw unity as the fundamental principle of nature," he ventures, "then its most visible manifestation in architecture was a continuity of material or a plasticity of form, wherein all parts appear to flow into each other or to be geometrically related" (201). Thanks to its concrete construction and unit system of building, Wright's binuclear design achieves this goal, which in turn reflects the goals of the era's progressive religious thought. Again, the structure works perfectly without need of explanation. But the very success of that structure prompts the congregant and even the mere visitor to think about how it was achieved, and the answer is that the architect himself was definitely thinking—thinking in terms of the culture he lived in and its developments to come.

Uncle Jenk's initial architect was Joseph Lyman Silsbee, in whose studio young Frank Lloyd Wright first found work when seeking a career in Chicago. And like Frank's uncle, his earliest employer was involved with cultural thought of the day, particularly as advanced by a cousin, art critic and collector Ernest Fenollosa. Arguing for the convergence of European and American with East Asian civilizations, Fenollosa urged an appreciation of Japanese art and culture as a path toward achieving Unitarian hopes. From prints seen in Silsbee's office in 1887 and architecture viewed at the 1893 Columbian Exposition to the planning of a trip to Japan in 1905, Wright explored Fenollosa's thinking during this important first stage of his own architectural experience.

Allying Japanese art and culture with Unitarian thought is a different approach than critics take when exploring Wright's affinities with the East. But then he himself would never tolerate the notion of "influence" when it came to the very real properties his work shared with this or any other country, unlike borrowing his family's religious motto as his own for both person and profession. More common is what Julia Meech observes in *Frank Lloyd Wright and the Art of Japan: The Architect's Other Passion* (2001). She quotes with admiration Wright's comments to the Taliesin Fellowship at a print party in September 1950, that the great printmaker Hiroshige "did with a sense of space, very much what we have been doing with it in our architecture. Here you get a tremendous, limitless space, instead of something confined within a picture. . . . That's a great lesson for you boys to learn" (230). Once more, the groundwork for Wright's manner of thought runs much deeper than contemporary trends. Such trends only make their contributions when they complement his fundamental orientation, something his architecture may suggest but which only an understanding of his manner of thought can prove.

Frank Lloyd Wright's public expression of thought begins in 1894, when he is just one year out of Louis Sullivan's office (with its after-hours conversations that included talk about the master's latest letter from Walt Whitman), seven years removed from Silsbee's practice (and the Japanese woodblock prints), and eight from the Wisconsin pastoralism that read Emerson and Thoreau as contemporaries. Through all of this the young architect had shared the thoughtful world of his Uncle Jenkin Lloyd Jones and was being ushered into a world rich with the era's lively progressivism. What's remarkable is that the architect's 1894 talk could have been delivered just as appropriately in 1959, the year of his death. Not that Frank Lloyd Wright's thought doesn't grow. It entertains European modernism in the 1920s, anti-urbanism in the 1930s, world conditions in the 1940s, and new horizons of design in his last decade of life. But throughout there is a basic coherence of thinking that for all its development and complexity never reveals a contradiction or even inconsistency. Wright, of course, was a great egotist, with no small measure of what he called an honest arrogance (as opposed to the hypocrisy of a false humility). When he cared enough for an idea to give it public expression, he knew he was right or could at the very least present a convincing argument to that effect. Never simply repetitious, he articulated his core beliefs with an eye to changing conditions. Organic architecture had different battles to fight in the 1890s and each subsequent decade, and hence successive essays in its advocacy would take different forms. But the issue was always there, and remains so today.

Yet as a thinker as well as an architect, Frank Lloyd Wright needed company. While some feel it was simply to impose his will, others, such as Myron A. Marty, believe the man needed like-minded innovators (and only later obedient followers) to reinforce his creative productivity. Marty's *Communities of Frank Lloyd Wright* (2009) finds the architect most happily at work among others: with Cecil Corwin in Silsbee's studio, with Louis Sullivan himself and then a young George Grant Elmslie in the same office, and locating his own first practice at the center of a group of Chicago architects, "The Eighteen," who would make their own contributions to the Prairie Style even as they met professionally and socially near their respective offices downtown. When Wright built a studio connected to his Oak Park home in 1898 and moved his practice there, a remarkable pool of talent came to work with him as associates. Foremost was Marion Mahony, one of the first women architects in the United States and as enthusiastic as Wright for a new, organic architecture; anecdotes from the studio during this first decade of the twentieth century describe a special magic that took hold of the drafting room when the two would work together. Much of Wright's success at landing commissions at the time and the beautiful picture his early designs present today are due to Mahony's gifted delineations of his work. Mahony stepped in to complete some of Wright's commissions and do others of her own when in 1909 the architect left for Europe with Mamah Borthwick Cheney. Joining her was an associate who had left Wright's studio earlier, angered that his employer would repay a $5,000 loan with a selection of culls from an otherwise valuable collection of Japanese prints. Walter Burley Griffin had other complaints as well, including how his innovative uses of corner piers and ideas for what Wright would call the "Fireproof House for $5,000" were never fully credited to the mind that conceived them. (Two decades later, practicing in Australia, Griffin—since married to Marion Mahony—would claim responsibility for Wright's textile blocks as well.) But Griffin was an exceptionally gifted architect with special talents in landscape design, and alongside Barry Byrne and William Drummond was an essential part of the studio in the early 1900s.

Working in the company of others definitely spurred Wright's creativity and productivity, as Marty demonstrates. But it is also well to consider a more basic fact about such collegiality: that throughout his workday the architect would have people to talk with, young architects eagerly receptive to the ideas being exchanged as their work at the drafting tables took place. True, Frank Lloyd Wright was notorious for working alone as well, late into the night, where final plans would coalesce. But in the process he'd had the chance to verbalize his concepts, communicating his thoughts to others while they shared their own. Even in the relative isolation of the early years at Taliesin Wright would attract and benefit from the company of bright younger architects, now coming from Europe and Asia to work in his studio, individuals with such subsequent commanding fame as Rudolf Schindler and Richard Neutra. By 1932, when he and Olgivanna started the Taliesin Fellowship, Wright was able to surround himself with younger and perhaps even brighter minds. Many of them joined him in the rotating authorship of a series of columns titled "At Taliesin" that appeared in *The Capital Times* (Madison) and other Wisconsin newspapers between

1934 and 1937, as collected by Randolph C. Henning (1992). The great success of his "second career" is attributed in large part to this supportive environment—and not just supportive in material ways. Even though the members began as apprentices and paid for the privilege, how could Wright not profit from his hands-on involvement with persons such as John Lautner and the hundreds of others passing through? True, at print parties and Sunday morning talks the Taliesin Fellowship provided listeners. But as any teacher knows, one's own thinking benefits immensely from an informed and productive audience. The advantage of restating one's ideas and keeping them flexible by answering questions that come largely from people eager to learn and understand is self-evident. Although in the last decade of Wright's practice some of his designs may have declined in quality due to his isolation from criticism, and even though some of his self-published political tracts in the series called *Taliesin Square-Papers* (1941–1953) became strident under the pressure of international events, it is indisputable that from his professional beginnings in 1887 to his final days of work in 1959 the man existed in a context where the articulation of his ideas was a regular feature of life.

While there are indeed some "frou-frou" aspects of late designs such as the Grady Gammage Auditorium (1959) and the mid-1950s projects for Baghdad (including allusions to Persian culture more appropriate to colonialist fairy tales), his last years are among his best. At age ninety-one the architect could still be fully active, superintending the construction of New York's Guggenheim Museum as a 1943 design reworked through thirteen years of challenges by site, client, and city regulations. In *The Guggenheim: Frank Lloyd Wright and the Making of the Modern Museum* (2009), Neil Levine joins Hilary Ballon and seven other contributors to measure this building's success at its fiftieth anniversary of service to the art public. Here was a structure opened in 1959 designed by an architect born in 1867 who had acknowledged his first commissioned work in 1893 after several years of planning homes by moonlight so as not to anger his employer. And what is the critical verdict for the Guggenheim after all these years? First, that it is a boldly original work, well ahead of its time for the late 1950s, and startlingly innovative even now, half a century later. Second, that the essence of thought behind it squares with the major principles of the architect's career. "Of all Frank Lloyd Wright's architectural work," says Neil Levine, "the Solomon R. Guggenheim Museum, with its tall, spiral-ramped main gallery, most vividly embodies his ideal of spatial and material continuity. First identifying this ideal in his mentor Louis Sullivan's curvilinear ornament, Wright proposed to realize it in the three-dimensional totality of his architecture." Here too was his concept of "plasticity," so crucial to organic form, "which opposed the rectilinear architecture of the classical tradition and the International Style" (40). Did Wright's work in Sullivan's studio of the early 1890s leap past the yet-to-be-articulated modern in favor of something even newer?

The art of Frank Lloyd Wright's architecture is evident in his buildings, and architectural historians have met the challenge of explaining its effect in terms of space and form. A vast library of resources exists to help people understand why Wright's structures look the way they do, and why being in them generates the feelings people have attested to since the first resident of one of them moved in. Yet other questions have remained unanswered, questions that make Wright's career and the man himself difficult for theorists to deal with. How can it be, for example, that the most famous "modern" American architect decried modernism itself, and his work contradicts both the spirit and practice of modern architecture as typified by the International Style, modernism's iconic representation? How can it be that Wright's most fervently held and enthusiastically proclaimed principle, that of organic architecture, is an issue for the twenty-first century even more pertinently than it was at the end of the nineteenth? Distrusted first as an irresponsible radical and dismissed later on by some as a self-promoting showman, Wright suffered the fate of many great artists: that he was looked at but not always listened to, and that even his admirers did not fully understand his purpose. Only an examination of his thought can provide the basis to understand those principles that underpin his career.

There is a precedent for Frank Lloyd Wright's thinking that predates even his first years of working for Louis Sullivan. Meryle Secrest identifies it as a biographical item in her *Frank Lloyd Wright* (1992), something memorable to the architect as his mother's favorite lines from Shakespeare. "And this our life, exempt from public haunt / finds tongues in trees, books in the running brooks / Sermons in stones, and good in everything" (58). These words from *As You Like It* could serve as another motto for Frank Lloyd Wright, for in them is a nascent sketch of just what organic architecture would be. Here is how his mind worked, and how he would express himself, as stated in an unpublished essay of 1930: "So there is little to be done except write one's best thoughts (if one has thoughts) and, as may be, build that best thought whenever and however it can be built" (*CW* I: 346).

1

Architects and Machines

"THE MORE TRUE CULTURE A MAN HAS, the more significant his environment becomes to him." These first public words of Frank Lloyd Wright, spoken to the University Guild in Evanston, Illinois, in 1894, make him sound like very much the nineteenth-century gentleman. More than half a century later modernist detractors would give him damning praise as being the most famous architect of the nineteenth century—this at a time when his designs for Fallingwater, Johnson Wax, and his own Taliesin West were marking a great period of innovation and ascent. But the line he had used in the Victorian era, and continued to use through the modern and into postmodern times, raises questions to this day.

Mention "culture" in 1894, and the books of John Ruskin come to mind. *The Seven Lamps of Architecture*, for example, which Wright had first read as a child, or *The Stones of Venice*, which, as a young man, he had sought out on his own. Ruskin's was a very Victorian belief: that culture is beauty, and beauty involves the moral choices that legitimize both emotion and the loftiness of thought.

But before this first line comes Wright's title, "The Architect and the Machine" (*CW* I: 20), which raises another concern: how will the architect's opinion of the machine square with his concerns for culture? Again, the reference is timely, but once more in a way that fights against the image Frank Lloyd Wright developed for himself in coming decades, when he would win great fame for such striking developments as the Prairie House, the Usonian homes, and the Guggenheim Museum. Saying the word "machine" in 1894, especially in an architectural context, would bring to mind the Arts and Crafts Movement. Popularized by William Morris in the 1880s, this movement too was a product of Victorian England. For it, the machine was an enemy, the prime tool in the Industrial Revolution's suppression of individual talent and artistry. Anyone in Evanston who saw Wright's lecture publicized or heard its title announced might suppose the speaker was another in the line of architects that included C. F. A. Voysey, Charles Rennie Mackintosh, C. R. Ashbee, and others who had been looking back to Ruskin's ideals as a way of fighting for the principles of craftsmanship in an age that threatened to efface them. Wright's audience would certainly have thought that when they heard his first line, gentlemanly culture and all.

Instead, "The Architect and the Machine" presents a critique not just of bricks and mortar but of the "so-called artistic house" as well, a domicile that had become a freak of preposterous ornamentation. How could this kind of residence, possibly William Morris's own Red House that had initiated the trend and remained as the prime example of Arts and Crafts living, share Wright's disdain for the cardboard box with scissored windows "and whitewashed for luck" (*CW* I: 21)?

The answer isn't found in Ruskin or Morris, but in one of their American popularizers. Throughout Frank Lloyd Wright's career the influences he displays are less from philosophers and poets and more from the impact of philosophy and poetry on general culture. For Wright, as a citizen of Oak Park, Illinois, whose most immediate moral influence was that of his uncle, the prominent Unitarian minister Jenkin Lloyd Jones, thoughts on Ruskin's aesthetics and Morris's practical applications would most immediately come from one of Reverend Jones's friends, the Reverend William C. Gannett.

Gannett's sermon-like essay, *The House Beautiful*, was a popular publication in the 1890s, going through several editions. It addressed directly—more directly than anything by Ruskin, Morris, or other sophisticated writers—the notion of just what made a house beautiful and how that beauty was a major force in helping one live a happy, rewarding life. For an already noteworthy architect who had just opened his own practice, Gannett's text was a natural for publication as a beautifully crafted, hand-printed volume from The Auvergne Press, a hobby enterprise pursued by Wright's first independent client, William Herman Winslow. The Winslow House, in the adjacent suburb of River Forest, was designed and built in 1893–1894, and soon after its architect joined his client in designing and producing elegant small press editions. Gannett's *The House Beautiful*, running about five thousand words, was printed in an unpaginated edition divided into six chapters. In Wright's format, each page held roughly 150 words, set in fifteen relatively closely spaced lines that allowed for a thickly designed border such as the architect may have been drawing for Louis Sullivan just a few years before. The border itself was sufficiently centered so as to leave a second area of open space all around. The clear intent was that the words on each page be not just read but contemplated. And the notions therein were much like the ones Wright asks his listeners to ponder in his own essay of about the same length, "The Architect and the Machine."

As the son of a preacher, Frank Lloyd Wright always favored a manner of delivery that seemed straight from the pulpit. And so as he begins his lecture to the University Guild in Evanston, it is no surprise that he sounds a bit like Gannett in the sermon he was preparing to print. Opening with a caution, he warns his listeners that their homes may be lying to them, their front parlors calling everything else in the house insulting names. Even worse, their home was calling residents themselves bad names, as if the owners had harbored the worst elements of society, elements that condemn one simply by association.

In his own sermon, the Reverend Gannett has done much the same, characterizing a typical house in terms similar to Wright's—"four walls with a lid, to box in a little of the blowing wind" (Ch. 1, second page). Like the architect behaving as a preacher, this preacher carrying on like an architect is making a point: it is not just how space is constructed but how it is occupied that needs attention in the transitional world of 1894. Both authors emphasize that while hoping to live lives filled with good and beauty, people are foiled by the nature of their Victorian parlors, for that is not where they actually live. "The heart cries, 'Take me where the people stay. I didn't come to see the chairs,'" Gannett laments, feeling a "homesickness for the back parlor" (Ch. 2, third page). Furnishings and decorations in a room not lived in but used only for making impressions wind up giving the worst impression of all. Both agree that if the money spent on the largely unused front parlor were distributed throughout the house, even the humblest abode could be a paradise, supporting in a much more effective way the quest for a happy life within.

Both Gannett and Wright proceed by emphasizing the positive, that the best home is filled with beauty, every object contributing to the family's sense of happiness. To the extent that these objects enhance life, they are true; if just for show, they are false. When one impulse works against the other, the result is discord. When all work together for the inhabitants' happiness, harmony is achieved, what Wright calls the truthfulness of integration that is the same for a house, a person, or a picture. Good design is a design for life. This is less Ruskin the idealist, or Morris the artist, and more one's own minister (or local architect) advising that it's the quality of life at home that counts. It is a quality not for rarified aesthetes but for the practical citizens of a democratic nation, for readers not of *The Stones of Venice* but of Walt Whitman's *Leaves of Grass*. "Eyes and ears are eager to be fed the harmonies in color and form and sound," Gannett urges; "these are their natural food as much as bread and meat are food for other parts." From this he calls on a larger sense that "For in proportion as the eyes and ears are fed, we are not sure, but apt, to see a fineness spreading over life" (Ch. 3, third page).

Simple harmonies as found at home may reflect Ruskin's thought at the lowest level, but in the emerging architecture of the time they suggest a step beyond the ways William Morris applied Ruskin's ideal to hearth and home. The trend was certainly evident elsewhere in Chicago. Soon to take employment at Frank Lloyd Wright's office in Steinway Hall and studio out in Oak Park was a young architect named Walter Burley Griffin. He would stay with Wright from 1901 through 1906, and after that make his own name as an innovator in the Prairie School before winning an international contest to plan the new Australian capital city of Canberra and moving his practice to Australia where other opportunities awaited him. Although politically and socially a Progressive, Griffin never mounted the bully pulpit. But because he spoke so clearly about how changes in architecture affected the quality of daily life, his thoughts are worth considering here. In a lecture entitled "Architecture" first presented in 1915 and collected in *The Writings of Walter Burley Griffin* (2008), he notes how the difference between annoying noise and pleasurable music—in other words, what constituted harmony—could not be explained (and hence fully capitalized upon) "til the law—a purely mathematical one—of the conservation of rhythm was understood." Noise resulted from the interference of sound waves with each other, while "the sounds we derived pleasure from were such combinations as reinforced each other so that they went on to infinity." This understanding, still fresh from the past one hundred years of research, has its parallel in the even more recent understanding of certain principles in architecture based not on time but space:

> Music is a time art measured by rhythm. To satisfy the human soul these units must be preserved and must be so used as to reinforce each other, for destruction is painful to us but evidences of continuity are a joy and inspiration. Architecture is a space art. Let us search for its basic law. Is it not the conservation of space? As in music we rejoice in being made conscious of time, one of the great fundamental elements in our present creation, and in being made aware of infinity through the preservation of rhythm, so in architecture and landscape architecture, which are but interdependent elements of one field, we rejoice in being made conscious of space, and can be satisfied only when the space units we use reinforce each other, and a feeling of spaciousness is obtained. In a building or in a community, a huddle and clutter of unrelated units is as distressing as a harsh sound. (*WWBG*, 212)

To illustrate this principle, Griffin describes how a family can best find harmony in its home. His details are based on Wright's and Gannett's more dramatically expressed sentiments voiced some twenty years before, yet are expressed more levelly—otherwise in 1915 he would be preaching to the choir.

Both Wright and Gannett praise simplicity and repose, qualities held in esteem since the days of Michelangelo. And both agree that there is a causal path to this status, which involves stripping away ornamentation to get down to a "more useful form" (Ch. 3, fifth page), which is in turn bound to be more beautiful. There are so many correspondences that one has to assume Wright had Gannett's presentation in mind when he drafted his own. The latter quotes a prophet: "If a man should find himself with bread in both hands, he should exchange one loaf for some flowers of narcissus, since the loaf feeds the body indeed. But the flowers feed the soul" (Ch. 4, second and third pages). Wright, a prophet in his own land, speaks for himself, but to the identical point, that if there is just twenty cents for a meal, it is wise to spend three of those for a flower whose presence on the table will feed the family much better in the long run. Yet Gannett's own phrasing would stay with Wright for a lifetime; more than half a century later he would carve it as a motto adorning the fascia board overlooking the seating in the Unitarian Meeting House (1947) designed for Shorewood Hills, Wisconsin. This church included clear glass windows looking out on fields of prairie grasses and flowers, and in the same paragraph of his Evanston address Wright suggests such flora as a simpler and cheaper choice for table arrangements, even if they are considered weeds. His studio was filled with them, albeit in striking pewter holders he had designed; Griffin and other associates would remember being summoned from their drawing boards to undertake prairie weed hunting expeditions in the fields across Chicago Avenue from the Wright Home and Studio. Gannett presumably spared his own acolytes from this task, but does admire a woman, "among friends counted for poor" (Ch. 4, first page), who won praise for decorating her plain house in this same manner.

Beyond these incidentals, there are correspondences between the two presentations that link even Wright's most pioneering ideas to those homely practices Gannett recommends. "The house we live in is a building of God, not a house made with hands," the Reverend would have his readers know (Ch. 1, sixth page), a recommendation that lies at the heart of Wright's thinking, given that throughout his life he always insisted that the church he worshipped in was Nature, spelled with a capital *N*. Nature is the best model for a builder of houses, he urges. Homes must grow comfortably from their site and blend with whatever natural forms are there—and if there are none, emulate them in a manner that is organic. This is the first use of the term "organic" in Wright's work, and considering how central the idea would be to his architecture and how often it would recur in published examples of his thought for the next sixty-five years, it is not surprising that he stays with it for the rest of the page. Over the years, it would be expanded to become almost synonymous with "integrity," wherein all elements of a design derive from a central governing principle that encompasses conditions and context. Here Wright uses it to counter the Victorian propensity for ornamental excess. Simplicity is not something like the side of a barn, he counsels, but is rather something that is beautiful from which all discord has been removed. Perfect adjustment of everything to the whole assures repose, which is the serenity Gannett promises, if similar rules are followed. The first is to make one's home livable according to the best hopes people have. What Wright says here, Gannett has preached on every page: that if a home has the sense of being lived in, the life within it will be rewarding.

At the time of delivering this first address in Evanston, Frank Lloyd Wright had been in independent practice for just a year. Before this he had designed several houses behind Louis Sullivan's back, some of them credited to Cecil Corwin (to cloak Wright's identity) and many in currently fashionable styles (to please the clients of a yet-to-be-established architect, and keep Sullivan's suspicions at bay). Yet architectural scholars have noted elements of an emerging organic architecture in each, from the opening of views and interpretation of inside and out in the George Blossom House (1892) to the loosely arranged interior of the Chauncey Williams House (1895), one of Wright's first independent commissions but a home whose exterior still displayed fashionably historic period references. *Exterior* is the key, for on the inside, as with the Blossom House, the young architect was working wonders with a new grammar of space. Indeed, some of the earliest projects involved not new-builds at all but rather remodeling of interiors. How appropriate it is, given his emerging thought, that Wright begin his innovative work on the inside, linking what had been the boxes of Victorian-style rooms with wood screens and banding in a freshly fluid way. The reason why Frank Lloyd Wright was setting off like this is clarified by his first pronouncements in Evanston, and having those pronouncements associated with a famous sermon by William C. Gannett does not by any means make his thought retrospective. Instead, what Gannett (in his moral way) and Wright (as an architect) say anticipates what recent scholarship identifies as a late-twentieth-century trend setting terms for the twenty-first: that in organic architecture, as defined today, space is to be valued as lived in, a quality achievable when the nature of its design is not so much conceived as perceived—or, as Richard Weston puts it in his *Twentieth-Century Residential Architecture* (2002), a matter of acknowledging "the primacy of perception, not concepts, in the shaping of form" (216).

So many classic Wright principles follow from these two presentations that simply citing them would be tantamount to reprinting the full pieces, but it is remarkable the extent to which his comments in 1894 reflect those ideas manifested in his life's work. How should a house be? Simple, with as few rooms as fit the conditions under which one lives, simplicity being one of Gannett's basic tenets. Will all these houses look the same? There should be as many types of homes as there are people, Wright allows, for it is the occupants' personal traits that create the nature of the place, another point Gannett makes several times. The organic house, or *The Natural House* as Wright called it in his 1954 book, may not be exactly *The House Beautiful* that Reverend Gannett proposed, but the reasons for building and living in each of them are much the same, which is the same reason that we teach children to speak the truth and make their lives as beautiful as possible.

In the same year that Frank Lloyd Wright presented "The Architect and the Machine," his small-press partner-to-be, William Herman Winslow, moved into the River Forest home he'd had Wright design. This was the first "honest" commission the architect had acquired and completed after leaving the firm of Adler and Sullivan in a flurry of recriminations for having designed several "bootleg" houses on his own, in violation of his contract with Louis Sullivan. The Winslow House is an emphatic step forward in Wright's development, with its clean lines, smooth finish, rectilinear massing, and design elements that enhance a sense of the horizontal, thus anticipating the Prairie Houses of a decade later. The home's sharpness as it faces the street suggests the "machine" of Wright's title, but its other elements, inside and from the back, correspond to both Wright's and Gannett's pronouncements, and once in the door human elements of the "house beautiful" prevail. The entry space is both inviting for guests and protective of its residents. The axial nature of the fireplace unites the family on one side while on the other side allowing for room configurations that serve individual family members. Life at this site on Auvergne Place (for which Winslow's press was named) was not monological. Although the street-side view speaks for its owner's stature and authority, the roofline conveys a feeling of shelter, a value Wright and Gannett find essential and which the architect achieves by forgoing the typical Victorian roof that reached skywards, suggesting heavenly ascent if not social striving.

From the back, the Winslow House conveys an even homier mood. Because of family-related elements on the second floor, including a hearthside sitting room that overlooked the privacy of a rear garden, this façade is anything but regular. Instead, its shape conforms to the room's internal functions, which are family oriented. Here, one story up from the building's more public rooms for reception and social dining, was for Wright the true index of a home's success at facilitating happy family life. There is no reason the second floor should be less thoughtfully designed than the first, he exclaims, taking Gannett's suggestion that all rooms be considered as important as the front parlor had been for Victorian society. The architect's metaphor is sermon-like, asking his listeners if they care more for their neighbors than for themselves. This makes no more sense than tolerating poor undergarments in favor of showing off a top hat. The plan he provides for Winslow makes the ideal lifestyle Gannett proposed much easier to accomplish on the second floor, which is another anticipation of the Prairie House.

With "The Architect and the Machine" in mind, one sees how the Winslow House's design anticipates the principal feature of an even later development in Wright's career, the Usonian House of his last two decades of work. In each, the home opens to and embraces the privacy of a back yard. From the front the Winslow House, like Usonians coming forty to sixty years later, is all straight lines. To the right, one can glimpse the shallowest of bays coming off the living room, while to the left a delicately structured porte-cochere does nothing to disrupt the impression of rectangularity from the street. But passing into the back yard one encounters a veritable explosion of shapes and angles as the home's rear façade reveals the nature of family life that has been going on inside. Gannett had urged that the house generate its sense of space from within rather than be defined from without, and from the privacy of the back garden this purpose becomes apparent, so different from an act of public display.

For the Winslows, Wright provides everything needed to live according to Reverend Gannett's moral precepts from *The House Beautiful* and his own artistic imperatives voiced in "The Architect and the Machine." This moralism cannot be overemphasized; when the time comes to relate Wright to this era's more properly intellectual thought, his strong affinities will be with the religious thinker William James rather than with the philosophical pragmatist John Dewey. Even here, ethics coming from the pulpit rather than from the salon make Wright's ideas more accessible than John Ruskin's and more practical than those of William Morris. If there is a pragmatism to Wright's thinking at this stage, it is in the way he takes impulses from both ethics and aesthetics and puts them to work in an exceptionally functional house.

In choosing domesticity as a key for the improvement of life, Wright and Gannett find a way of making morality and art fit together in a comfortable and sensible way. This uniquely American interpretation could soon be contrasted with the emerging modernism from Europe that would be coldly intellectual in the service of a good seen in much broader social contexts. As the era evolved, Progressive thought in the United States would take on all aspects of life, public and private, but it is important to see how in Wright's world of the 1890s, this matter of home life could assume such great proportions. In 1889 Wright designed and built his own home and over the next nine years made major changes and additions to it twice. Because the property was his own, he could experiment with a freer hand, making structural alterations and devoting Sunday afternoons to incessant rearrangement of furniture, probing for different practical and artistic effects. In a similar manner, his business with the bootleg houses gave him greater flexibility than working under the direction of Louis Sullivan; and he was also free from the inhibition of having his name connected with a property when his ideas were at an early stage of development and when his junior status in the profession made him more beholden to a client's whim. He also continued to speak, again to the University Guild of Evanston, and to publish in increasingly important venues.

Presented in 1896, "Architect, Architecture, and the Client" dates from a time when there were still considerably more projects done for Sullivan and bootlegged in the moonlight than commissions fully acknowledged as by Frank Lloyd Wright. Moreover, two of the ones Wright did acknowledge speak less of Wright's ideas and more of his clients' tastes—tastes he seeks to improve in this new Evanston lecture. These two homes, designed in 1895 for Nathan G. Moore and Chauncey Williams, join the earlier properties conceived undercover in drawing on the full stylebook of the times, making Wright's production to that date less progressive than it was exploratory. Exceptions were the Winslow House and the single major project done with Sullivan for which the younger architect would claim major credit: the Charnley House (1891), built on the near north side of Chicago in an urban neighborhood quite different from the leafy suburbs of Oak Park and River Forest, yet sharing a rectangular shape and cleanness of line that characterized the front of Wright's first genuine masterpiece on Auvergne Place.

By 1896 Wright was three years into independent practice, and had learned well that architecture needed to be addressed not just on its own terms but with the relationship of architect and client in mind. Indeed, in his second lecture to the University Guild one of Wright's imperatives, announced self-consciously as "play[ing] the part of preacher" (*CW* I: 27), is that once clients decide what is wanted and who should provide it, they should trust their architect as they do their doctor or any other specialist who is expert in appraising their needs. Wright himself is aware that all clients are different, and therefore factors their uniqueness into his planning: to underscore this he repeats the point from his previous Evanston lecture, that there are as many types of houses as there are types of people. That Wright was making good on this promise is evident from the wide variety of houses he designed between 1889 and 1895 — starting with his own, already modified to reflect changes in his life. But Wright preaches something beyond submission to the architect's expertise and that is how architecture itself can best provide not just shelter but an environment in which all aspects of existence can be improved.

Not surprisingly, elements of Reverend Gannett's *The House Beautiful* reappear in this lecture, delivered as it is by an architect preaching the goal of moral as well as aesthetic betterment. Choosing a type of house not to impress one's friends but to suit one's self is proper, because it is this self that a true friend treasures above any advertised image. Furnishing that home as simply as possible, even decorating it with dried grasses and weeds — these suggestions from Gannett's sermon inform this second bit of Evanston preachment as much as they did the first. But now Wright elevates the discussion by showing that when architecture is practiced as art, the results are even more rewarding. Art, after all, is simply a practical example of beauty, and the most inclusive way of introducing beauty into one's life is by making one's home a work of art.

How is that beauty discerned? By reading the souls of his clients, Wright argues, and building a house for them in which anyone can see a legible inscription of who the owners are and hope to be. Unfortunately, clients may retain likes and dislikes from their former environments that prevent the plan from fulfilling their deeper happiness, a happiness an architect like Wright can perceive even when they themselves cannot.

I know my clients better than themselves, this rhetoric suggests. *They tell me what they want, but I know what they really want.* Much later in his career, when his striking innovations as an architect and flamboyance as an outspoken media personality had made him so eminently quotable, Frank Lloyd Wright would say things like this to chide his critics. But even from the improvised pulpit of the University Guild in Evanston Wright argues for the essential soundness of this position and its importance in achieving the goals he'd set. Therefore he turns these initial premises on art, beauty, and the more happily lived life into a disquisition on the state of architectural design as it exists in 1896 — and, at least implicitly, how the problems of serving clients in this state of affairs influenced the type of work he had been doing.

Great architecture no longer exists, Wright complains, and lays the blame on Gutenberg's printing press and primacy of literature over architecture that followed. Does it all just come down to the book replacing the cathedral? As with his inspirations borrowed from Reverend Gannett, Wright again shows his self-educated background and predilection for the popular by summarizing an argument made not by Ruskin or Morris but by Victor Hugo. Throughout his life the architect would look back to a favorite chapter, "The One Will Kill the Other" in *The Hunchback of Notre Dame*, as the source for the idea presented here.

As with his use of Gannett, Wright takes the idea much farther than does Hugo, or at the very least applies it more specifically to the present time. When books replaced the cathedral as manifest expressions of spirit, one great model for style was replaced by an infinity of pages presenting a range of styles as long as history and as broad a human conduct. A perceptive architect can see these representations for what they are. But for impressionable clients, the results can be disastrous. Wright considers what in these circumstances the architect can do: he can study his client's best qualities and design a home he can grow into, or else he can just give him what he thinks he wants and be done with it. If the latter happens, is it really the architect's fault?

Like a preacher, Wright chides his listeners with shameful characterizations of their conduct. Wanting one's home built in an historical style is like dressing up in others' clothes borrowed from a different time. Do this, and nothing fits. Whether Colonial or Renaissance, chateau or chalet, the choice is damning of the client, who has chosen something that is not American, something Wright regretted when surrendering to the whims of Nathan G. Moore the year before. Could the architect give him a good enough half-timber type short of selling out? The problem is pondered in *An Autobiography*. It was worth trying, Wright concludes, albeit with a sigh: "I tried . . ." (*CW* II: 189, ellipses in original).

The Wright canon from 1889 through 1895 makes gestures in various directions. Both as a worker by moonlight and as a young independent who could be honest about needing to support his growing family, the architect had excuses for trying out alternatives. His Evanston lectures professed a sincere desire to give his clients not only better homes but a better way of life, and in these early works, subtly suggestive of his emerging thought, one sees a variety of approaches with a common goal, which is to open up the spatial reality of interiors no matter how diverse the outside shape may be.

In calling architects to do a better job for their clients, Wright demands honesty on both sides. "A Philosophy of Fine Art," read in 1900 before the Architectural League at the Art Institute of Chicago, engages listeners on a casual level, transposing the Idealism of Thomas Carlyle to the wisdom one learns from a mother and finds reinforced by a wife: that the practical and the Ideal are one, that beauty cannot be applied but must emerge from the thing itself. A false use of ideal beauty is made by those who advertise their riches in vulgar display. If Americans want examples of success, it is far better to look at the plain manner of Abraham Lincoln; everything about him spoke of the genuine. What does a simply honest work of art look like? No matter what the medium, it must be "true to the conditions of its existence." A painting, for example, "must be a thing made with a brush, dipped in paint and applied to canvas," and not a piece of literature that tells a story. If a picture of a cow looks irresistibly lifelike, do not buy the painting, Wright advises— buy the cow (*CW* I: 42). Listeners at the Art Institute were surrounded by one of the best French Impressionist collections in the country, and thus had no problem understanding Wright's meaning. But even here his emphasis on the medium's physical substance and action as opposed to its subject anticipates an aesthetic as innovative as his most forward-looking architectural projects to come: Harold Rosenberg's description of abstract expressionist painting two generations later. Rosenberg's *The Tradition of the New* (1959), published in the same year Wright's Guggenheim Museum would open as a venue for such art, draws its conclusion from what Wright proposes: that a painting is not a surface upon which to represent but rather an arena within which to act.

What some people asked of abstract expressionism could be asked of Wright and his theories of art in 1900: is all this just art for art's sake? The 1890s and its Oscar Wilde aesthetics were still fresh memories and the question is fair. But Wright has equal enthusiasm for what art should do, which is to conventionalize natural things so as to reveal the poetry of their nature, a poetry that reveals an identity of form and function with life that constitutes civilization itself. *Conventionalization* was the term Wright used for abstraction, and like later theorists his intentions have a moral tone. Civilization is nothing less than conventionalizing nature, he reminds his listeners, and is what keeps the light of human progress alive. And whose business is it to keep that light burning? The architect, of course, for only music can approach architecture as an index of the civilized. Here Wright once again takes advantage of the location where he is speaking, drawing on the appreciation of all the arts likely to characterize an audience at one of his city's leading cultural institutions. Just as music provides delight in temporal rhythms and harmonies, he indicates, so does architecture with space. What a tragedy to have one's appreciation of music limited to the prosaic spectacle of program notes, where sounds are presumed to inspire just pictures. And what an even greater loss to live the better part of one's life in a building, one's home, that fails to provide happy harmonies of spatial occupancy.

Are these thoughts innovatively educational? Because of his aunts' experience with the extremely progressive Hillside Home School operated from 1887 to 1915, Wright is assumed to have been shaped by the ideas behind this undertaking, which eventually found a national voice in the theories of John Dewey. Yet in all five massive volumes of Wright's *Collected Writings*, there are only two references to Dewey, and quite passing ones at that: in a prospectus for the Taliesin Fellowship and in *An Autobiography*, both dating from 1932, he mentions his aunts as having learned of Dewey only through Francis Parker, a predecessor who had introduced Froebel's blocks and other ideas for early childhood education to American schools in the 1870s and for whom the aunts had taught before establishing their own school. Education does not surface in Frank Lloyd Wright's thinking until a generation later, when he becomes an educator himself. For now, his architecture and the thoughts behind it show the inspiration of people like Reverend Gannett and a Lincoln of homespun mythology.

As the nineteenth century drew to a close, Wright's work in Chicago concentrated on designs completely his own. The most impressive of these include homes for Isadore Heller (1896) and Rollin Furbeck (1897), and while their narrow verticality shows none of the Prairie House's innovations just a few years away, neither is done in anyone else's style, as were the bootlegs. At this point another address to the Architectural League presented a few months later in 1900 takes on special pertinence. In "The Architect" Wright faces his profession directly, as only someone who finally feels established in it could hope to do. He makes overt reference to the machine that lurked behind the title of his first Evanston lecture and was mentioned obliquely in the second, as one of the tools science has placed in the hands of architects who haven't yet learned to use them. By 1900 Wright feels architects have found a way to use the machine, but improperly: to mass-produce styles and pile them up in a plan-factory that makes plan-making central rather than incidental to the profession. When that happens, the architect abandons his primary responsibility to his clients, which is to provide a dynamically shaped design for living that brings out the best in one's life.

How can this situation be remedied? In coming up with an answer, Wright speaks in general terms that summarize the progress of his career to date. He begins with praise for the type of person who would rather build a summer cottage than build a city, a description of just what the young employee of Adler and Sullivan had done by designing a pair of Gulf Coast cottages in Mississippi for Louis Sullivan and his friends the Charnleys (1890) instead of lusting after work planned for the classically themed White City in the 1893 Columbian Exposition. He expresses regret over the older European styles that infect America like a contagious disease that children bring home from school. The reference is deliberately homely, so that the argument may be developed on an educational level. Can new architects be taught better? Only if they start learning within two days of birth and are well-schooled growing up with nature, as was Wright by his mother's thoughtful decoration of his nursery and his active involvement with the work of his uncles' farms. From there the education of an architect must involve moving into the hustle and bustle of the city to learn how civilization thrives (as did Wright when leaving Wisconsin for Chicago), and there being mentored by a "loving Master" (*CW* I: 50) as was Wright by Louis Sullivan. These specific references are never stated, but the implications are clear, for this is the only way to get a proper architect, one capable of finding the poetry inherent in his work, an architect who is in fact a boy with the heart of a king. If that sounds egotistical, it is no more so than Wright's future statements would be. Granted, this is the stuff of the nineteenth century, expressed in a romantic manner that approaches sentimentality. But to guarantee success Wright looks forward as well, to a world in which architects will use modern methods rather than be used by them.

"The Architect" does not end here, not on this lofty note. Recalling how his previous essay's initial aspiration to Thomas Carlyle and the Ideal had been brought down to earth with the homeliest of filial and uxorial analogies, Wright concludes with poetry at its most accessible level: a full-length recitation of a piece of doggerel straight from the popular culture. Its subject is how a new manner of poet is needed to sing the power of modern railroads—the same type, Wright concludes, which is needed for architecture. A laughable spectacle? Not in context, for throughout these early lectures Wright has consistently fashioned himself as a preacher, and a staple of any preacher's methodology is the "double proof" whereby a truth from one realm is underscored by the parallel proof from another: material for spiritual, common for uncommon, mundane for the lofty, and so forth. Wright also knows, and surely feels this way himself, that an argument from everyday life will carry more persuasiveness than one grounded in abstraction. To his listeners and to himself, the Reverend William C. Gannett will sound more convincing than John Ruskin, and Thomas Carlyle's pronouncements on the Ideal will come across more effectively in the voice of one's mother or wife. Where is Frank Lloyd Wright's image of success: in the ostentatious manners of the business and social elite? No, it's in the homespun virtue of Abraham Lincoln.

There is also humor involved. Wright genuinely loved popular expressions of great truths, a sign of the self-educated person. But he could also joke about it. He'd tease his friend Carl Sandburg that the poet's greatest work was his *Rootabaga Stories* and would recommend it as an example of what good literature should be. That would always get a laugh from Sandburg and others, because the architect was having a bit of self-deprecating fun with his own taste. That's what is happening at the end of his lecture as well, as Wright takes the inspirations of architecture and its future and uses them to conclude with a rousting doggerel poem that makes the most of this occasion.

The architect also has a good time with the home he designs in the flush of early success. He has earned his reputation by taking the stylistic desires of early clients and introducing spatial elements that made their homes not only more attractive from the outside but more livable within. Now at the end of the 1890s he wins commissions that let him show what can be achieved by designing from the inside out. Two homes do this in the vertical manner—not the direction Wright's Prairie Houses would take in the next decade, but for that all the more suggestive of how working with interior spaces comes first: the Isadore Heller House (1896) and the home for Rollin Furbeck (1897). These residences contributed to Wright's reputation as the most important architect in the suburbs, and when he completed the studio addition to his home (1898) and relocated his practice there, keeping just a small business office in the city, his status as a local hero was assured.

It is a hometown issue that prompts the last of Wright's 1900 lectures. "Concerning Landscape Architecture" is a pleasantly informal address to the Fellowship Club, one of Oak Park's several women's organizations that the civic-minded Catherine Wright supported with her membership and volunteer activity. Its opening statements show how entertaining Wright could be, his wit and the subject serving as good stand-up comedy. And laugh his audiences should, given how ridiculously their suburb's landscape planning had evolved. Bucolic leafiness had been its original attraction, but now it has devolved into a place where people might wander lost until they starved to death, so shaded that "little children grew thin and pallid like potato sprouts in a back cellar" (*CW* I: 54). Like an improvising comic riding the laughs of his audience, Wright riffs through several more situations, having good-natured fun with the state of things in Oak Park. He describes the new decorative trend of topiary with the equally extreme examples of a box shrub crafted as a crowing rooster and a hedge trimmed with a locomotive, tender, and cars rushing along its top.

Then, with his audience won over to his side, Wright gets serious, explaining how such new styles come about. For this he departs from landscaping for a moment to consider a presumably higher art, that of stained glass decoration. He names the universally admired Louis Tiffany and asks if his later projects haven't been a bit extreme. Having worked in color all his life, the designer loses interest in normal effects and is tempted to the "ragged edge of discord" that is so abnormal, so unbearable, that it "can please no healthy eye" (*CW* I: 55). Wright further emphasizes his point with familiar examples: the discordant colors currently popular in women's fashions and extremities of taste for food. Whether garish hats in uncomplimentary blues and greens, gamey meats, or smelly cheeses—the decadence of taste is all around us, Wright and his listeners agree. As for better taste in their gardens, he reminds them that it is the landscape architect's job to harmonize growth and environment without marring the natural grace of either. He can recommend a good book on the subject by an English woman, Gertrude Jekyll's *Home and Garden*, a recently published volume that belongs in every library. Wright's voice is hardly a cry in the wilderness.

Walter Burley Griffin, a gifted landscape architect with beliefs like Jekyll's and Wright's, would the next year be taken on as an associate, joining a group of exceptionally talented young architects that included Marion Mahony. Five years later an angry Griffin would leave Wright's studio, and by the decade's end Mahony was out of it as well. The two would marry, and share bitter memories of the man whose selfish ambition had, they believed, betrayed them. But in 1901 all was happiness. Griffin was the closest thing to a valued and respected partner that Wright would ever have, and Mahony's aesthetic sense was a great benefit. Its author supported by talent and enthusiasm, Wright's "Concerning Landscape Architecture" looks forward to the first decade of the twentieth century, a decade that would be graced by his Prairie House masterpieces, wherein landscape architecture becomes an important factor. These were years when Wright cooperated most comfortably with others, delegating work to those who had the greatest gifts for it: Walter Burley Griffin for landscape design, Marion Mahony for delineations, George Mann Niedecken for furnishings and interior details, Richard Bock and Alfonso Iannelli for sculpture. The large compound-complexes done for Darwin T. Martin in Buffalo (1904) and for Avery and Queene Coonley in the southwest Chicago suburb of Riverside (1907) cannot be imagined without these cooperative efforts. The plan for the Martin project hung above Wright's workplace for the balance of his long career as testimony to how all elements of a design are properly integrated. And not just for visual beauty. In his address to the Fellowship Club Wright stresses how the beautiful ways that art can improve our environment are as influential on our lives as the cultivated conduct of good society. This connection is what he and Reverend Gannett had been preaching for the past seven years. Environments inside the house and outside of it accurately reflect the society inhabiting these realms. If it looks ugly and stupid, Wright asserts, you can be sure it is the bottom of society.

"Concerning Landscape Architecture" would be Frank Lloyd Wright's last small-time speech. The next, delivered to an influential audience at Chicago's Hull House, seat of the innovative and influential organization directed by social reformer Jane Addams, is titled "The Art and Craft of the Machine." Presented in March of 1901, it takes Wright out of the pulpit (and away from the garden club) and places him among the most pertinent group of listeners of these times: activists devoted to improvements in life that would begin with the basic infrastructure Wright himself had been striving to reform. In fact, the piece looks less to the future than to the past. Later this same year Wright would publish two essays that did predict his emerging work with the Prairie House, and a certain machine aesthetic is involved in that. But for his Hull House audience the architect is more concerned with how the machine has been resisted, even demonized, by the same people who are otherwise most dedicated to reform. There is no preaching to the choir here, but rather a soberly stated argument that the idealists of the Arts and Crafts Movement—famous figures such as Morris and Ashbee and others sure to be admired among the Jane Addams group— have been counterproductive in turning completely away from the machine. Wright's thesis is that the machine is in truth their friend. Their ideals have been admirable, but in throwing out all possible benefits from machinery the Arts and Crafters have not just made their own work more difficult but have placed themselves in opposition to the greatest means of improvement at hand for the lives of ordinary people.

For twenty years William Morris and his followers had been condemning the Industrial Revolution's degradation of craft and the replacement of craftsmen by workers enslaved to their machines. Wright's counterargument is that the evil lies not in the machine itself but in how it is used. If it simply replaces expensive handcrafts with mass-produced items that drive down prices and discourage fine artistry, machinery is bad. But if used to make work easier and more pleasurable, to eliminate the drudgery of a job and leave more opportunity for the creative, then it is good. But of even more importance, especially to Wright, is that the very nature of machinery brings out the simple, natural qualities of the material being worked with, whether wood or steel. Rather than simply rejecting the Arts and Crafts ideal, Wright reminds his listeners that William Morris valued simplicity as the basis for all art. This same quality could just as easily underlie the art of the machine. From here Wright moves through all aspects of what the machine can do, aligning them first with Morris's goal (simplicity) and his own (the organic). Granted, this transformation from the handcrafted to the machine-made is revolutionary, but such is the age at hand. The transformation, however radical, is a good one, because it not only preserves human creativity but enhances it by allowing an easier way to embrace the natural for one's own benefit.

Wright concludes this lecture not with doggerel poetry, but with an invitation to his audience of serious social workers to look from atop a tall office building across the city in all its glory and menace. There below is a monster leviathan, stretching out in a complex image that has Wright not just painting with words but constructing with analogies that are almost too much to bear. The huge range of the city is like fleshy tissue, tied together by nerves and pulsing as an organism through which flow the fluids of life. As the metaphors compound, flywheels whirl like the impulses of nerve ganglia, machines murmur like whispers and breaths, while any number of urban activities are ablaze with passion.

Though not so identified, this vision matches what Wright encountered as a nineteen-year-old arriving at night on the train from Wisconsin, seeing a metropolis for the very first time. It certainly motivates the raptures he now, as a thirty-four-year-old professional established as one of Chicago's leading architects, feels to be appropriate curtain music for the symphony of ideas he has just concluded, the most profound of which is that the machine's essence is simply "the principle of organic growth working irresistibly the Will of Life through the medium of Man" (*CW* I: 68).

2

The Prairie and the World

AS THE TWENTIETH CENTURY GETS UNDERWAY, Frank Lloyd Wright's family motto of "Truth against the World" takes on a prospective dimension. As his first decade of practice demonstrated, Wright had no trouble whatsoever innovating within established nineteenth-century forms, whether Queen Anne, Shingle, or Colonial Revival—or, for that matter, the perennial favorite of wealthy lawyers and financiers, the Tudor half-timber. But in 1901 he reorientates to the future, developing an architecture that not only gives Midwest America its first totally original style but wins its maker an international reputation. In America, Europe, and eventually Japan his work would be seen as truly revolutionary.

Unlike "The Architect and the Machine," prepared for listeners at Hull House this same year, three important essays published in 1901 in *The Brickbuilder* (later called *The Architectural Record*) and *The Ladies' Home Journal* look forward rather than back. And what a remarkable future they foresee. Wright's move from the local lecture platform to the national press may have been enabled by what biographer Robert Twombly (1979) calls the "terrific boost" (37) given to his career by fellow architect Robert C. Spencer, Jr., who in June of 1900 published an illustrated essay on Wright's work for *The Architectural Review*. A Steinway Hall neighbor and, according to H. Allen Brooks (1972), the person who had "supplanted Cecil Corwin as Wright's best friend" (28), Spencer praised elements that Wright would soon be foregrounding in his own essays: the quiet simplicity of family life that results from the three-dimensional opening of space, the natural growth of design elements in a manner identified as "organic," and the belief that any ornamentation be *of* the surface and not *on* it. With the confidence that this essay surely inspired, Frank Lloyd Wright could now expound to a large readership just what he intends for both commercial and domestic architecture.

In "The Village Bank Series" Wright presents his concept of what small town banks should be. Louis Sullivan would design them as jewel boxes, but the younger architect here proposes something else: a combination of strongbox and temple to the God of Money. It is in the notion "temple" that Wright shows how his thinking has developed. Although not stemming from religion, the desire of bankers to have a significant and therefore monumental building leads to unfortunate associations with mausoleums, most of which are neither significant nor monumental: rather, they suggest a memorial, where memories of life and hopes for the afterlife are enshrined. Wright by contrast gives his bankers a temple to the God of Money. This particular bank was never built, but a real temple was: the structure Wright would design in 1904 for his own Unitarian congregation in Oak Park, Unity Temple. Here the solid cubic shape and great interior openness serve religion even better, at the same time making people feel as they would have hoped for a place of financial safety, that this place is here to stay.

Useful space and happy occupancy typify another new building, the headquarters done in 1903 for the Larkin Company of Buffalo, New York. But as much as he wanted to win big commissions for major buildings, Wright would spend most of this decade working on houses. Therefore it's appropriate that his two other essays published in 1901 be written for *The Ladies' Home Journal*. The first appears in the magazine's February issue and bears the title that would name not just a style but a movement: "A Home in a Prairie Town." Accompanied by a perspective drawing, a floor plan, and a proposal for siting such houses in a quadruple block arrangement that rotated each home's direction so as to maximize both privacy and space, the essay describes a structure much like that built later the same year in the Chicago suburb of Highland Park for Ward W. Willits.

The Willits home is a fine example of the Prairie House, a term applied to most of Wright's domestic production for the next dozen years. The house itself is famous for what would become familiar Prairie features, including a strong horizontal aspect, main floor set atop a short but clearly defined base, interpenetrating internal spaces that flow into one another, an axial sense deriving from a centrally placed fireplace, a central chimney that anchored the home's cruciform arrangement of wings, a feeling of the outside world coming in, and a strong sense of shelter provided by the broad projections of a low, overhanging roof. "A Home in a Prairie Town" presents appealing reasons not just for building such a house but for locating it on a lot 400 feet wide by 400 feet deep—immensely larger than the 60-by-120 foot suburban building lot or the fifty and even thirty-foot frontages common within the Chicago city limits. Wright knew very well how much space was available, having seen the commuter lines extend to Oak Park and beyond. Throughout his career his advice to clients was that they seek land as far out as they thought they could possibly move—and then go ten miles farther. In 1901 he urges a larger site not just in a lust for space itself but for how this extra room outside can enhance a home's internal design.

In the plan for the "home in the prairie town," long bands of casement windows swing open; low terraces along the wall ease any sense of confinement. From outside, the house associates itself with the prairie, quiet and level. Inside, its floor plan invites an equally simple and easy lifestyle, keeping the family together yet allowing plenty of space. Inside and outside flow together and internal spaces are offered with the option of a floor-through arrangement that extends living room space into the second story (enclosable for an extra upstairs bedroom). Even finish details are meant to enhance this easy, natural mood, with interior walls plastered with sand finish and trimmed minimally in Georgia pine. Life in a Prairie House is meant to be a pleasant experience, inside and out.

These innovations are presented without the least sense of preaching, because the perspective, floor plan, and block siting speak for themselves; all Wright needs to add are the details. Those details include a cost breakdown, bringing the home in for under seven thousand dollars, quite competitive in the 1901 market. Most of what he'd done in the 1890s cost a great deal more.

Even more affordable (at $5,935) is "A Small House with 'Lots of Room In It'" described in Wright's essay for *The Ladies' Home Journal* in July. Again, there was a real-life home on the architect's books at this time that conformed in image and details: the Warren Hickox House (1900) in Kankakee, Illinois. It looks quite different from the Willits House, and therefore is not characterized as fully Prairie in style. Wright acknowledges this in his essay's first line, crediting the average client's preference for the gabled roof, which the Prairie House, as introduced in this same magazine five months before, does not have. But to satisfy the prospective homeowner and himself he has come up with a gable that flares gently from its eaves, raised at the peaks for better perspective, all of which makes the outlines "crisp." *Crisp* is good, but not just for itself; beneath this visual effect is a floor plan in which the dining room and living room meld easily while each maintaining its own function. Thus in the architect's manner of thinking, visual attraction is valuable, but only as it enhances function, suggesting that in his mind the two are one. Wright is emphatic that the living room stands at the house's center, but not in any sequestered manner. Instead, status is won by virtue of the room's access to both interior and exterior features, including a peek at the stair landing as one enters. For Wright, *heart* is not a static concept but rather the source of circulation, and the Hickox House makes movement open and easy. The living room's broad rectangle has its fireplace located midway along the long wall opposite the terrace, a rear-facing structure that stretches the full length of this room—its size and accessibility effectively double the living space in fine weather. But this same living room gains added spatial dimensions at each end, where a library and dining room extend the respective lengths by projecting out (via five sides of an octagon) into the side yards.

Natural is the term Wright uses most often to described effects whether external or internal. Its natural feel and open circulation ally this "small house with lots of room in it" with the Prairie House per se and make it an integral part of the Prairie Movement. As the essay's title promises, it is an eminently practical home. But the most stunning visual effects are found in the more formal Prairie House, making it not just a wonderful place in which to live but an object of great visual beauty. In Frank Lloyd Wright's book, and of course in the Reverend Gannett's, these aspects are mutually reinforcing. But in harmony with the general tone of these *Ladies' Home Journal* essays, there is no need to preach. Beautiful pictures are worth more than any number of sermonized words, and the Willits House especially has generated stunning photographs, showing how lovely Wright's work can look both inside and out, most effectively so when the two realms interpenetrate.

Mrs. Willits would prompt the architect's next piece of writing by suggesting the Wrights accompany her husband and herself on a trip to Japan in 1905. Her motive was to rekindle Frank's romantic interest in his then-wife Catherine, and to douse the same for another client's wife, Mamah Borthwick Cheney. The voyage enhanced Wright's enthusiasm for all things Japanese and inspired the first of his many essays on this country's art, an art sharing affinities with his own architecture and beliefs.

"Hiroshige" (1906) is Wright's critical introduction to a catalogue (without illustrations) of the Chicago Art Institute's exhibition of this artist's work. Just four hundred words long, it mimics the aesthetics being praised: that of subtraction rather than addition, the attractiveness not of content itself but how that content occupies a space without crowding it. A comparison of the Willits House with the Robie House, conceived and realized after the trip, makes this same point: that the ultimate form of the Prairie House is a reduction to its ground-hugging line that holds without ostentation expansive volumes of internal space.

Utagawa Hiroshige (1797–1858) was Wright's favorite of the Japanese print artists because his work concentrated not on society's elite but rather the artisan class whose inherent poetic grace was portrayed as delightful. This distinction mattered to Wright, because by virtue of it he could claim all of this artist's restraint, chasteness, and delicacy of balance as essentially democratic traits — the same qualities Wright sought for his own architecture. He also appreciated how Hiroshige's work is representational without being literary. Like a Prairie House, there's no story to unravel, no secret meaning to decode; the substance of each composition is immediately perceived.

In 1913 Wright would travel to Japan again, pursuing a commission for Tokyo's new Imperial Hotel. More thoughts on Japanese art would follow this visit, but a piece of writing on Japanese prints derived from the first trip merits attention within the context of developments in his work and his personal life.

His marriage with Catherine did not survive the decade. In 1909 he left for Europe in Mamah's company. Making a brief return visit to Oak Park in 1910, he arranged for the support of Catherine and the children and returned to Italy to live with Mamah. Catherine had promised to grant his request for a divorce if he waited a year, but when the time arrived she reneged, hoping against hope that he would eventually tire of Mamah and come back as a dutiful husband. In 1911 the lovers returned to America, Mamah to finalize the divorce her husband Edwin sadly granted, Frank to salvage what remained of his architectural practice. For himself and Mamah he'd build Taliesin, a hillside home in his ancestral valley near Spring Green, Wisconsin that bore suggestions of the Tuscan-style villa they had rented in Fiesole. But he also continued to collect and deal in Japanese woodblock prints, an activity that was outstripping his disrupted architectural practice in earnings. From this experience, and with memories of his 1905 adventures in Japan still vivid, he would write a short book called *The Japanese Print: An Interpretation* (1912).

Published at the same time the architect was underwriting books on European feminist thought translated by Mamah, the volume lacks illustrations. This lack is richly compensated for by Wright's insightful prose—eight thousand words of it. His enthusiasm for the Japanese aesthetic had grown since his brief statement on Hiroshige. Inspiration came from the familiar belief that beauty itself is the finest morality, an ideal popular since Ruskin but parsed by Wright for architecture. Beauty comes from structure, structure comes from organic form, and informing it all is the vital whole of life itself. All this is said in the six hundred words that precede Wright's interpretation of the woodblock prints: that for all its grace, Japanese art is above all structural. At the heart of structure is design, and at the heart of design lies geometry. "Geometry is the grammar, so to speak, of the form," Wright concludes, paralleling (albeit coincidentally) the method of Saussure's *Course in General Linguistics* (1907–1911) that would inspire, more than half a century later, the thinking of a different era entirely. Wright's appreciation of geometry's "spell power" (*CW* I: 117), such as the circle's suggestion of infinity, the triangle's sense of structural unity, the spire's aspiration, the spiral's organic progress, and the integrity of the square are not in themselves forward-looking, but neither are they Ruskinesque. They are instead aspects of Frank Lloyd Wright's manner of thought, here taking shape in Japanese art.

Wright believes that, more than other artists, the Japanese understand this sense of syntax and demonstrate a mastery of the grammar, grasping form by probing its underlying geometry. Having found the core of reality, the printmaker can express an inner harmony that determines outward form and character. The colored woodblock prints that the architect praises show this quality, which is nothing less than a Platonic ideal. This distinction between psychological and metaphysical may remind readers how Frank Lloyd Wright comes a generation after Ralph Waldo Emerson and is in fact sharing the times of William James; here is the idealism not of *Nature* (1836) but of *Varieties of Religious Experience* (1902). In this discourse, the practice of art is not primarily a spiritual affair but is rather a physical involvement with objects that are played as comfortably as a pianist might play a keyboard. Grammar and syntax, notes and melodies, harmonies and rhythms: these are Wright's keys to instructional truths, and their very palpability speaks for the physical and psychological dimensions of his thought, a quality his friend Robert Spencer saw derived from Wright's childhood exercises with the spatially dimensional Froebel blocks.

Appreciating how the core of Japanese art lies in eliminating the insignificant so that the simplest reality remains, Wright begins moving his argument in an at least implicitly architectural direction. For her *Frank Lloyd Wright and the Art of Japan* (2001) Julia Meech has sifted through Wright's comments in later years to the Taliesin apprentices and the apprentices' reactions. Beginning in the early 1930s "print parties" were a frequent exercise for the Fellowship, one of the few teaching devices this unteacherly master used. At one of these parties in 1950 he pulled out some Hiroshige prints and praised their "tremendous, limitless space, instead of something confined within a picture." Meech notes the printmaker achieved this through "abrupt cropping and diagonal asymmetry," and how years later Curtis Besinger, now a practicing architect in the organic manner, would intuit that just as the subjects of these prints seemed to extend beyond the unframed margins, a house could be designed to feel larger by reaching out into the space around it (Meech, 230). An abundance of space, of course, is available only because the extraneous has been eliminated—by the printmaker and by the architect. In each case it is accomplished by an act of *conventionalization*, Wright's term for an abstraction that strives for a holistic sympathy with nature. Once again, there's grammar at work, for dramatizing something conventionalizes it, which is in turn to simplify along geometrical patterns. This mathematical basis makes those patterns symbolic, woven as the woof builds on the warp. Eliminate the insignificant and you thereby emphasize the real—in a print, in a house.

The richness and depth of Wright's analysis shows how far he has come since his "Hiroshige" piece appeared in 1906. But the conclusion to his argument in 1912 indicates how his life itself has fared in the intervening years. What distinguishes these years from the period before 1906 is his involvement with Mamah, and specifically how that initial involvement with a client's wife turned, after the 1905 visit to Japan, into an abiding romance and intellectual experience that would shape his personal values and orient his career. In 1915, he'd write about it in a brief piece titled "On Marriage," but some of that essay's thinking is present in the closing pages of *The Japanese Print: An Interpretation.*

Many of the classic figurative Japanese woodblock prints draw their subjects from the Yoshiwara, the licensed entertainment quarter of Edo. These works celebrate the geisha's sexuality, Wright states, in a manner innocent beyond western comprehension. Although in Japan as in America the family was the principal unit of civilization, the Japanese people of this era (1603-1868, the Tokugawa period) did not make sex the essence of marriage; moreover, the Yoshiwara served literary and artistic needs as well, for the rising commercial class of Edo. Here the geisha was honored as a living work of art and a poetic refinement of life, a crowning example of what Wright considered an exquisite civilization.

It was Wright's and Willits' doings in just such a pleasure quarter that convinced Mrs. Willits that Frank's marriage with Catherine was beyond saving, and that Ward had best be taken home. In fact, Wright's appreciation of this district echoes the feminist beliefs of the Swedish reformer Ellen Key, whose books the newly divorced Mamah Borthwick had been translating and for which Wright had arranged American publication. Key's work advances the same idea that Mamah had been espousing, with Wright in firm agreement: that love was not the chattel property of marriage, but was rather a personal emotion worthy of existing and being shared on its own terms. When challenged by the Chicago newspapers to explain his apparently sinful cohabitation with Ms. Borthwick at Taliesin while Catherine Wright of Oak Park was still his legal wife, Frank responded with a Christmas Day 1911 press conference at Taliesin and made the same points as his 1915 essay: that the form of marriage means less than the life of a marriage, and that marriage without love was an empty form. Conversely, love itself brought life to any relationship, legally sanctioned or not.

Wright's comments to the press were published the next day in the *Chicago Tribune*. "On Marriage" appears only in Wright's *Collected Writings* (I: 138), but sentiments from it are used to make his final point about Japanese art: one must love a thing before it can be truly known, and such deep sympathy has a spiritual dimension that puts the life into art. This is an eminently practical demonstration of how something spiritual can be made material, with the abstract ideal being a means and not an end. Wright admires it in the Japanese print and practices it in his architecture. And while there is a spiritual element to such work, it is neither the foremost nor the conclusive element. Rather, it is a stage in the larger human process that is emphatically physical, psychological, and emotional.

Architectural writings in the years following Wright's first visit to Japan reflect on the decade's accomplishments. Like many things Japanese and all things Frank Lloyd Wright, "A Fireproof House for $5,000" makes good on its title by simplification, subtraction, and an open sense of space. Appearing in the April 1907 *Ladies' Home Journal*, it takes principles espoused in his first two articles (1901) for this magazine and applies them to a much smaller and more economical dwelling. He begins by citing the recent steep rise in building costs, tacitly admitting that his Home in a Prairie Town and Small House with Lots of Room In It might be financially out of range for average clients. Costs are high, but new building techniques make materials such as concrete and steel affordable—and Wright has just the way to use them. By a process of elimination he reduces the main floor to just three rooms: living, dining, and kitchen (with pantry and cabinets built in). Ornamentation is limited to flower boxes and concrete urns with trailing plants; in winter the building's sense of proportion is its own decoration. Although the kitchen and an upstairs rear bedroom (brightly lit for use as a sewing room) protrude a few feet, the home's four sides are equal, so that the same forms for pouring and setting concrete can be reused all around.

Architects such as Robert Spencer and Walter Burley Griffin had been opening up space in their own designs during this decade, but it is Wright's manner of addition by subtraction that distinguishes his contribution. Seeing his beliefs confirmed in the art of Hiroshige, he makes bold moves with the constituent elements in home construction, shifting the fireplace to main floor center so it could bear the weight of floor and roof. With the need for bearing walls removed, it becomes apparent that the main floor's openness is not an L but an abbreviated U, as the dining room continues unobstructed until a built-in hutch and door mark off the kitchen. The unity of flow is underscored both outside and inside: by the wood bands that wrap the exterior and by its echoed motif inside as a shelf that runs beneath the living room ceiling and continues into the dining room, an effect seen most dramatically in the George Stockman House (1908) in Mason City, Iowa.

The Stockman residence and another for Stephen M. N. Hunt (1907) in LaGrange, Illinois, are the main examples of Wright's design, which turns out not to be fireproof because stucco rather than concrete would be a more practical building material for structures this small. Unity Temple in Oak Park, however, was the size and shape for building with concrete. In its cube-shaped sanctuary Wright's vision fulfills itself perfectly; the "fireproof houses" are meant to suggest a cube, but are in fact a bit wider than they are tall.

Unity Temple also figures in Wright's major essay, "In the Cause of Architecture," appearing in the March 1908 issue of *The Architectural Record*, accompanied by eighty-seven photographs and drawings of Wright's work, already built or projected. Here was the chance for the architect to review his two decades of practice. Fame and the greatest number of commissions had come in the past seven years, but to claim credit for his foresight Wright begins with a tip of the hat to his own Evanston lecture of 1894, in which he set down propositions that now, in the light of experience, may be judged concisely.

Quickly Wright marks them off: simplicity and repose achieved by reducing the number of rooms while making openings between them integral features of structure and form, complemented by lack of inorganic decoration and use of built-ins for furniture and appliances; no single type of home, but rather as many kinds as there are different clients; building naturally from the site; natural colors; materials used true to their own nature; and the belief that a house with character will ultimately outvalue any currently prevailing mode.

This new succinctness of purpose benefits by dropping the preacherly tone of the 1894 address. As befits modern times, moral reasons for building this way need no longer be cited. But two other imperatives are developed at length. One is that a building should grow comfortably from its site to harmonize with its surroundings—with natural features if they are present but, if they are not, in as peaceful and organic a manner as if Nature herself were doing the construction. This proviso is a key one, answering in advance how a so-called Prairie House could be built where there was no prairie in evidence. It's the mood of the prairie Wright seeks, not any decorative effect. Its quiet level is the architect's goal, achieved with the now familiar gentle slopes of the roof, sheltering eaves, terraces that lead inward and rooms that reach out to private gardens. Here is the Prairie House that may have been in the back of Wright's mind in 1894 but would not be built until 1901. Another aspect expanded upon from its mention in the title of Wright's 1894 speech is how the machine is the normal, practical tool of present civilization that challenges the user to choose it for work that can be done with integrity.

In addition to refining his aesthetic and letting it stand on the basis of beauty rather than morality, Wright can by 1908 identify who will seek this style of housing. Fifteen years into independent practice and with the Prairie House established as his unique contribution to the architectural milieu, Wright looks to his client base and finds not Reverend Gannett's loving family nor those of the Arts and Crafts commune but American businessmen with unspoiled instincts and untainted ideals. The architect knows this type well, having socialized with them in Chicago suburbs such as Oak Park, River Forest, and Riverside. Men like this form their own personal and professional judgments and common sense appeals to them. Culture in terms of prettified historical styles is of no interest. Like Wright himself, they are interested in such new devices as motorcars, and some will have dabbled in inventing versions for manufacture. Others will have manufactured and marketed new forms of ornamental metal, window glass, soap powder, and the like. One of them, the remarkable Darwin D. Martin, reorganized a rather homely mail-order firm, the Larkin company, along lines that would become characteristic of twentieth-century efficiency, productivity, and marketing. Their favorite politician was Teddy Roosevelt, himself an image of the era's ideals when it came to intelligent, forward-looking action. They were a coherent group, and Wright was ready to give them what he believed they needed for their home life and work.

Leonard K. Easton contrasts Wright's remarkable clients with the more conventional buyers of the day in *Two Chicago Architects and Their Clients: Frank Lloyd Wright and Howard Van Doren Shaw* (1969). While Shaw's homes were not quite the period monstrosities Wright describes, they bespeak tradition in both function and form—in other words, with little or no correlation between the two. Wright's designs express a natural harmony between ground plan and elevation and an integration of the whole that makes any of his houses a practical pleasure and an aesthetic joy to live in. Wright's businessmen are Progressives—in politics, social thought, and in the modern ways they have developed their enterprises and industries. Their wives fit this type as well: educated not in finishing schools but at universities, conscientious about social reform, and in many cases militant about women's rights, starting with the right to vote, a major issue of the time. At least one would distinguish herself as a feminist. In some cases it was the wives who chose the architect: the Coonley House (1907) commission owes as much or more to Queene as to Avery, for it was she who wanted Wright's integrity of design. In similar manner, the Cheney House (1903) stands as much for Mamah's thinking as it does for Edwin's—with tragic consequences for both the Cheney and Wright families. The businessmen stand out not for their riches or social connections, but for innovations at work and in their personal lives: Frederick C. Robie, for example, a man with no consuming interest in the arts, was told repeatedly "you want one of those damned Wright houses," and who in Frank Lloyd Wright found a man much of his own type, someone he could talk with and be both understood and inspired by.

Future decades would produce more clients who kept up with or were ahead of their times, including Edgar J. Kaufmann for Fallingwater (1935) and Herbert F. Johnson for the S. C. Johnson Administration Building (1936), Wingspread (1937), and the S. C. Johnson Research Tower (1944). Even in Wright's next phase, providing Usonian designs for those with fewer resources, his clients would be noteworthy for their progressive work in such fields as journalism (Herbert and Katherine Jacobs First House, 1936) and education (Jean S. and Paul R. Hanna House, Honeycomb, 1937). That Wright could gauge a client's suitability is shown by his ultimate success with a unique taproot design for a seventeen-story skyscraper. In 1929 the client was the Reverend William

Norman Guthrie, socially progressive rector of St. Mark's in lower Manhattan who was seeking efficient housing for his parishioners as well as devotional space. The stock market crash put a halt to the project, but twenty-three years later Wright would resurrect the design in radically different times for a startlingly different purpose in a distant and distinct part of the country: in Bartlesville, Oklahoma, as an office tower (1952) for oil pipeline builder Harold C. Price, Sr., whose openness to innovation matched Guthrie's. Today the Price Tower thrives as an arts center and boutique hotel, but through all of its uses the design speaks for Wright's canniness in finding clients who could share his vision.

And so in 1908 Wright stands confident in mastery of his design and familiarity with the type of client he can expect to work with. The world he builds in is certainly no longer Victorian, but neither does it partake of the emerging modern — and is nothing like the International Style of modernism that would emerge in the late 1920s and be a powerful architectural mode for decades to come. In fact, the architect's thinking looks to an era well beyond the modern, to a time when theorists were finding the same flaws in a lapsed modernism that Frank Lloyd Wright voiced about it when it was still a nascent style. One cannot call Wright's architecture postmodern, for in this field the term refers to a specifically self-conscious use of historical features with quotability in mind; his buildings look nothing like the postmodern architecture built in the 1970s and 1980s. But when one considers postmodernism in the broader sense of a manner of thinking that informs philosophy and (most dramatically) literature, then some of Wright's comments from 1908 skip over the modern era entirely in order to embrace the organic school of design that has reemerged in the early twenty-first century. His work is more celebrated now than in the decades immediately following his death, when what was called "postmodern architecture" lagged well behind the innovations of postmodern thought.

When "In the Cause of Architecture" calls for "a significant grammatical expression" that makes "the whole, as nearly as I could, consistent," both the organic and the intellectually postmodern come to mind. Grammar and syntax are linguistic terms, and were used that way by Saussure in 1907, but in much later times these words and the principles behind them start being used as a way of discussing ideas, whether of reason or the imagination, in what would be called literary postmodernism.

An integrity of grammar produces an integral whole, Wright believes, and continues with another anticipation of postmodern thought by considering how the newly democratic nature of his age not only broadens education and raises intelligence but allows for the existence of not just one dominant style but any number of individual styles. The more individual the better, for if the motive is genuinely organic the result, however various, will have the beauty and integrity of good design. At that point nobility in architecture becomes possible, but only because Americans will have demanded it from new practitioners as they come on the scene.

What can inhibit demand? Satisfaction with inorganic architecture, of course. Here is where the most common practice of late twentieth-century thought clarifies what Wright is not only arguing for but reasoning against over sixty years before. The central analytical practice he anticipates is called Deconstruction, introduced by the French philosopher Jacques Derrida and since the late 1960s used widely by American academics both in philosophy and literature. Deconstruction, like the semiotic belief in the value of working with culture on the level of signs, is obvious, calling as it does for the interrogation of what underlies any assumption. Admitting that a belief is nothing but an assumption is a revolutionary idea, growing slowly from the notion first advanced in anthropology that one culture's reality is simply a description or an account, and that any valuation can be made not in universal terms but only in judging the persuasiveness of that account. Deconstruction applies this method to beliefs that have stood as absolute, often finding that behind these absolutes are the most conventional of assumptions. It is just these assumptions that Wright uncovers in his study of how an inorganic architecture has been resisted for what he calls literary reasons.

His buildings have a sound preparation at ground level, Wright indicates, "and it is the first grammatical expression of all the types" (*CW* I: 93) in his canon that he now surveys. The integral workings of grammar and syntax hold them together and identify them as a self-apparent system, *his* way of doing things as opposed to others. Supports for these buildings, for example, are placed inside the wall rather than outside so that the outer base can appear for what it really is, an essentially horizontal element. Fenestration is handled differently too, with windows grouped rhythmically in horizontal bands. Casements replace sashes and more than compensate for any reduction in ventilation, illumination, and view. Indeed, there is as much of those features as any client could wish without making empty stylistic gestures. Floor plans are axial and order the space according to specific units for each structure. Never is a pretty picture the goal, but rather a scheme making sense in all three dimensions. Wright has great faith that if the building is put together with all the proportions being derived organically the picturesque will take care of itself in an appealing manner. In truth, there is no choice, no way extraneous concerns can rightly interfere, because the design's generating principles have determined how things will come out. A perspective drawing will agree that the organic design is correct, but there is no proof residing in the drawing itself.

Taking advantage of the magazine's eighty-seven illustrations of his buildings, Wright shows how his design is a matter of grammar and syntax by reducing their groupings to three. There are those with low-pitched hip roofs (such as those for Winslow, Willits, and Coonley), others with low roofs and simple pediments sitting on long ridges (such as Hickox House and Dana House), and a third group topped with a simple slab (for which Unity Temple and the fireproof design for *The Ladies' Home Journal* serve as the best examples). Wright presents this same three-part grouping two years later in his Introduction to the Wasmuth portfolio, an even more imposing presentation of his work, and its distinctions encompass key elements of his work to that date. But even for the great art museum that opened in 1959 on upper Fifth Avenue, the organic principles espoused in this 1908 essay hold true; it is just the shape that differs, and that because of the building's purpose: it is a comfortable way to walk through an art exhibition. The Guggenheim, after all, spirals *down* for the ease of its museum-goers, while at the same time it reaches up to complete its form. Form and function are one, here in complementary dimensions, just as the three styles of roofs differentiate the three groups of smaller buildings. Each group grows from its base in an integral manner, because the particular type of roof tops off its organic growth.

Having identified his clients and described his manner of building for them in an organic manner, Wright pauses to consider how customer and architect can best work together. Because the nature of each already has been clarified, there should be no trouble. After all, an individual shows his or her true character in the choice of an architect, and trusts that in the relationship with the architect this character will be revealed. That's how close the bond between the two is. Put to work, the latter will idealize the former's personality and taste, providing a house felt to be uniquely suitable. Yet that house, so intimately representative of its owner, still speaks for the character of its creator, just as any portrait by a great master will be as forever recognizable for its painter as for its subject. Wright has argued before that clients should trust him, but here he goes so far as to say that in serving that trust he is designing for the ages.

Familiar thoughts round out the piece. Any decorations should be *of* the surface, never *on* it. Limitations are any artist's best friend. Coping with the machine opens new avenues of democracy. Simplicity is not an end, but a means. A good sense of that end, an integral fashioning of the whole, is suggested by the qualities of Japanese woodblock prints. How will these elements shape Wright's work in the future? He predicts a simplicity of expression that says more with fewer lines, accomplishes more with less work, is more plastic and fluent and therefore more coherent, which is to say organic. As Frank Lloyd Wright lists these qualities, it is easy to foresee the textile block houses in California, the labor-saving Usonians, the soaring plasticity of the great workroom at the S. C. Johnson Administration Building, the remarkable fluency of Fallingwater, and even the more organic shape of the Guggenheim. "In the Cause of Architecture" is a statement from an architect having great current success with the Prairie House, but the essay expresses what would be a lifetime of developments.

1909, the year that separates this essay from Wright's Introduction to the Wasmuth portfolio, would be the first of several traumatically disruptive years in his life. Far more dramatic and tragic incidents would follow, but in terms of all he had achieved the events of 1909 qualify as life- and career-changing. His family was a large and apparently happy one, the children bright and lively and wife Catherine uncommonly devoted—to him, but even more so to the children, which was one source of Wright's problems. His architectural practice was flourishing, and in the 1908 essay he proudly lists his busy group of young associates—two more areas of concern, both the heavy workload on Wright and the growing difficulties in keeping such a stable of talent under control and unthreatening to his ego. Not mentioned in the essay, of course, is his affair with Mamah Borthwick Cheney. But in the stature he now accords himself, not just as an architect but as an artist, an artist of great genius to whom clients have been drawn as if by magic and to whom they should concede their every desire, it is hard not to see the type of person who would abandon wife, children, and work for a great love, no matter how scandalous and destructive that abandonment might be.

Personally, the events of 1909 comprised a flight to Europe with Mamah. Professionally, they involved putting what remained of his practice in the care of Hermann von Holst (after the more appropriate Marion Mahony and several others declined it), meeting in Germany with the publisher of his architectural portfolio, and settling in Italy where he, his son Lloyd, and his draftsman Taylor Woolley prepared drawings, with Mamah present as a housemate. Many friends and clients terminated their relationships with Wright; a few key people stayed with him, through this and much worse to come. On his and Mamah's return to the United States in 1911, he'd build Taliesin, a complex of structures that would exercise his talents for organic architecture in a manner so dramatic that only Fallingwater, designed a quarter century later, could even begin to approach its amazing achievements with domestic space.

Yet through all of this his thinking as expressed in the 1908 essay for *The Architectural Record* remains consistent, as evidenced by his Introduction to the Wasmuth project, *Ausgeführte Bauten und Entwürfe von Frank Lloyd Wright* (1910). The portfolio features seventy-two drawings of Wright's work, both built and as projected (as the title says). In 1911 the same publisher would issue a collection of photographs depicting Wright's structures as they appeared at the time, but it is the 1910 volume, known as the Wasmuth portfolio, that crowns Wright's achievement and publicizes it to an eager European audience. Among its readers would be the leading young architects of Holland, Germany, France, and Austria. In the portfolio they see not inadequate photographs but renderings drawn appealingly in the manner of Japanese prints. Some had been done by Marion Mahony, traced over in ink by Wright and his helpers in Fiesole so that printer's plates could be made. And introducing it all was a nine-thousand-word treatise by Frank Lloyd Wright showing that despite all the changes in his personal and professional life he was still in absolute control of his canon.

The basis of that control is actually broadened in his initial comments, which flatter his European readership. As always, he encourages architecture that harmonizes with the happiness of life, but now he adds a new locale to those celebrated in *The House Beautiful* and old Japanese prints. Italy has been his proof positive for the joy of living, he reports, having reposed so pleasantly near Florence this past year. All the things art can make, from paintings and structures to buildings themselves, "sing themselves into being," like wildflowers. His romance with Mamah surely contributes to this enchantment, but it is an organic (and not romantic) principle he senses at work, with the growth of their love being "the very music of life" (*CW* I: 103). The principle, after all, is a universal one, common to primitive structures and achieved in civilized building when the natural impulse to build is not corrupted by what Wright would disparagingly call "the literary." What he has seen in and around Fiesole, where he and Mamah have been so happy, confirms his hope for the organic. Italian buildings rest easily, he attests; everything is content with its factors of existence and comfortable in its surroundings. And what lovely surroundings, Wright enthuses. A cypress tree grows into a perfectly balanced composition, making all complete. In Wright's Italy, life and art are one, perhaps because his own existence was now proceeding that way.

These words are apt description of the love nest he shares with Mamah; photos of the Villino Belvedere in the Wright Archive show how the architect framed his views to convey these qualities. The nearby Villa Medici, with its dramatic wrapping of the hillside, "of it and not on it" as Wright liked to say, would inspire his drawings of a fancied home in Tuscany and a very real one in Wisconsin, an estate he'd name Taliesin ("shining brow" in Welsh) and build the next year. For now, it is helpful to see how these attitudes and plans are foregrounded in this most important Introduction, the testament around which would be built his international fame.

His principles, familiar to readers of his *Architectural Record* essay of two years before, come quickly and naturally from his context established in the hills above Florence. Beauty expresses fundamental proportions in color, line, and form. These are the conditions of its existence, and that existence is a natural phenomenon. What corrupts it? False education, Wright announces, a matter of confusing curiosities with objects of beauty. The low point for this was the Renaissance: what's needed is

a return to harmony with nature such as the Gothic had achieved before the Renaissance undid it, an action that was less a development than
a disease. Harmonies are internal; they cannot be imposed. The best
chance for organic architecture to flourish now is in America, where
democracy empowers individuals to have their homes built to please.
And the ideal clients Wright identified in his 1908 essay are people in
his part of the country, where open-mindedness and independent thinking help common sense prevail in art as well as life. These are Wright's
own people, and are his partners in making organic architecture possible. As lovely as Tuscany has been, the architect's greatest sympathies
remain back home. There he and his clients share a bond that will get
them the homes they deserve. Yes, he is an artist, but part of that art
resides in a sensitivity to a client's nature. Each party educates the other,
each having "something to grow into" (*CW* I: 110).

There has certainly been growth for Wright, and he has been careful
to parallel his changes in material circumstance with his developing
ideas. From the happy world of Fiesole that marks the beginning of his
Introduction to the example of where his hopes for architecture can best
be realized, he has taken his readers through the present phase of his
life: a flight to Italy, where he has found happiness, and an impending
return to America, where that happiness can be built into a harmonious
personal and professional life. These are hopes, of course, and reality
would present challenges that could not be foreseen. But Wright would
overcome those challenges with his principles for architecture intact,
just as they have survived this first set of changes in his life and practice.

The Wasmuth Introduction concludes with thoughts of how organic
architecture can be taught—by approaching the beautiful from within—
and a review of the three groups of buildings that manage to harmonize
into a coherent canon. The last word is saved for America, and surely
reflects Wright's plans for returning to his ancestral homeland, the
Helena Valley near Spring Green, Wisconsin, and building his notion
of a perfect home. From his retreat in Fiesole, Frank Lloyd Wright describes Taliesin as it would rise in Wisconsin. But there is a temptation,
grounded in the view anyone can take today, that it is not just Wright's
1911 home but his entire estate, added to and built up over coming
decades and modified on an annual basis until the year he died, that was
in his vision.

The Helena Valley, sometimes called the Jones Valley or "the valley of the God-Almighty Joneses" as locals fancied it and Wright's youngest sister titled her 1965 memoir, consists of land once farmed by the architect's grandfather and uncles. As a boy, young Frank would come out from Madison and work all summer on his Uncle James's farm. In 1876 a nine-year-old Frank Lincoln Wright, who would not substitute his mother's middle name for his own until after his parents divorced in 1885, could walk down the lane from Uncle James's farm to where the valley opens to view and enjoy the panorama stretching invitingly to the north. Nearby sits the Lloyd Jones graveyard, where in 1886 a friend of Uncle Jenkin's, the Chicago architect Joseph Lyman Silsbee, designed a meeting house named Unity Chapel. As an aspiring architect taking engineering courses at the University of Wisconsin, Frank would be invited to help with the interior. Another quarter mile down the road is the site of Frank's first complete building, a large shingle-style Queen Anne housing his aunts Nell and Jane's Hillside Home School I, which Wright would design in 1887 from the Silsbee Studio in Chicago where he'd taken work. Behind it in 1902 he'd design a second Hillside School, which in the 1930s would be adapted and enlarged for the Taliesin Fellowship. Straight ahead young Frank could see another hillside, this one a site for the Midway Barns he'd design to serve his estate in 1938. And to the right, a third hillside, a commanding feature visible a mile away from Uncle James's lane: the place where in 1911 Frank Lloyd Wright would build the house named Taliesin.

In *An Autobiography* (1932), Wright stops short of allowing himself this vision as a nine-year-old, but given his egotism and precocity readers would not have been surprised if he had. As is, the book opens with the boy accompanying his uncle on a hill-climb through fresh winter snow. There's a lesson involved, as the uncle has set his sights on a distant hilltop and is heading straight for it, with little Frank beside him. But when the summit is reached, their tracks in the snow reveal how Frank's course has departed from his uncle's straight line, zigzagging this way and that with almost every step as distractions beckoned. The treasures he's been seeking are weeds, the dried stalks of prairie flowers sticking up through the snow. In subsequent pages he describes this same hillside in spring, where the fresh blooms of pasque flowers reach up through melting snow. On lovely summer days he flees there to escape work and revels in the joys of nature. He loves the spot, as will Mamah in 1911, a Fellowship of hundreds in the 1930s, 1940s, and 1950s, and countless visitors since the property was opened to view in 1991. The spot young Frank has been seeking in all seasons is precisely where he'd build when reorganizing his life and work. Its siting and materials help make Taliesin an especially appealing example of organic architecture. Today it continues to function as an icon of Frank Lloyd Wright's achievement.

Wright's major essay from this period that brackets his building of Taliesin in 1911 and the fire that destroyed its living quarters in August of 1914 reflects his changed conditions. As visualized from Italy, life with Mamah in rural Wisconsin would be paradise, and the home he designed fit that purpose. But scandal dogged him; newspapers in Chicago kept his reputation in tatters, and while some people in Spring Green were kind to Mamah, others were not. A trip to Japan in pursuit of the Imperial Hotel commission got him many fine prints but not, quite yet, the job, and work on the Midway Gardens entertainment center in Chicago was impeded at times by the client's inadequate capital. It is from this context that "In the Cause of Architecture: Second Paper" emerges. Appearing in the May 1914 issue of *The Architectural Record*, it strikes a very different tone from its 1908 predecessor and the 1910 Wasmuth portfolio Introduction. Those pieces overflowed with confidence and optimism. Now in 1914, for the first time in his career, Wright is something else, something that does not befit him: he is defensive.

The last time this journal's readers had heard from Frank Lloyd Wright he was not only showing off his personal successes but crediting the associates in his Studio. Budding architects had been drawn to him by sympathy with his work, with which they have loyally assisted, Wright had boasted in 1908, and went so far as to list their names and seniority in "our little university of fourteen years standing" (*CW* I: 99), an impressive list that included Marion Mahony, Walter Burley Griffin, Barry Byrne, and William Drummond, among others. Now, six years later, they are all gone, just as the Oak Park Studio is no more, having been converted to living quarters for Catherine and the younger children so the Home itself can be rented out for income. That's not mentioned in the new essay, of course, nor are the former associates' names, even though several have become well-known architects in their own right. This, Wright feels, is the problem: they have gone off to exploit a new school of architecture that confounds the master himself.

Wright still has his ideals, but now they are expressed negatively. Corrupting a young country's architectural future is to damage what is most precious to it, he warns. On the positive side, he still believes in the ideal of an organic architecture, but also knows that only integrity of instinct and intelligence can move this ideal forward into practice. In beginning his own practice many years before, he'd had the advantage of going into domestic architecture, an area his own master, Louis Sullivan, had left virtually untouched. Therefore Wright could say now, with no small pride, that he broke new ground and did what he needed "alone—absolutely alone" (*CW* I: 127).

One gets the feeling that he would like to be alone now as well. As a result, he claims far too many vulnerabilities and, even worse, gives himself far too much credit for a movement that has been much larger than himself. Claiming to have launched the movement, he now lacks strength to protect and direct it. The field of architecture has become awash with imitations that trade on the movement's name but in fact weaken the cause as mere novelty. Integrity and core values are set aside in favor of bald-faced careerism. At least Wright knows who is responsible for all this: himself! For he's the one who in the Studio's unique situation provided just the right innovations at precisely the right time, and never in doses too strong or too soon.

Wright does not mention the projects that in the New School of the Middle West are losing touch with organic ideals, but the most grievous error is that they "*trade long on mere forms*" (*CW* I: 130). Those forms were once an outgrowth of the original work's integrity. But now they are being repeated ad nauseum. It's a fair guess to say which projects Wright had in mind: the development in Decatur, Illinois, on Milliken Place, completed by Marion Mahony with assistance from Walter Burley Griffin and Hermann von Holst beginning in 1909, and perhaps more homes in Mason City, Iowa, where Griffin (again with Mahony's help, and later Barry Byrne's) developed the larger Rock Crest / Rock Glen community. Wright does not name them in his essay, nor does he analyze just why any of the structures in them fail as organic architecture. He certainly exceeds the limits of even alternative history by supposing that both projects could have been his own and would have been had he not left for two years in Europe just as their planning was to begin. The formulation is implied, but simple: the developers had wanted Wright, and when they lost him turned to associates from his Studio who could please them just as well—with a copy of Wright! And by definition any copy is *not* organic architecture. No matter that Griffin and Mahony initiated the Iowa project and that Griffin's house for Joshua Melson (1912) was more organic than Wright's copy of the Isabel Roberts House (1908) as proposed to this same client. When personally piqued, Frank Lloyd Wright and his thought do not show well.

With this, written expressions of Wright's thinking are put on hold by the tragic events that overtook Taliesin and its occupants on 15 August 1914. Frank Lloyd Wright was in Chicago, at work with his son John on Midway Gardens. But Mamah was not alone. Her children, a son and a daughter, were visiting her from Oak Park. After serving lunch, a deranged servant sealed all but one exit, spread gasoline, set the house on fire, and murdered Mamah, her children, and four others from the studio and estate as they tried to escape the conflagration. Receiving the ghastly news in Chicago, Wright returned to a scene he would later describe as the death of all his dreams.

It is a cliché to say that Wright assuaged his grief by throwing himself into work, but that is exactly what he did, clearing the rubble and beginning at once to rebuild. Not until *An Autobiography* was published in 1932 would he comment publically on the murders and his loss; the five hundred words he titled "On Marriage" (1915) were saved for himself, and speak to his and Mamah's quest for reform without any mention of the previous year's tragic event. The idealism of their love is what he wishes to preserve, and does, just as the rebuilt Taliesin would be a living example of the world they had hoped to continue sharing.

Yet Wright's behavior continued to generate scandal. Among the many condolences he received was a letter from a total stranger, Miriam Noel, expressing not just her sympathy but attesting a great affinity she shared with Wright as an artist. They met in Chicago and soon became lovers, all of this just four months after the murders and fire. Miriam was now the mistress of Taliesin in both senses of this term, and once again Chicago newspapers and Spring Green locals clucked in disapproval. To make things worse, the relationship was tempestuous. Miriam was a morphine addict and subject to great swings of mood. Wright himself was not the easiest person to get along with, and Catherine's refusal to grant a divorce added more tension. When she finally relented and Frank and Miriam married in November of 1923, things only got worse. Miriam was soon threatening divorce herself, on increasingly preposterous and vituperative terms. Soon after the two separated, Frank met Olgivanna Ivanovna Lazovich. Nearly thirty years younger than Wright, she was recently divorced from a Russian architect ten years her senior, Vlademar Hinzenberg. In Europe she had been a disciple of Georgei Ivanovitch Gurdjieff, participating in his dance ensembles and allied mystic activities. Still legally married to Miriam, Frank nonetheless began a relationship with Olgivanna, who'd bear him a daughter, Iovanna, late in 1925. Taliesin now had its third mistress. Miriam threatened lawsuits, criminal prosecution, and deportation (for Olgivanna, not yet a U.S. citizen). To complete the spectacle, the residential portion of Taliesin burned again, this time the result of an electrical short during a thunderstorm in April 1925.

Needless to say, during this period of the 1910s and early 1920s Frank Lloyd Wright was better known for his unconventional life than for his innovative architecture. He needn't have worried that his former Oak Park Studio associates would cheapen and destroy the Prairie House; by 1915 it had gone out of fashion, replaced by renewed interest in the eclecticism of period styles, with members of what Wright had called the New School of the Middle West either adapting to current fashion or leaving the profession. One last piece of writing from these years speaks for Wright's interests as they had developed over the past decades: the "Plan by Frank Lloyd Wright" published in the May 1916 issue of *City Residential Land Development*. In it he actually turns the table on a former associate by devising an exercise in town planning, the specialty of Walter Burley Griffin, whose "Competitive Plan for a 'Scheme of Development for a Quarter Section of Land in Chicago'" (1913) and "Trier Center Neighborhood and Other Domestic Communities" (1913) drew much attention in Chicago even as the younger man was preparing to move to Australia (*WWBG*, 182–97). Wright's and Griffin's plans are similar, in that within the urban grid they devise new street systems and siting of houses that create much more pleasant neighborhoods. Griffin staggers his houses, while Wright's are rotated 90 degrees so that each home provides a different perspective for its occupants and sits differently as viewed by others. While the senior architect relates his design to principle, that problems are solved not by working from the outside but from within, his former associate devises an even more attractive plan by means of better circulation and occupancy (his own mantra) in which a few more building lots are provided even as space is reserved for neighborhood parks.

As for Chicago itself, Wright did not have much work there during these years, beyond Midway Gardens. His attorney, Sherman Booth, commissioned a small development in the Ravine Bluffs area of the far north suburb of Glencoe (1915), but most of Wright's business was in Wisconsin: an impressive residence for Frederick C. Bogk (1915) in Milwaukee, a program for pre-cut housing to be marketed by another Milwaukeean, Arthur L. Richards, from 1915 to 1917, two sets of duplex apartment complexes in Milwaukee for Richards and Arthur R. Munkwitz (1916), and the imposing A. D. German Warehouse (1915) in Richland Center. Yet the architect maintained a small Chicago office and never let the city forget him. In 1917 the Arts Club of Chicago hosted an exhibition of his Japanese prints, and the next year he presented an address to the Women's Aid Organization. Whether the women liked what they heard was less important to Frank Lloyd Wright than the fact they were hearing him out about a controversial topic, "Chicago Culture."

As always, he speaks on principle, here the one that culture like art itself is a matter of expression from within rather than the application of something from without. It must be realized, Wright argues, not just accumulated; produced, and not merely purchased. But instead of a scathing attack on this practice, he prefers amusement: he tells a story about Howard Van Doren Shaw, an architect of a different manner entirely but a friend nevertheless. One of Shaw's richer clients was well traveled and had become infatuated with the Petit Trianon at Versailles. She wanted it for a house, but it was too low. "So Mr. Shaw put another story in the Trianon for her. If he had not done it someone else would have and probably would have done it worse," Wright allows, adding that Shaw himself disagreed with the generosity of this appraisal (*CW* I: 155).

After a few more funny examples, Wright woos his audience by naming Chicago's great legitimate cultural successes. Everything from Margaret Anderson's *Little Review* to Jane Addams's Hull House gets praise, along with a few of the city's architects: Louis Sullivan, of course, but also John Wellborn Root and Daniel Burnham. Plus one more, unnamed, but described by a person no less than Hendrik Petrus Berlage—when this giant of European architecture came seeking evidence of American culture, what impressed him most were Niagara Falls and the Larkin Building. And guess who designed the Larkin Building?

Wright had found in Chicago's neighborhoods and suburbs a welcome environment for his innovations of the previous decade, but these present years were demanding that he look elsewhere for better work. And he had been, looking eastward for a great opportunity. Not to America's east coast, or back to Europe, where he'd found shelter and a sense of respite, but all the way around the globe to the Far East. For more than ten years, from 1913 to 1924, Japan would claim the center of his attention.

3

Japan and After

THE ART OF JAPAN IS NOT AN INFLUENCE *on* the work of Frank Lloyd Wright, but has an affinity *with* his work, as he insists throughout his career. This claim is not surprising, because Wright likes nothing that is applied. A house such as Taliesin is *of* the hill, not on it. A style of art comes from *within* the artist as a manner of expression, and cannot be adopted from without. This is the organic principle, and when considering the art of Japan Wright is consistent with his key belief.

Although his written comments on Japanese art first appear in 1906 and reach a fullness of expression by 1912, his thinking about the subject becomes creative (rather than simply reflective) after 1913. This is the year he returns to Japan not as a tourist, collector, or student of architecture but as an architect in search of work—work that will be *of* Japan and not just another Western imposition on it. In 1913 he is accompanied by Mamah. On his subsequent trips through 1922 Miriam will accompany him and share his household, which consists of an apartment he designs for an annex of the old Imperial Hotel he intends to replace with a striking new one. When he takes ill, his mother Anna crosses the Pacific to care for him. Even more so than in 1905, Wright immerses himself in Japanese art and culture, but never in a sense of imitation or even absorption. Although enjoying home life in Wisconsin, business in Chicago, and the fascination of a new commission in Los Angeles, in Japan he can be himself in a context where the surrounding world seems to share more of his own values.

In 1917, with the commission for the Imperial Hotel in hand and work already underway, he takes time to organize an exhibition of his Japanese art collection for the Arts Club of Chicago. Its catalogue is not

62

illustrated, but the architect supplies a text: "Antique Color Prints from the Collection of Frank Lloyd Wright." This initiates his creative thinking about the medium of print-making, thinking that will reveal even deeper affinities with his sense of the organic in architecture. Because these prints have been stamped on a medium subject to change and by a means that could not copy itself, the product is unique—and therefore alive. Any Hiroshige prints of the same subject are so differently executed that each is its own design. This new appreciation for the vital nature of the art informs an unpublished essay from the same year, "The Print and the Renaissance" (1917). Here Wright quickly reviews his credo of how art from the Far East escaped the literalization of art imposed by the Renaissance and offers hope for a regained sense of the organic—and then announces that the principle of the print interests him more than any particular examples of it.

Growing from his exhibition catalogue comments, this interest focuses on the print's medium and production. As always, Wright values the integrity of a means that reaches an end, but now he can add that the Japanese woodblock acknowledges itself as a print and wishes to be nothing more. Of importance to today's readers is Wright's regret that such an aesthetic no longer exists. It is rare for 1917 and continued to be throughout the era of high modernism. But in the 1950s and 1960s the critic Harold Rosenberg would celebrate a newly emergent self-apparency in the medium and production of abstract expressionist painting, notably that of Willem de Kooning and Hans Hofmann. And in the 1970s writers such as Ronald Sukenick and William H. Gass would fight against the same sense of literalness that Wright decries, urging instead a style in which words function less as representations of a subject than in their own existence as made objects, or at the very least as signs existing in the theory of grammar and syntax known as semiology.

We know how much Frank Lloyd Wright values the integral workings of grammar and syntax in organic architecture. It certainly set his thinking apart from the Victorian tradition into which he was born. But in his essays we see him complaining that architecture by and for others is not developing as he thinks it should. Indeed, by the time "modernism" is widely established Wright becomes one of its most vocal opponents. But not because he wants a return to anything Victorian. Instead, he calls for something even modern literature would not have, which is a comfort with its own medium and means of production in the service not of representation but of itself. The Japanese print could do this, but it is a creature of a century and more before. American painting and fiction writing would eventually do this, but not until times had changed and a new manner of thought emerged.

Wright's praise for the nature of the Japanese print reads much like Harold Rosenberg's advocacy of abstract expressionism in *The Tradition of the New* (1959) and *The Anxious Object* (1964). It also fits comfortably with what William H. Gass and Ronald Sukenick say in *Fiction and the Figures of Life* (1970) and *In Form: Digressions on the Act of Fiction* (1985) respectively. Sukenick's use of the word "act" rather than "art" reflects his book's point: that fiction is not about something, but rather is that something itself. Consider how similar is Wright's appreciation of the print, especially how color "is used for its own sake," how "every circumstance of its making is delightfully confessed in the result," and "the craft of the print is integral with its Art" (*CW* I: 150). Art and act are the same, just as "line has a language of its own regardless of a sheep or a hearse or any picture of anything" and just as "color has qualities all its own akin to music and that color like sound has notes precious for their own sake" (*CW* I: 151). Lines and color stand a better chance of being accepted like the notes of music than do words, but the innovative fictionists of the 1960s and 1970s strive for it nonetheless. As William H. Gass admits, "That novels should be made of words, and merely words, is shocking, really. It's as though you had discovered that your wife were made of rubber: the bliss of all those years, the fears . . . from sponge" (*Fiction and the Figures of Life*, 27, ellipsis in original).

Story commands a powerful sense of fascination. It can overrule all else, not just in fiction but in any form of art or even in the notion of art itself, as Wright rues damage done by the literal as imposed by the Renaissance. Hence his delight with a Japanese master who works with color and line, who discovers that they can be arranged to generate wonderful moods without having to tell a story—even though music itself sometimes perversely and unnecessarily mimics a narrative. Consider Ronald Sukenick's similar endorsement of the nonliteral purpose of fiction: "It transmits feeling, energy, excitement. Television can give us the news, but fiction can best express our response to the news" (*In Form*, 242). None of this is art for art's sake, a charge possible in light of what

Walter Pater and Oscar Wilde had done with John Ruskin's aesthetics and one actually made half a century later against the innovative fictionists. "Art for art's sake" is in truth "art for the artist's sake" and not the viewer's. Instead, both Wright and Sukenick emphasize the response to such work, the moods created, the feeling and energy and excitement, even the spirituality aroused. And how is this done? Not by privileging the artist's self-expression, but rather by acknowledging the materiality of his or her medium of art in a way the work's audience can share.

At the time, Frank Lloyd Wright's principal work is in Japan, and this time not as a print collector but as an architect. Yet he still has the culture of America on his mind, especially its wellbeing in the future. And here is where his thoughts on Japanese art and culture become pertinent not just in 1917 but for the entire century that follows. Why must things be patched on? he sighs. Is it not better to develop from within, making it stand for nothing other than itself? A new country, such as is Japan for him, becomes a fresh opportunity to do things right. This familiar call for the organic has now been enhanced by an appreciation of how art happens not by telling a story nor by effusing some personal sentiment, but by working with the materials of the medium *as materials*. By 1928, with his work in Japan not only completed but intact after surviving nature's greatest challenge, a major earthquake, he will be subtitling his habitual "In the Cause of Architecture" essays with a qualification, "The Meaning of Materials." The development of his thought is significant, for now he sees that he is creating not as God but in God's manner, making his work of this same kind. Has Japan enhanced Wright's ego? Probably so. But his understanding of just how art operates has been deepened as well.

The Imperial Hotel in Tokyo carries a design date of 1916, for that is when he is officially hired. After an initial trip in 1913 and the opening of an office in Tokyo in 1915, Wright will spend much of the next six years travelling to and from and living in Japan. He writes about the hotel in 1922 (as it nears completion), in 1923 (after it survives the massive Kanto earthquake that leveled most of Tokyo), and in 1925 (for the Dutch publication *Wendingen*, seven issues of which are devoted to Wright and collected as *The Life-Work of the American Architect Frank Lloyd Wright*). But other things happen as well. Aline Barnsdall commissions a huge home and surrounding theater complex in Hollywood, California, which prompts Wright to open a Los Angeles office and look into relocating his practice there. But he also stays active in Chicago culture, organizing his print exhibition and speaking on "Chicago Culture," as noted. At this time, in 1918, he reconciles with his former master Louis Sullivan, from whom he'd been alienated since leaving Adler and Sullivan in 1893 for having taken bootleg commissions that violated his contract. Although Sullivan makes the first move toward reconciliation with a phone call, it is Wright who over the next six years will attend to his old mentor through hard times and personal deterioration, until the man's death in 1924. One year before that, Sullivan is able to repay the favor with a pair of essays on the success of Wright's Imperial Hotel. All these texts and activities must be considered as one piece, for they demonstrate an important transition in Wright's thinking.

His essays on the Imperial Hotel are written for three different publications and thus cover much of the same ground. Even the fact of the building's surviving the great earthquake on 1 September 1923 is not cause for anything significantly new, because Wright has been present for a smaller but significant tremor the year before, the worst in fifty years. He notes the hotel's imperviousness to this event in the first essay, which appears in Tokyo's *Kagaku Chishiki* for April of 1922, but only as confirming his integrity of design. The major point of this and the other pieces is that the Imperial departs from commonly imported styles of architecture, whether nineteenth-century grandeur or modern American skyscrapers, with earthquake survivability in mind. This is the major point of his pamphlet published in 1923, *Experimenting with Human Lives*, but all of Wright's commentaries on the hotel emphasize the unique suitability of its design and construction, based on a cantilever resting on supports sunk deep into the site's underlying mud. Seismic shocks are absorbed at base, while the structure itself has sufficient flexibility to withstand any shifting. In fact, the Kanto earthquake works for rather than against Wright's building, settling it into a natural position that closes fissures that had opened earlier during construction.

Another innovation equally pertinent to where it is built is the Imperial's purpose. Less than half of its space is for hotel rooms. The other portions serve the social needs of the Japanese as they meet and entertain foreign visitors. Here Wright's thinking takes another step not just out of Victorian style but beyond modernism itself. The Imperial is not a single structure, he explains, but is "laid out as a group of buildings in a system of gardens and terraces" as opposed to the manner of American hotels, which are more like office buildings. The beauty of the whole derives from each unit's integrity within the greater plan, as loggias and gardens share enough space that one can become the other. There are sunken gardens and even roof gardens, appropriate because "Japan is Garden-land" (*CW* I: 177). Repeated seven times in one sentence, the term "gardens" becomes exponential as if to infinity, Wright's prose giving readers a sense of what this "Garden-land" is. In 1954 Donald Barthelme, the son of a Wright-inspired architect and on his way to becoming a boldly innovative fictionist, would visit the hotel time and again when on leave from his duties as a soldier in Korea. "Don spent hours wandering the Imperial's halls, delighted by their unpredictable curves, admiring—with his father's eye—the way Wright had designed the floors to be supported by centered joists, like a waiter balancing a tray on his fingertips, so earth tremors wouldn't yank down the walls," says Tracy Daugherty in *Hiding Man: A Biography of Donald Barthelme* (2009, 104). The young Barthelme also thrilled to the interpenetration of gardens and the complex's varied entertainment spaces, including private function rooms, a cabaret, a big theater, and a banquet hall that could seat one thousand guests without sacrificing social intimacy. Barthelme's fiction of the later twentieth century would take the fragmentation of modern life and reshape it with a pleasing harmony, using the principle of collage whereby each element contributes to an integral whole without losing its own identity as an object. This is just the effect the young writer-to-be admires in Frank Lloyd Wright's Tokyo masterpiece.

As in Barthelme's fiction and that of other short story writers whose work would come to prominence during the years when this architect's work was being freshly reappraised and most deeply appreciated, Wright's structure asserts itself boldly with no suspension of disbelief. For the Imperial Hotel, there is no illusion, such as there would be if it had a façade. Façades make sense in two dimensions but not three, and the Imperial Hotel is most definitely a three-dimensional building, designed in organic fashion from the inside out, thrusting upwards and outwards to shape the space its functions need, much like Midway Gardens.

Wright's innovations of construction and design come together to serve his greater purpose, which is peculiar to this instance. He is especially careful to preclude any simplification of its origins and this purpose. The Imperial is not an American building dropped into Tokyo. But neither is it a Japanese structure. It is quite simply Wright's tribute to a nation he has found to be quite special, respecting its tradition while still expressing its individuality in friendship.

But Wright does not stop there. As always, like the preacher citing a double proof, he seeks confirmation for his thought in a higher principle, higher than that of historical record. It is true that even the greatest earthquake to that time in Japanese history could not bring Frank Lloyd Wright's Imperial Hotel down. He does not dwell on this fact, confident as he is in the manner of its design and construction. But in his 1923 pamphlet he does profess his belief that working in the manner of the great Japanese print-makers is akin to the Creator's own art. As always, Wright's religion is nature, and when a structure violates nature's principle, nature herself will bring it down. He does not need to add that his creation has survived the test and that he has been proven right.

Reunited in friendship with Frank Lloyd Wright, Louis Sullivan would repay the moral and financial support his former associate was providing by publishing two essays in *The Architectural Record*. Both are collected in the 1925 *Wendingen* volume appearing a year after Sullivan's death. The first, from 1923, celebrates Wright's accomplishment in Tokyo. The second, in 1924, responds to how that accomplishment survived the Kanto earthquake. Each is helpful in seeing how a former pupil's thinking measures up a third of a century later in the eyes of a "beloved master," Wright's favorite term (usually expressed in German as "*lieber Meister*").

Sullivan's greatest praise is that Wright's thinking is itself organic. It is "in the nature of any organism that it wishes to be free to grow and expand," he advises, understanding the frustrations the younger man has faced. "This instinctive desire for freedom has been held in check and dominated by the intellectual idea of fear, resulting in unnumbered inhibitions and suppressions, which have led to an obscuration of the minds of men of the two ideas of slavery and freedom" (*W*, 101). Wright has fought against this obscuration, arguing for "the true status of man not as creature but creator; an enlarging view of man's inherent powers and a growing consciousness that his slavery has been self-imposed" (*W*, 102). Sullivan relates this quest to his own architecture, specifically the Auditorium Building, the Adler and Sullivan project in which Frank Lloyd Wright was schooled. Here forms are "eloquent expressions of a something that must reside within them and justify them, upon logical grounds, as forms developed from functions of utility" (*W*, 104). The Auditorium Building is not a group but a single mass, yet its flow anticipates what Wright would achieve in Midway Gardens and the Imperial Hotel, specifically in how "the differences of levels . . . favor also the interpenetrations and the easy accessibility of the larger units" (*W*, 105), in the same manner as the terracing of the Imperial Hotel. From here Sullivan proceeds with an enumeration of the design's features—the flexible foundation, the cantilever structure, the nature of the building's materials—but returning at every point to the fact that it is Wright's idea, his manner of thinking, that has brought this project to completion.

Sullivan's second piece is more topical: "Reflections on the Tokio Disaster." But again the emphasis is on Wright's thought. "This man, a poet, who had reduced thinking to a simples, began his solution with the fixed fact of earthquakes as a basis and made an emotional study of their nature and movements," Sullivan points out. "The second move was the resolve never to relax his grip on the basis fact of earthquake as a menace, and to devise a system of construction such as should absorb and dispose of the powerful shocks, waves and violent tremors, and yet maintain its integrity as a fabricated structure." Note Sullivan's choice of words: not "basic" fact but *basis* fact. Wright's "thinking in simples" is just this, an organic growth from a specific basis. The Imperial survives not because it is stronger than an earthquake but because the earthquake's nature is built into its design. As Wright notes in his own essay after the quake, it is as if nature's seismic tremor is not countering his work but completing it. In a mind where thinking is as holistic as is its organic subject, principles can be expected to relate. "It may be remarked in passing," Sullivan adds, "that the quality and power of emotion dramatizes the power of thought: that the poet is he whose thought, thus enriched, imparts telling power to the simple and the obvious, bringing them into the field of vivid consciousness" (*W*, 128). Here *emotion* means the physical nature of thought, expressed by architects in their buildings. As Frank Lloyd Wright emphasized in his 1894 lecture, "The Architect and the Machine," soon after he'd left employment with Adler and Sullivan: The point of education is to make one more alive to things, to let one appreciate the world as Shakespeare described it in *As You Like It*, a realm where one heard "sermons in stones, and symphonies in running brooks." Now, three decades later, a proud Louis Sullivan sees the effect accomplished in the Imperial Hotel, its lava stone and water feature giving the words of poetry physical shape.

"Thinking in simples" is a radical idea, Sullivan admits, especially to academic minds whose training has inhibited any measure of freedom. "I go further and assert that such idea may be repugnant to such minds— may even alarm such minds—it is too disturbing in its ominous sugges- tion that thoughts may be living things—Now!—Here!" (*W*, 129). The thought is sufficiently novel to create a new poetry about this same time, the poetry of concrete encounters pioneered by William Carlos Williams. His notion of "no ideas but in things" runs counter to the modernism of Ezra Pound and T. S. Eliot and serves as the foundation for work of a later era by Kenneth Koch, Gilbert Sorrentino, and many others to come. For now, Sullivan can be satisfied with what has been accom- plished in the Imperial Hotel. "This vast sumptuous building, in all its aspects: structural, utilitarian, and aesthetic," he notes, "was the em- bodiment, and is now the revelation, of a single thought tenaciously held by a seer and prophet, a craftsman, a master-builder." It "stands today uninjured because it was thought-built, so to stand" (*W*, 131).

The inseparable nature of "Form and Idea" (*CW* I: 196) is what Wright identifies as the master-key to Sullivan's architecture. In these comments following the older man's death his former pupil takes a broader perspective, putting aside his own dislike of the skyscraper— Sullivan's triumph of form and idea—in favor of the more general point, one that the master had now identified as the key to Wright's success in Japan. Wright himself would soon propose a radically different structure of his own, the St. Mark's Tower, for lower Manhattan; it is for Tokyo and Los Angeles where new work is underway that he feels skyscrapers are inappropriate, because of geologic conditions. In time even Broad- acre City would include in its plan a tower or two—seventeen stories, as originally proposed for the St. Mark's project, and as eventually built in Bartlesville, Oklahoma in the 1950s. The tall buildings Wright dislikes are those that waste the advantages of structural steel by draping the building with anachronistic effects, and the people he detests are landlords who overbuild simply to multiply rents. "Pig-piling" (*CW* I: 218) was the term Wright used for these practices, and never thought Sullivan guilty of either.

Attempts to relocate his practice to Los Angeles would prove unsuccessful for Frank Lloyd Wright. The struggle to save Taliesin from mortgage foreclosure and to protect his relationship with Olgivanna from harassment by Miriam Noel were constant distractions, and delegating responsibilities to his son Lloyd Wright and former assistant Rudolf Schindler (both of whom were becoming successful Los Angeles architects in their own right) proved troublesome. The biggest project— a home, a theater, a children's theater, and several support buildings, including homes for staff—would be for Wright a major headache thanks to the stubbornness of his client, Aline Barnsdall. The massive Hollyhock House (1917) was completed, but not to Barnsdall's liking; she soon moved out of it into one of the two much smaller supporting houses Wright designed (Residence A and Residence B, 1920) and made plans to donate Hollyhock House and the grounds that would have held her theaters to the City of Los Angeles as a cultural park. Four "textile block" houses would follow, for Alice Millard in Pasadena (1923), John Storer in Hollywood (1923), and Samuel Freeman and Charles Ennis in Los Angeles (1923). The block system was promising, offering many advantages favored by Wright: on-site manufacture from local materials, ease of construction (even by the owners themselves, if desired), and incorporations of ornament as part of the functional design. But a fire at Taliesin in 1925 would redirect much of the architect's efforts and rebuilding costs would lead to such desperate acts as a massive sale of Wright's prints. Wright emphasizes in his introduction to the sale catalogue issued by the Anderson Galleries in New York (1927) that he still believes Japanese prints have much to teach Western culture, but market conditions require him to promise that any requests for refunds will be promptly honored.

The prints did sell, but Wright's share would not be enough to forestall creditors. Taliesin was saved, after a brief eviction, by a corporation set up by old friends and sympathetic clients. Wright's huge fee for the Imperial Hotel had been spent (on art) before leaving Japan, and the four textile block homes in California were not enough to live on. Big projects such as the National Life Insurance Building in Chicago and the Gordon Strong Planetarium and Automobile Objective in Maryland fell through, and no new commissions were in the offing. At the decade's end, there may have been hope that the St. Mark's Tower might work out, but the 1929 stock market crash ended that, along with any likelihood of other chances to build.

At this point editor M. A. Mikkelsen of *The Architectural Record* comes to Wright's aid, commissioning a series of articles developed from the series "In the Cause of Architecture" of 1908 and 1914. At five hundred dollars apiece, they would earn Wright a total of seven thousand dollars in 1927 and 1928, years in which architectural income was limited to a consultant's fee for helping a former assistant with the Arizona Biltmore Hotel (1927) and expenses covered by Dr. Alexander Chandler for work on San Marcos in the Desert, a resort nearby that the 1929 crash halted at the design phase. Hence there was little to distract Wright from working on the essays. He fancied that at completion they might be collected in a volume, but by then Olgivanna would be pointing her husband toward a different kind of publication, *An Autobiography*. Yet *The Architectural Record* was the type of magazine that is saved, and the essays' proximity of appearance makes for a continuity that Wright's *Collected Writings* confirms.

Other than a short piece for the *Wendingen* project, which tied in earlier principles with their recent manifestations in the California textile block houses (*CW* I: 213), Frank Lloyd Wright had not written on general architectural topics for over a decade. Now, he turns with relish to the subject of his larger ideas and does better than picking up where he'd left off, for the 1914 essay had been defensive and even petty. Instead, he goes back to the start of his writing career and its subject of how architecture benefits from the machine, a discussion that in the intervening years had been advanced by European architects such as Ludwig Mies van der Rohe and Le Corbusier. "In the Cause of Architecture I: The Architect and the Machine" repeats the title of Wright's 1894 address in Evanston, but now history supports the narrative, beginning with the acknowledgment that like it or not the machine has become the architect's tool; either the architect will master it, or it will master the architect. Is this a cause for worry? Not at all, because machines when perfected are simply extensions of human ability, Wright counsels, clarifying that they are new not in principle but only in means. Therefore the Machine is given a capital letter, as he does for other principles like Art and Beauty. But it has no life of its own, Wright offers in gentle reminder. Whether it emancipates or enslaves is up to the person who uses it.

This endorsement of principle is far more than Wright has managed in his much earlier essays on the topic, and now he goes even farther toward integrating it with his larger beliefs and manner of thought. Tools must be mastered by learning their nature and using them for what they do best. He stays with the subject for his next month's essay, "In the Cause of Architecture II: Standardization, The Soul of the Machine." Standardization is no detriment, he must remind his readers; it has always existed, and in the right hands is the agent of democracy. At the heart of standardization is an ability to discern the life of a tool, what makes it natural—in other words, organic. Here is where Wright parts company with the Europeans. The benefit of machinery is that it brings out the best in the nature of materials: pure grain in wood, clean lines (as opposed to grotesque carvings), even the ability to inlay, fret, and enhance natural plasticity. The same is true with glass, thanks to the freedom of plated form. And steel, which deserves its own essay.

Steel exemplifies this age, Wright pronounces at the start of his third installment, and the question now is to recognize it for what it is and use it to the best advantage. Here Wright pulls out all the stops in his writing, summoning both epic and personal effects to speak in an entirely different manner from his European counterparts. He draws an analogy from classical history, comparing the Romans' discovery and mastery of the arch with what he hopes may happen with steel in the present era. Wright marvels at the great power of steel waiting to be fully born and sees it as the perfect material for an architect. Bereft of decorative qualities, it depends wholly upon the artist's imagination for any sense of life. Used honestly by engineers, steel has the beauty of mathematics, and the architect is wise to recognize this material property. Combined with concrete, reinforced steel speaks for a liberation of the idea, eclipsing limitations of the old restrictive forms of masonry, lintels, posts and beams, even the arch itself. Yet Wright's argument does not take the direction toward reason and rational purity that was being followed at the present time by Mies and Corbu. Instead, he pursues the liberation of thinking from such obstructions to its natural, organic form that Louis Sullivan had praised in Wright in the first of his *Wendingen* essays. Here Wright sees concrete and steel as the materials that make this liberation possible. Overcoming the weight of taste that still ties minds to dead forms, Frank Lloyd Wright's imagination is alive and free of such restrictions. Steel and concrete have given him the slab (Unity Temple), the cantilever (the Imperial Hotel), and the splay (the Gordon Strong project). One can feel the architect itching to build. But for now, he can design—and write.

Writing brings forth the best of Wright's thinking, and his next installment, "Fabrication and Imagination," shows what he has been putting his mind to. Imagination distinguishes humans from animals, and is moreover what made the Gods. "A creative being is a God," the architect advises, adding that "There will never be too many Gods" (*CW* I: 241). This is the essay in which Wright introduces his most recent example of built success: the textile block system that produced four strikingly beautiful homes in the Los Angeles area and was at the time of the essay being used to great effect in the Arizona Biltmore Hotel and its cottages (1927). The textile block system fulfilled his requirements of simplicity of form, naturalness of function, and ease of technique. Indeed, the manner of building with these blocks is as simple as weaving a rug, here done with a uniform material which lets the building virtually build itself. Fashioning the blocks is a simple task the clients can do themselves, for which Wright provides instructions. The outer shell serves as the exterior, the inner shell as the interior, with an insulating space in between where piping (cut to order in the shop) can be run. Windows are similarly fabricated in advance. Consider all that is saved, from form work and masonry to carpentry, plastering, painting, and even decoration. Everything is integral and offers a peaceful simplicity that benefits the persons who live there. Reverend Gannett could not have said it better, and it is all made possible by material that is abundant everywhere, awaiting transformation via imaginative action. Wright the democrat thus joins forces with Wright the artist.

Subsequent essays for *The Architectural Record* treat designing with a thought to the three dimensions of space (rather than the pictorial representation of two), the logic of the plan as an idea within the creative mind, and how articulate buildings such as the textile-block Ennis House (1923) resemble the music of Bach, master of true form that he was. Having started this series with its basis of thought in the machine, Wright carried his thinking through all aspects of design until coming to that most recently expressed. But unlike his initial lectures of thirty-odd years before, he is no longer preaching. Instead he is thinking, and with that thought putting himself in the position of being a model for how architecture should be worked out. As the second year's pieces (freshly numbered) proceed, there are references to how the young man in Architecture might benefit from Wright's example, how richer that vision might be if such disciplinary power is developed. Find the essential geometry of pattern, Wright urges. Learn to see the room as expressed in the exterior as space. These are principles that, once grasped, will let prospective architects grow as creative factors empowered by ideas. It is easy to foresee the Taliesin Fellowship and all Wright would hope for in such statements.

For now, Frank Lloyd Wright is thinking, and using the occasion of his series to get various ideas in order. Not all were for publication. Though headed with the same short title, "In the Cause of Architecture," two were for himself. The aptly subtitled "Purely Personal" (1928) is unpublished as such, though comments on Le Corbusier and Fiske Kimball would be incorporated later in book reviews. Like his 1914 essay, the piece is defensive. Once again the offenders are architects who have taken certain ideas of his and applied them in a superficial manner, ignoring the integral growth from within and the spatial elements of a third dimension in favor of externally administered effect. These complaints would soon develop into a reasoned critique of the emerging European modernism known as the International Style, but for now Wright just wants to get them on paper—for himself, as it were. More impressive is a second unpublished piece from 1928, "In the Cause of Architecture: Composition as Method in Creation," which Bruce Brooks Pfeiffer identifies in his headnote as one of Wright's most cogent essays on the use of materials and the machine. Like the articles in his published series, this piece is about three thousand words long, the unit of expression Wright seems to have found comfortable at this time. Concise, it locates the source for organic growth in the "life-principle expressed in geometry at the center of every Nature-form we see" (*CW* I: 259). This is a newly expressed idea for Wright, and it's wise that he work it out for himself before presenting it as a model for others.

It is a new idea, but Japanese art provides the best model for it. In this case it is the printmaker Hokusai's theory that every object as commonly perceived emerges from a geometry that can be drawn with a T square, triangle, and compass. In these hidden forms lies the architect's world. Wright recommends penetrating this world of forms by discriminating the patterns of oak trees (as opposed to pines), the distinctive shapes of "curling vine, flowing water, curving sand," and "the easily characterized chrysanthemum," while appreciating how a "rock or a rose is difficult" but no less ultimately discernable (*CW* I: 260). There is a discipline to such power of seeing from which the architect cannot help but profit and Wright promises that "a habit of thought arises from such eye-minded exercises to make constructive effort natural, 'design' spontaneous" (*CW* I: 261). Such is the facility he himself could demonstrate on demand, amazing both the Taliesin Fellows and the public alike. Not as a teacher, but as a master—working from models, with the ultimate model being his own conduct and practice.

From this encouragement Wright moves to a negative example, how what he calls modernistic buildings mistake this geometric vision for an easy sense of decoration that plays with proportion and shape for its own sake. "Such buildings do not grow," he warns. "Such buildings happen. They are made" (*CW* I: 261), products of deductive reasoning rather than of organic creation. He then reminds readers that not until abstraction discovers the underlying pattern can any building become "the constitution of construction itself" (*CW* I: 262), which is the inductive way.

The balance of Wright's "In the Cause of Architecture" essays address specific points, serving more as clarifications than models or exhortations. "What 'Styles' Mean to the Architect" distinguishes singular from plural. *Style* per se is not a manner but rather the practice of building according to the organic principle, starting from within and following through according to the nature of what has been initiated. There can be as many examples of this as there are architects who pursue it, a reminder of Wright's early assurance that there are as many different kinds of houses as there are different kinds of people. Humanity itself owes its development to the individual's creative power, each person seeking Truth and Beauty in expansive rather than reductive ways. "The Universal speaks by way of the Personal in our lives," Wright offers, perhaps remembering Whitman's *Song of Myself* in his appreciation of how "we can only understand the message in terms of ourselves" (*CW* I: 263). An individual works in a style—organically, creatively. "Styles" become an issue when the organic achievement of one architect is adopted, in an external manner, by another, applying it from without rather than developing it from within. The disposition is a familiar one for Wright, but no less essential here. And once again he anticipates the goal of a Taliesin Fellowship, where expressions of human life could grow as handsomely and healthily as great trees in good soil, flourishing in sunlight and maturing by inner principle, formed as the citizens only democracy can produce.

"*Style is a quality of form that character takes*"—here is Wright's ultimate distinction between a style from within and styles applied from without, and it will be character that his Taliesin Fellowship intends to foster, as opposed to being in the narrow sense any sort of architectural school. Character itself cannot be taught; it is everywhere, in any flora or fauna, and in this sense one does not learn character itself, but only how to perceive it as an inward force that takes form according to its nature.

Wright further characterizes the nature of materials architects work with, and for these he has sensuous feeling, starting with the pencils on his drafting table. He loves to grasp a handful of them and let them lie loose on his palm, he writes, the light striking each color with the message of "its own song . . . Each has a story" (*CW* I: 270). Stone also speaks in its own language and it is in this essay that Wright first describes his manner of working with the medium, laying it up in strata with natural edges facing out. Wood is even more sensuous, especially now that its inherent beauty is preserved by the machine. Wood is also crucial to the definition of line, a principle Wright will dwell on later. For now, he notes how articulations of design can be accomplished at times by the dividing lines of wood alone, prompting readers to recall the way horizontal banding unifies elements in structures such as the Stockman House inside and out. Wright also looks forward, as so few of his contemporaries did, to the matter of conservation, regretting how much wood has been wasted and how much can be saved once his own principles are followed.

Terra-cotta as a material merits an essay because of Louis Sullivan's success with its ability to trace natural forms. Glass is praised for its contribution to integral lighting, and is also suggested as a building material itself, combined with the spider's web of steel to be like a diamond set in gold. Wright would do just this the next year in the residence built for his cousin, the Richard Lloyd Jones House (1929) in Tulsa, Oklahoma, though the steel was used to reinforce narrow piers of concrete block that lace the dominating walls of windows.

Concrete wins more appreciation, especially as steel has expanded its possibilities. This plasticity makes reinforced concrete more useful than stone. No matter that it is a plain material, for this allows the architect's imagination to be responsible for aesthetic effect. The same goes for sheet metal, which Wright compares to the brain in motion. When a material itself has beauty, as does copper, a project such as the National Life Insurance Company (1924, unbuilt) in Chicago becomes especially inviting, its walls disappearing in iridescent copper-bound glass. Wright's description makes the building sound beautiful, and it certainly looks so in the color presentation drawings, among the loveliest in Wright's canon. Decades later he would finally have the chance to incorporate key elements of this design with others from another project, the St. Mark's Tower (1929, unbuilt), in the Price Tower for Bartlesville, Oklahoma (1952). Wright recalls the principle as first being worked out in 1923, in time for him to discuss it with Louis Sullivan a few months before he died. The old master admired the building as beautiful, but also genuine, a contribution to a true "Architecture of Democracy." Sullivan also added, as Wright notes here, that "I never could have done this building myself, but I believe that, but for me, you never could have done it" (*CW* I: 309). Wright therefore dedicates the design to him.

"In the Cause of Architecture IX: The Terms" (1928) completes Wright's series as published, with five essays in 1927 and nine numbered freshly for 1928. Having shown how the nature of materials provides clear direction, he feels confident that he has roused the imaginations of the young architects reading him to adopt at least a few practices that he himself has found successful. Wright has done much more, in fact, propounding a philosophy not just of architecture but of art, and demonstrating the expression of its principles with plain and practical examples. In either event, he draws back for some quiet reflections, such as remembering childhood hours after bedtime listening to his father play Beethoven on the piano. Here lies the material proof for his thinking. Even as a youngster he recognized that this music was speaking a language beyond words. As an adult, he learned that architecture did the same, expressing truths of the heart.

The challenge has been to find words for it. Poetry in architecture, he knows, means finding nature's harmony and expressing it in visible form. To attain such poetic expression in wood, stone, cement, glass, and steel, he urges a move to architecture's third dimension, admittedly hard to fathom within the two dimensions of the drawing board and difficult to imagine for minds trained since the Renaissance to think in terms of the literal and pictorial. The way out of this box is appreciating how it is in the third dimension that qualities exist *of* the thing rather than *on* it. Once this sense of within is grasped, the architect can realize the result in *form*. Because it is a PRINCIPLE, as he emphasizes in capital letters, its effects are extensive, entering into every action taken, every use of materials, and every choice of method. Needless to say, three-dimensionality informs and characterizes every form that results, deriving from the integral interpretation behind it. It is, Wright stresses, an integrity in anything and everything done, from building a chicken coop to designing a cathedral.

Thinking in the third dimension is a gift, and those who would work at Wright's side and witness his manner of creation attest to it. Edgar Tafel, one of the first Taliesin Fellows and a productive architect in his own right, recalls how structures such as Fallingwater and the S. C. Johnson Administration Building took shape over many months in Wright's head, with designs put to paper only at the very end of the process—for the Kaufmann home, in the two hours it took Edgar, Sr., to drive out to Spring Green from the Milwaukee airport. Wright himself always argued against the academic practice of starting with a sketch. This was by definition beginning from the outside. Start from within, he would urge; do it often enough and it becomes second nature, which is probably how this habit of thought had developed in him. Can the young architect hope to achieve it? They are given this benediction: create with love and work by principle so that Beauty will prove their joy in work.

As his series concludes, Wright continues publishing elsewhere, including pieces that show a growing irritation with the emerging International Style—specifically how its emphasis on surface and mass are by definition external qualities rather than principles of growth from within. In an unpublished essay from 1929, "The Line Between the Curious and the Beautiful," he finds in the line as properly drawn not only a safeguard for civilization, but civilization itself. It is interesting to see him here undercutting the theoretical purity of Corbu and the rationalization of Mies by citing eminently practical, even homely examples. With gratitude he sees this proper use of line in such current accomplishments as the airplane, the automobile, and the ocean liner, even in common kitchen utensils. Such streamlining has avoided both the affectations of ornament and "the sterility of ornaphobia" (*CW* I: 341) apparent in the surface and mass distraction of the International Style as Wright describes it in a subsequent essay.

Frustration with the International Style would bedevil Wright from now on. His exasperation with how Henry-Russell Hitchcock evaluated his work for *Cahiers d'Art* (26 November 1928) and anger that Philip Johnson was granting him less than superior status in the Museum of Modern Art's *Modern Architecture: International Exhibition* (1932) would fuel suspicions that Frank Lloyd Wright was becoming a curmudgeon. But these years also catch the architect at a point of transition. His "In the Cause of Architecture" series had been motivated by his successes with the Prairie House and the Imperial Hotel and underwritten by a belief in the organic principles that had generated each. Two years after the series concludes, he drafts for himself "In the Cause of Architecture: Confession" (1930), an unpublished piece that to unknowing eyes might appear wistful. It posits that great architecture is more essential to the modern age than ever before, but more than ever before its progress has been retarded by selfishness and cruelty—enough to break the heart of anyone who loves it.

Does he indeed feel forsaken? This confession, so unlike the liveliness and commitment of the published essays, is in fact motivated by the realization that all these sorrows and joys characterize "an Architect's full lifetime" (*CW* I: 348). Perhaps for the first time in his life, and certainly for the first time on paper, Frank Lloyd Wright is admitting his age. 1930 is the year he turns sixty-three. His career spans four decades. By this point in their lives and careers most architects have fulfilled their promise. But here in this "Confession" is a man who has been speaking with the young as if he is still an idealistic youth himself. And what has it brought him? After sailing home from Tokyo, his big commission already spent (on art), the balance of the 1920s were difficult years, and now in 1930 the Great Depression promised even worse.

At sixty-three, Frank Lloyd Wright had not been building a great deal in recent years. "So there is little to be done except to write one's best thoughts (if one has thoughts) and, as may be, build that best thought whenever and however it can be built" (*CW* I: 346), he allows. And if there can be only writing? Well then, he will write in the same spirit in which he has built.

It is the imaginative spirit and fervor of that writing, published so prominently and extensively in the influential *Architectural Record*, that helps Wright turn the corner not just into the 1930s but into a whole new career, one that would eclipse the Prairie House and Imperial Hotel in ways that not even Henry-Russell Hitchcock and Philip Johnson could have imagined a younger generation of Internationalists accomplishing. A bit later in 1930 Wright can sense the change, for Princeton University has asked him to prepare six lectures to be given in May for the prestigious Kahn series, with the Art Institute of Chicago requesting two more for presentation in October (both sets published in 1931). Now, in another unpublished piece from 1930, "Poor Little American Architecture," Wright looks back to Hitchcock's essay that had angered him so much and has a bit of fun with it.

At this point he knows the author only by virtue of a picture of the man picked up at *The Architectural Record*. It's a poor image, but no worse than the bad photographs of Wright's work he presumes have generated the critic's thought. Hitchcock has called him the greatest architect of the present century's first quarter. The statement is meant as praise, for about this time Philip Johnson (Hitchcock's friend and associate) was prone to calling Frank Lloyd Wright the greatest architect of the nineteenth century. Wright takes both statements not as a personal or even professional affront, but as a matter of principle and belief, knowing that his work is far from over because the principles of organic architecture have not yet been sufficiently accepted. Rather than weep or sigh, Wright makes a promise, phrased with wit and good humor. He will not only be the greatest architect so far but the greatest who will ever be, Wright boasts—to himself, but in a piece of writing he saved. He repeats the claim and affixes his red square and signs his name to it. Even ordinary bootleggers serve twenty-five years for less, he laughs. Wright's oath is peculiarly American, similar to Melville's claim for Hawthorne ("He says 'No!' in thunder") and Huck Finn's similarly Faustian challenge that if his compassion for Jim damns himself, so be it. Critical advocates of Hawthorne, Melville, and Twain accept these attestations as valid, just as enthusiasts for Wright's work would come to appreciate the grandness of his claim—not on face value, perhaps, but certainly as a measure of his immense ambition and an honest appraisal of all he had yet to do for the cause of organic architecture.

Wright's fun with Hitchcock (who would later become a friend and collaborator) and even more so with himself indicates a new role for the great architect: as performer. The Kahn Lectures, published as *Modern Architecture* (1931), are much the same, even to the extent of having fun. No longer an essayist for *The Architectural Record*, Wright is now appearing before an audience—a very specific one, the students of a great university. He relishes this fact, and begins his series with a performance piece, reading for them a text he claims was first delivered in 1901 (before any of them were born) at Hull House in Chicago. "Machinery, Materials, and Men" is in fact quite different from the original "Art and Craft of the Machine," probably because Wright had modified it over the years for other audiences. He now declares this its last presentation. This serves to emphasize what he feels nearly thirty years later is most important among the thoughts he'd shared with Chicago's Progressive Era social reformers.

As Wright delivers the lecture, he wants his listeners to picture him in 1901—not as the old man he is today, but as a relative youth in the profession—and consider the battle he faced back then and would be engaged in ever since. His description of the city, with its stirring imagery and grandly extended metaphors, comes earlier in this Princeton version, part of the performance that moves the audience to take his initial thoughts on the negative aspects of current style and let them be redirected toward a celebration of all the machine can accomplish. As he has explained in *The Architectural Record* series, that accomplishment is centered on the nature of materials—here, how the machine brings out the best in them. But beyond specifics is Wright's insistence that by embracing the machine, human thought is changing forms from something old to something new.

Wright's second lecture, given the next day, is on another familiar topic, "Style in Industry." Once again his point is the one made in previous essays: that attaining a sense of style involves working against the notion of styles, plural. For his audience of university students who are there not to learn the specific practices of a trade school but to comprehend the greater principles that direct such specifics, Wright is patient with his explanation. Understanding the nature of anything means grasping the principle that lives within it, giving form and character. Life itself is too complex to comprehend, but its effects and consequences can be perceived if one knows what to look for. This visible world is external nature; within, there is an integral structure that produces this life organically. Grasping that integrity is more of an artistic than a scientific process, based on the imagination's ability to see the various materials for what they are. As listeners may have come to expect, Wright praises Japanese art and culture for having the greatest success with this. After *nature* and *organic*, the third key term to understand is *plasticity*, a word that implies an absence of constructed effect. Here the nature of materials is seen as growing into form rather than being joined together from bits and pieces.

With his terms for discussion set, Wright moves to his thesis as announced the previous afternoon: that style itself has nothing to do with *the* style or *a* style, and certainly not with style*s*. Had he not been so careful with his first three terms, especially in their finer nuances of language, he might not have been able to count on his listeners to discern the difference articles make and the distinct meanings of singular and plural. Styles are the result of imitation, whereas style comes from understanding a principle. The Japanese have reached this understanding with the help of what he calls standardization; Wright points out with pleasure how the conventional size of a floor mat determines the size and shape of a typical house. All such practices are then accorded the dignity of ceremony, so that the doings of everyday life can be raised to the level of art. For his own country's culture, he recommends a simplicity that comes from the heart rather than the head. One way to do that is to discard the pictorial sense of art introduced in the Renaissance, for pictures are concepts, not feelings.

This second lecture ends with the first published description of the school Wright would be trying to organize, at this stage somewhat different from the Taliesin Fellowship that did get underway two years later. To the Princeton students he speaks of a school of the allied arts (glassmaking, textiles, pottery, sheet metal, woodworking, casting, and reproduction) with resident masters in charge of each specialty. Part of each day's work would include agricultural field labor, a practice the eventual Fellowship did adopt, as it would adopt Architecture as the background for everything, just as it had been in ancient times. This qualification speaks for the essential nature of Wright's concept, that it is not a school that offers instruction in design and building but rather will be a haven, in the beautiful countryside, where an entire way of life can be modeled on the organic idea. Wright admits that creative art cannot be taught, but knows well what inhibits its development. His school would remove the inhibitions and put the students to work with the nature of materials under the guidance of a master at each craft. From the abilities that followed might come real art, but that would be a matter of each student using the best of his or her imagination.

The Hillside Home School of the Allied Arts would never happen, dependent as the plan was on industrial affiliation (impossible under the rules of education accreditation and unlikely in the Great Depression). Nor was the facility for it ready. When the Taliesin Fellowship's first members arrived two years later, one of their initial tasks, in addition to harvesting their sustenance, was to begin repairing and rebuilding the actual Hillside Home School that Frank had designed for his aunts thirty years before—and which had deteriorated after a family financial crisis and the tragedy with Mamah forced its closing in 1915. Yet it is important that Wright mentions it in this lecture, for a major part of his argument about style is that it cannot be nurtured in either the architectural or educational climates of the present.

Wright's third lecture in the Kahn series is one of his most personal, drawing on anecdotes from his life and experience to underscore the most important points of his preceding talks. The students have got to know him, after all, and in this lecture he makes the most of that. The first anecdote is a scene presented as dramatically as anything from his in-progress *An Autobiography* (1932). The subject is a technical and historical one, "The Passing of the Cornice," but Wright makes it personal. His instincts, he reveals, had always been to hate the shallow pretensions of the Renaissance, instincts confirmed when reading Victor Hugo's indictment of that setting sun all Europe mistook for dawn. In this formulation, architecture would die, to be replaced in the human spirit by literature. Wright says he found the consequences of this reformulation unbearable, reinforced by an incident in his life from this same time. It involves an accident during the construction of the new west wing of the old State Capitol in which the stone basement piers, meant to support the structure's interior weight, including the cornices, collapsed. As a youth he witnessed the scene, a traumatic event he could recall in vivid, terrifying detail more than half a century later. It starts with the bucolic image of walking past the green park under shade trees, hearing the roar of the collapse and turning to confront clouds of lime dust rising in the air, the cries of the casualties resounding. Sick with horror, he stands transfixed as workers stagger from the ruins and fall dead on the grass now strewn with rubble and the dust of lime. From this world of the walking dead Wright carries the color image forward, looking up to the boldly projecting cornice now hanging in space, and beneath it a workman dangling upside down, his foot caught by a falling beam. The red line of his blood streaks down the wall beneath, starkly hideous against the stone. The young architect-to-be is stricken with the scene's terror, and it stays in his mind as a matter for dismay and eventual reflection. What has caused the tragedy? Not anything valid in its own right, but rather a pointless fabrication of sheet iron masquerading as stone. Why was the imitation necessary? With the personal immediacy and human mortality in mind, Wright turns to his lecture's general topic.

Why have such a cornice? Simply to privilege local American building with a sign of culture. Why should he object? Because the cornice itself had nothing sensible to do with the construction, but was simply a sign from the era of Classical Greece meant to dignify contemporary structures with a reference to ancient temples.

That much is obvious. But to emphasize and reinforce his point Wright tells another anecdote, this time from his own viewing of the ultimate model for such design, the Parthenon in Athens. Standing before it, he uses his imagination, recreating the scene when its original colors were bright and vibrant. He restores the arris of the mouldings, sharpens the cornices, and creates in his mind the building as it would have appeared two millennia ago. Then he stands and looks at it.

Perhaps at this point in his lecture he would pause, letting his listeners think back to the last time he mentioned looking at a structure—the old State Capitol in ruins, with the ghastly devastation and agony of the workmen recreated for the imaginations of these Princeton students. What he wants his audience to see now is that, while the Parthenon's crumbling ruins are of stone, they were originally meant to look like a painted temple made of wood. Stone was only a model for this, the original form that the Greeks wanted to emulate. Even the cornice itself, that would come down to current times as the exemplar of culture, was for the Greeks themselves a sham, a stone projection pretending to be the overhang of a wooden roof (as it would have been on the original temple).

The argument has been structured with Wright's listeners and his immediate presence in mind. On the strength of two anecdotes, two dramatically recounted personal stories that make both the tragedy and the futility of the cornice strikingly clear, he is able to move to his concluding point: that just as democracy expresses the dignity and worth of an individual, organic architecture—*unfolding* as opposed to *enfolding*—promises the best truth for dignity and worth. This is his hope for the future, the reason why he is speaking to students at Princeton, and why he will be founding the Taliesin Fellowship in short order. The fact that American architecture is at this time both small and immature works in favor of growth. Wright's intention is to foster an architecture that will not sculpt buildings but grow them, such growth expressing the nature of humankind. Thinking perhaps of the fields and pastures that are part of Taliesin, he qualifies this architecture with one of his favorite terms, here distinguished from its customary misunderstanding as extremism: *radical*, meaning "of the roots," here the roots of architecture planted firmly in the soil that gives life.

Having been taken from principle to personality and back again, the audience is now ready to appreciate a specific example of Wright's work. His fourth lecture, "The Cardboard House," describes the most successful attempt yet to have organic architecture grow naturally from the soil: the Prairie House that distinguished the first part of his own career. The need for it is something Wright can now joke about, throwing out one-liners to an appreciative audience eager to laugh on cue. Access and fenestration, he mocks, were nothing more than big holes for the big cat and smaller ones for the little cat. As his listeners laugh, he feeds them more humor. There was no more architectural music to such design than the pandemonium of the barnyard. Cats running in and out; pigs snorting, sheep bleating, roosters crowing, cows mooing—what rusticity this homespun philosopher brings to the ivy-clad halls of the East. But all the so-called architect had to do was call out plan numbers for his clerks to pull, adding a bay window if the client wanted one.

The description of the Prairie House that follows is complete, adding nothing to what Wright has said about it in the three decades before but phrased with a sense of conclusion. The era of the Prairie House is a closed period. Frank Lloyd Wright no longer designs them as such, although for Herbert F. Johnson he'd present Wingspread (1937) as his last of the type, even as it includes most of the architect's innovations from the 1930s. For his audience at Princeton he uses the Prairie House as an example of not just what could be done but what had been done, with great success—one of the reasons Frank Lloyd Wright is there speaking to them. "What a man *does, that* he has" (*CW* II: 53), he intones, with the great Prairie Houses of the century's first decade standing behind him as proof.

Even here, he's good for a laugh. After working his way through the familiar list of Prairie House features, each of them related to organic principles and integral effect, he reflects a bit on the last one, that because all features should work together even the home's furniture should be architect-designed. Here Wright admits a challenge he sometimes failed, especially at making chairs that fit both the architecture and a person's body. He himself has been black and blue from interacting with his own furnishings. At least the good posture required for eating has allowed him to integrate form and function. Wright's dining rooms, especially those with his tables and chairs, are indeed some of his most attractive achievements; while joking about himself, he can take the sympathetic feelings he has aroused and direct them toward his genuine successes.

Plus the joke will live through history. It is today one of the most frequently quoted lines of Wright's, as are others that take obvious failings and treat them as comedy. His living room furniture is damnably uncomfortable; so it hurts him, too. His roofs tended to leak. Consider his frequently quoted response to Herbert Johnson, who phoned from his dinner table to say water was dripping right on his head. "Then move your chair, Hib," Wright laughed.

Lecture number five, "The Tyranny of the Skyscraper," starts with a joke as well, about Michelangelo building the first such structure when he "hurled the Pantheon on top of the Parthenon" (*CW* II: 59). A falsehood at the time, St. Peter's would become a travesty in the modern era as the symbol of authority for municipal buildings. What does this have to do with today's skyscraper? *Tyranny*, Wright explains, the tyranny of a false idea over the practical enjoyment of life. In the present world this tyranny is exercised by the landlord, reselling the same area again and again on each ascending floor, to the detriment of the crowded neighbors and at the expense of congestion below. Yet the architect is careful to distinguish structure from use, even structure from structure. There are good skyscrapers. Louis Sullivan's Wainwright Building is one of the best, thanks to its sympathy with the organic. As for proper usage, Wright again takes advantage of his performer's role and teases his audience with it. His set of lectures, he admits, has been developed and presented like one of his father's old-time sermons. Therefore he concludes in this manner, choosing as his text the admonition to do unto others as ye would have them do unto you. If skyscrapers and those who profit from them do this, there is hope.

Wright's hopes are founded on the changes in transportation and communication that in his next (and last) Kahn lecture will be designed for the city. For now he simply notes that the present crowding of skyscrapers thwarts any benefit from the automobile, whose contribution when combined with the telephone and telegraph should be helping people reject verticality and embrace the horizontal as a better orientation for happier lives. His prescriptions for more happiness in a world that builds skyscrapers are specific: limiting construction, widening streets (and hence the spaces between buildings) by placing pedestrian ways on a different level, burning coal not in furnaces on-site but at remote generating stations, and reducing the size of automobiles that are used in town (as opposed to cross-country trips). As for the skyscrapers themselves, were false dressing dropped the structure might find its own integrity as a work of steel and glass. Wright looks forward to Broadacre City and even farther ahead to his Price Tower when he suggests that a skyscraper could work in the countryside, where abundant space would give it a park-like setting. But trends must be reversed, he warns. There was a promise of light in the Wainwright Building that failed to hold true, as barbaric successors have been built with no thought for their environment or each other.

"The City" leaves Wright's listeners with a blueprint for a post-urban society. He posited the machine as the tool that would build structures and provide services for this new world, and in foreseeing what can be done Wright is remarkably prescient. His method is to conclude from the evidence presented that cities themselves will eventually die and be replaced by smaller communities dispersed across the land. This itself mandates changes that can be reasonably specified, involving new necessities to replace the ones no longer operative that had mandated cities in the first place. He predicts that people will be using cars much more to get around, and service stations will be there to fuel them—but also to sell groceries and serve as restaurants, restrooms, and neighborhood meeting centers. Forty years later these would exist as convenience stores. Other innovations proceed in line: chain stores for easy distribution, roadside motels for easy lodging, and homes reconceived to provide culture found in the city, but now with personal comfort and choice. The medium for this is television (which Wright knew was coming) and the internet (whose purpose he anticipated). Everything needed would be at home or within easy reach, including office parks in which to work.

How could Frank Lloyd Wright be so canny in picturing the next age pretty much as it did develop? By understanding human nature and having a deep sympathy for its wants and needs. People desire the freedom of space, and find it in the expansive horizontal line along which life proceeds—a line the city has taken away. This perception, which in the mind of a less practical thinker might wander afield into abstraction, is for Wright grounded in empirical observation. When transportation and communication were restricted, people had no choice. But consider what has transpired with the advent of electricity, telecommunication, and automobiles. An organic consequence of all this is the freedom of reach and movement best exercised on a horizontal rather than a vertical axis, as it is the former that widens the sphere of activity. Times are changing, the pace is accelerating, and pressures are mounting. Far better for human nature that the direction for this explosion be outward rather than upward, consistent with America's promise to her ideal.

Delivered in May of 1930, the Kahn lectures are published as *Modern Architecture* (1931). They are soon joined by *Two Lectures on Architecture* (1931), issued as a pamphlet following Wright's talks at the Art Institute of Chicago on the first and second of October, 1930. Scheduled to accompany an international exhibition of the architect's life work, they allow him to be both retrospective (for the first, "In the Realm of Ideas") and prospective (in the second, "To the Young Man in Architecture"). Trimming each perspective down to an hour's talk makes for concision but also compression; as with the Kahn lectures, it is interesting to see what Wright chooses to emphasize.

His first lecture restates a typical Wright motto: that what a man does, he has, which can be confirmed here by a stroll through the galleries. He reviews what houses typically looked like before his work began. These homes lacked human proportion and even human sensibility, being little more than boxes with holes cut in them for doors and windows. Wright's remedy finds the organic principle for designing a home, with its guiding principle that of simplicity—a topic he'd handled in technical terms for the students at Princeton, but for his general audience at the Art Institute something he could speak about as a genuine local son. He was instinctively drawn to the simplicity of the prairie, with its flowers and trees below the crowning sky. From these elements he makes his point: that "a little height on the prairie was enough to look like much more" (*CW* II: 85–86). What kind of house fits on the prairie? One that begins on the ground and projects a look of shelter, scaled to the human figure. No attics, no closets, just a whole new value to space based on a plasticity that treats the building as a whole. Walls, ceilings, and floors share a common growth, drawing continuity from each other and eliminating any overt sense of construction, much as Louis Sullivan integrated ornament not as background, but as part of the whole. The nature of materials would guide their use. *The internal order as integral* was for Wright the key to being organic, overriding all other ideas. Did it work? Evidence was on exhibit in the gallery.

From this first realization of the organic derives a second: that rooms themselves as interior space would shape the building's exterior—not the other way around, as had been the case in houses Wright abhorred. Once the space was opened to admit it, light could beautify the home and bless its occupants. To achieve this effect, the machine stood ready to free the individual to become just that, an individual. And how does that liberated person proceed? Once again, Wright's manner is to change abstract ideas into objective specifics, which in turn enhance his argument as metaphor. By benefit of casement windows, cement exteriors, steel-in-tension supports, and natural trim, that progress would be horizontal, ever the line by which human freedom extends. Whereas technical details laced with occasional humor worked well at Princeton, Wright knew a popular audience would need some poetry and enthusiasm, both of which his first Chicago lecture supplies.

With the story of his own success thus told, Wright in his second lecture looks to a future now in the hands of architects as young as he was when developing principles that produced the Prairie House. The essence of architecture is still the same, a quest for beauty based on order as intelligence apprehends and science executes. Form must be related to purpose, parts must work with the form, with methods and materials yielding a natural integrity of purpose and result. Achieving all this will be possible for the young architect, but only by developing a habit of thought that perceives the universe itself as architecture. The principle comes first; without it no ways or means can do the job.

Where can this habit of thought be learned? Not in school, but in the architect's office where these processes of thought are at work. Here one can observe material resources being applied to purpose, which is Wright's definition of power. Here too one can see that while principles are universal, they make sense only when approached from within. Doing so allows one to discard false notions picked up from conventions and bad schooling. The old master is giving his listeners a head start, for not until they have reached his age would a new era of thought popularize the notion of interrogating beliefs to discover any unstated false assumptions that corrupt them.

The temptation to make absolute pronouncements is tempered by this understanding. "Architecture is the very body of civilization itself,"

Wright proclaims in his familiar manner, but for these listeners he adds the caution that it takes time to grow, beginning to be architecture "only when it is thought-built" (*CW* II: 99). There is a language for such thought, and within it an alphabet to be learned from the nature of steel, glass, concrete, and machines used as tools. There can be distractions from this knowledge, such as the International Style's business with surface and mass. Citing Le Corbusier, Wright allows that a house can be a machine to live in, but only to the extent that a heart is a suction pump—"Sentient man begins where that concept of the heart ends" (*CW* II: 100).

Wright closes this lecture with a set of instructions for future architects. They vary from the sublime to the ridiculous, from beginning immediately to form the habit of asking "why" to going as far away from home as possible to build a first building (because while the physician can bury his failures, the architect can only plant vines). Within this range are the practical matters of avoiding "the shopper for plans" and shunning organized competitions that can only "average upon an average." The single most important piece of advice is to think in simples, as Louis Sullivan used to say, reducing parts to those that express first principles.

Thinking in this manner is what has brought Frank Lloyd Wright before them this day, in the company of an exhibition celebrating his life's work. In the last few years he had been thinking of his career achievement, urged to do so by Olgivanna, who believed it would not only set the record straight but get his mind off his recent string of personal troubles and professional disappointments. Even as he speaks to these aspiring architects he knows the materials have already been assembled that will tell his own story both more intimately and more grandly than can his remarks this day and the exhibits that have been mounted. It will be published in 1932 as *An Autobiography* and be instrumental in attracting young people to the Taliesin Fellowship formed later that same year. Together, book and Fellowship will begin a whole new career for Frank Lloyd Wright, a virtual second lifetime as an architect and thinker, a lifetime some consider even more important than the first.

4

An Autobiography and the Fellowship

FRANK LLOYD WRIGHT'S STORY OF HIS OWN LIFE begins in Wisconsin, not where he was born (Richland Center) or principally raised (Madison) but rather in the rural Helena Valley beyond Spring Green. The occasion is a walk up the snowy hillside overlooking several of the Lloyd Jones family farms. During the summers of his boyhood young Frank would work here, exhaustingly so—much of Book One of *An Autobiography* will chronicle his fatigue from these endless tasks and chores. But in this different season he's back for a visit with his Uncle John, who accompanies him up the hill. For Frank it has been an adventure, darting about to seize armfuls of dried prairie flowers sticking up through the snow. Uncle John sees it differently, pointing out from the summit that while his own tracks form a straight line, the boy's have wandered with wild deviations. "A stern look came down on him," Wright recalls, accompanied by "gentle reproof." The Uncle's meaning is plain: "NEITHER TO RIGHT NOR TO THE LEFT, BUT STRAIGHT, IS THE WAY." The older man is proud of his own adherence, and kindly emphasizes the positive. But young Frank looks at his own "treasure" and then at his uncle's pride, "comprehending something more than Uncle John meant he should. The boy was troubled. Something was left out" (*CW* II: 104–5).

As the sixty-five-year-old author of this memoir, Wright uses both his pen and drawing instruments to illustrate what was left out of his uncle's vision. In language, it's a matter of a line that runs like a vine, embroidering the straight one with its search for something else. In graphic form, represented on the page divider that subtitles Book One as "Family Fellowship," the uncle's straight course moves in a clear diagonal up across the page from bottom left to top right. By itself this line would be uninteresting. What merits its presence in the book is the boy's variations, a dance of acute angles that sometimes form triangles, other times branch out in parallel directions, and only at the end fall in line with the uncle's path. There, near the top, a series of tight contour lines indicate the shelves of exposed limestone characteristic of hills and ridge tops along the Valley, and only as these cease do the two tracks come to an end with a slight divergence, the boy taking two steps to stand at his uncle's side as they look back at the record of their progress. And we know what was said about that.

But one more feature climaxes Wright's design. In the upper right corner, just to the side of uncle and boy positioned to survey their tracks, is a large square. Standing apart from the line of progress and the embroidery of adventure, it is more conclusively solid than any of the other forms. As the lines running up the page are clearly an ascent of the hillside, the square near its top is a house. In the 1870s, when this scene takes place, there are no structures, just a favorite spot where young Frank would sneak away to avoid work and enjoy the beauties of nature. In 1932, however, a home does stand here, as it has since being built in 1911 and rebuilt in 1925. It is Taliesin.

If *An Autobiography* would codify Frank Lloyd Wright's importance to the world, it anchors such importance not in the buildings he would design, nor his ever-newsworthy exploits, but rather on this hillside where he'd learn about life as a youngster and then live it as a man striving to master his fate. Here he would build his refuge from the scandals of Chicago, and rebuild after tragedy. From here he'd design promising projects in the 1920s — and when most remained unfunded and unbuilt, he'd use his drafting room as a writing studio, producing the *Architectural Record* series of essays and the lectures for Princeton University and the Art Institute of Chicago, with the latter endeavors published as books. *An Autobiography* was the world's best advertisement not just for Frank Lloyd Wright but for Taliesin and all that could be done here. And within the same year as its publication a Taliesin Fellowship would be formed, an undertaking that not only gave the architect his first stable base in almost twenty-five years but provided support for what would be a whole new life and career, the achievements of which exceeded even his grandest successes so far.

The hill-climbing episode forms what Wright calls a Prelude to Book One: "Family Fellowship." His subtitle anticipates the Taliesin Fellowship, already being advertised, and the little adventure serves as an illustration in miniature of what it will propose as pedagogy. But from here the autobiographer moves into an extended treatment of family roots and experiences, with a much greater emphasis on his mother's side. They are Welsh (his father is English), and Wright begins with the Welshman who with his wife and children immigrated to the United States in 1844. More children would be born after they settled in Wisconsin, so that the Lloyd Jones family had thirteen members to take possession of the Helena Valley and rename it after themselves. Richard Jones was patriarch, and with Mary Lloyd as his wife the last names were joined for the children to carry. Richard was a farmer, and on Sundays a lay preacher. He had two gospels. One was the family motto of "Truth against the World," expressing the rebellious side of his Unitarian faith, a touchy issue both here and in Wales. The other was the gospel of hard work, in which young Frank would be schooled until it hurt. Yet Wright writes of his admiration for his grandfather, for teaching how to "add tired to tired and add it again," he notes in a phrase that will become one of his favorites, clearing the wilderness and replacing it with the best of human traits — or, as Wright phrases it, a "human smile, where before had been the Divine Countenance" (*CW* II: 107).

With Frank's birth the fictionalizing begins. He doesn't name the year, because by 1932 he would be equivocating about it, listing 1869 instead of 1867. 1869 is the date indicated on the marker above his grave in the Lloyd Jones burial ground — an empty grave, because his body would be exhumed and cremated after Olgivanna's death in 1985 and the ashes mixed with hers at Taliesin West in Arizona. Nor does he mention his middle name: not "Lloyd," as he would begin signing it after his parents' divorce, but "Lincoln," in homage to the recently slain president his father had admired.

What he does say is creative: that even before his birth his mother decorated the nursery with a set of engravings of English cathedrals from the periodical *Old England*. Were these illustrations published as early as June 1867? Some say not. But the nursery hangings are part of a legend: not only did Anna know she was to have a boy, but she knew he was destined to become a great architect. Even more creative, but no less moving, is a consequence of his birth, which creates a rupture between his parents. The mother's "extraordinary devotion to the child disconcerts the father," who "never made much of the child, it seems." Anna loved William no less, the son avers, "but now loved something more, something created out of her own fervor of love and desire. A means to realize her vision" (*CW* II: 109). This vision is of an architect who will build beautiful buildings, and to it she is uncommonly devoted.

To make this motherly devotion an even greater thing, Wright embroiders upon the straight line of the marriage's progress. It was a line going down, not up—Anna Lloyd Wright and William Cary Wright would divorce in 1885. Wright's biographers ascribe the deterioration to several factors, from William's position as a widower with children of his own for Anna to raise to Anna's displays of mental instability. In *Many Masks* (1997, 33) Brendan Gill illustrates the pathos of this first situation and the terror of the second by quoting stepdaughter Elizabeth Amelia Wright's unpublished memoir (deposited at the Iowa State Historical Society in Iowa City) detailing life in Anna's house. But as autobiographer Wright makes the bad conditions all his father's fault. His descriptions of Anna being stunned by her husband's desertion and pining for his return until his death many years later are at odds with family history and the details William Wright provided to the court in a divorce proceeding (1884–1885) that Anna did not contest (see Appendix). The uncertainty continues with Frank reporting that it is his mother who asks for the divorce rather than his father, as court records show. Of course a youth aged seventeen cannot know everything about such matters, but as the mature author of these memoirs Wright does build a detailed case that favors his mother. Why so? Personal reasons are just that, known only to Frank Lloyd Wright. But literary analysis of his rhetoric suggests that it is to enhance the sense of his mother giving special nurture to a child so he could become a great architect. In other words, he is favoring himself.

From this first section of Book One, "Family," emerge specifics of this special childhood. All conspire to make a life of fiction from the somewhat slippery materials of fact. There are the Froebel blocks that Wright himself and countless critics afterwards would describe as a kindergarten for architecture; it's his mother who is credited with discovering them at the Centennial Exhibition in Philadelphia (1876, when her son was well past kindergarten age), while in fact his aunts Nell and Jane, as professional progressive educators, would have known about the Froebel System before Anna. Story unity demands that its source be the mother. There is the Lloyd Jones motto, "Truth against the World," and its association with not just the "unity" of all things in Unitarianism but its working out in "the transcendentalism of the sentimental group at Concord: Whittier, Longfellow, yes, and Emerson, too" (*CW* II: 112). Of these, only Emerson was in Concord; "New England" would be a better cultural indicator, but that is where Frank's father is from. William Cary Wright did in fact profess these same ideals—and as an ordained minister rather than lay preacher. But again narrative coherence asks that they be associated with the mother's side of the family, reading this work on the farm in Wisconsin. By this point it is hardly a "side" but has become Frank's single family, a situation he acknowledges in life (though not described in *An Autobiography*) by changing his middle name from the paternally treasured "Lincoln" to the "Lloyd" that had been adopted for similar reasons by his grandfather, Richard Jones.

It is the Lloyd Jones family that both shapes young Frank as who he is and prompts him to flee in favor of what he'd like to become. Boyhood summers on the family farms provide much good material and another literary association with nineteenth-century America as celebrated in novels by Mark Twain and William Dean Howells. Working the fields and tending the animals are treated at length, the weight of attention meant to suggest the utter fatigue the child endured. He writes in such detail for several reasons, not just idealizing formative forces of his youth but enjoying the fact that as he writes these family farms are being reorganized into the Taliesin estate—to be worked by apprentices wishing to be cast in the mold of their great master. The cliché "gentleman farmer" can be used to mock Wright's agriculture of the 1930s and 1940s. He did not fight the image, but enhanced it, once again making self-dramatization an essential part of life. When riding equipment such as a cultivator or road grader he'd wear (as always) suit trousers, a fancy dress shirt, necktie, and stylish hat. Produce to be sold in Madison would be taken there not by truck or wagon but in the trunk and ample back seat of his car of the moment: a Cadillac Eight, a Packard Twelve, a Lincoln

Zephyr, or in the era's supreme example of automotive luxury, a Cord, custom painted in Wright's signature Cherokee Red.

Even as work forms him, the boy is forever running away. Uncle James calling him to come back is familiar, not just as the errant nephew has slipped away to hide from work but when he's wandered off mentally into a daydream. These meditations, which take him away from tiring labor, are an even more crucially formative force. When not working, he is thinking: how pastures are bathed in sun and rain, how trees stand like buildings more various than in all forms of architecture, and how what gives human style to architecture is the same as what gives character to trees.

As the boy grows, a rhythm emerges from his existence, with parallel themes developed from his lives in the city and on the farm. Madison, his home during the school year, is a delight of friendships, especially with young Robie Lamp. That Robie is crippled makes the affection he and Frank share all the more touching. They are inseparable, sharing the name "Frankenrob" as they christen the water-velocipede they've invented. Devouring the classic literature for boys, the two also acquire a printing press and do their own small editions. Summers in the country involve Sundays at the family's gathering ground (where just before his departure for Chicago Wright will assist with the interior design construction of Unity Chapel in 1886). For every morning of worship (and afternoon of picnicking with the clan, often numbering more than seventy) there would be six days of hard work during which Frank had to devise imaginative rhythms to ward off the monotony of repetitious labor. Any task, he learns, can be made interesting by discovering and exploiting such rhythm. The reward is confidence in one's own strength and physical dexterity that is as nimble as his thinking because the two are joined in a buoyant optimism that sees sunshine following the rain and success in the wake of failure. All this derives, he senses, from the balance of natural forces. Here may be the birth of the organic as a working principle. The interior sense of this balance would become a religion to the young man and serve as his place of refuge.

Study at the University of Wisconsin would lead to deeper reading, but out of class: Carlyle, Ruskin, Shelley, Goethe, Hugo, Blake. Wright exaggerates his university career—not graduating, as he admits, but coming much closer to it than the truth, which involved courses taken over a few semesters. For him, education was little more than emotional distress in which the inner meaning of anything never became clear. Instead, oppressive and threatening rules and regulations did little but hamper him. What he learns as an assistant to Professor Allan D. Conover, who was in charge of constructing the new Science Hall towering over Park Street at the foot of Bascom Hill, is more useful for what he will do in life and for anecdotal material. One task was fitting steel clips to the apex of roof trusses, which sends the young person climbing high up through this terrifying forest to retrieve the clips that the workmen had left dangling. This hardly seemed educational, he mocks. The scene comes right after one repeated from the Kahn lectures about witnessing the collapse at the State Capitol with all the terror of destruction and hideous loss of life, a story told this time not as a warning against false ornamentation but for the grave responsibility resting on an architect. This responsibility could be learned working for a master, as young Frank saw Professor Conover, with an emphasis on the educational value of work itself. College courses, on the other hand, dealt only with mass production, and Wright leaves the university feeling betrayed by having received so little of a true education.

Three lines conclude the "Family" section of Book One, each set for emphasis as a separate paragraph. The first states young Frank's desire for deeper knowledge. The second reveals him as a sentimentalist in love with truth. Only the third admits how tragic this situation may be. The answer to these regrets comes in the next part's title, "Fellowship." Sought beyond the naturally extended family of the Lloyd Jones clan and the contrived family of university life, fellowship is an ideal realized in the unlikeliest of places, Chicago. It is to this city that the young man flees in 1887, having pawned his father's finely bound copies of Plutarch's *Lives*, Gibbon's *Rome*, and several other books, plus the mink collar his mother had sewn into his overcoat. With just enough money for train fare and a few days' support, he arrives at night in a teeming metropolis. It hardly projects a warming sense of fellowship to the confused nineteen-year-old from Wisconsin, who is seeing electric lights for the first time and getting himself stuck on a swing bridge over the Chicago River. The abundant signage is overwhelming rather than helpful, an expressive text that claims his eye for everything, demoralizing it with an excess of vision. The next day he begins seeking work as a draftsman, but finds none available at present. Come back in a few months, he's told—hardly a possibility for a youth fresh off the train with only a few dollars in his pocket. After four days of this he tries the office of Joseph Lyman Silsbee, disguising his relationship to one of Silsbee's major clients, the Reverend Jenkin Lloyd Jones—hard to believe, given that less than a year before the youth had assisted Silsbee with the Unity Chapel for the Lloyd Jones family. But the point isn't crucial, for two reasons: Wright goes to the Silsbee office as a last resort, not first, and once there his point of contact is a fresh one, the young architect Cecil Corwin.

The relationship that develops is both professional and personal. Cecil becomes his new schoolmaster and his integration into the Silsbee firm is made easier by all that Corwin showed him. Beyond this they are feasting on the city's cultural delights. Corwin has lent Frank ten dollars to send to his mother so that Anna can learn not only where he is but that he has ample employment. Frank is taken to see Uncle Jenk's new church, the construction of which Corwin is supervising; when the uncle himself is encountered, Cecil makes it clear that Frank is now his ward, and not the family's. Wright had indeed left the "Family" of Part One. How the "Fellowship" of Book Two develops is a happy story.

Wright learns not only how it's done in Silsbee's office, but how there can be a better way as well. He appreciates that the architect's picturesque combinations of Queen Anne and Shingle Style features are a healthy contrast to the gimcrackeries so prevalent in this late Victorian era, but also regrets that his designs begin with an exterior sketch. This was just making pictures, Wright complains, with no perti-nence to what was real in the building. Nevertheless, he adores Silsbee for his style that shows through his imperfect methods. The young man is struck by the elder's somber mien with a hint of the tragic, the author-ity in his booming voice. "I learned a good deal about a house from Silsbee by way of Cecil" (*CW* II: 152), he concludes.

Although presented as an autobiography, Wright's narrative owes its form in these sections to a literary model, that of a Bildungsroman, the novel of young manhood so popular among nineteenth-century Romantic writers. Goethe's *The Apprenticeship of Wilhelm Meister* is the prime example, but well into Victorian days the style remained popular, as in exemplars such as *David Copperfield* by Charles Dickens. In this genre formative influence takes precedence, and so young Frank will spend time with Uncle Jenk as well. Here there is another "Fellowship" advantage. As one of the city's most progressive ministers and a widely read author, the Reverend Jenkin Lloyd Jones would be meeting regularly with other reformers, including the like-minded leaders of other faiths and social activists such as Jane Addams. Uncle Jenk's nephew was welcome at their dinners and occasions, getting an education in the age's developing thought. There were social activities for the congregation's young people as well, and at one of them—a costume party and dance themed on Victor Hugo's *Les Misérables*—Frank would meet his future wife. The meeting makes for a good story, as the two literally bump heads during the evening's lively commotion. The introduction is a fitting one, because their relationship continues as a series of jolts. Catherine Tobin (from the south side neighborhood of Kenwood, not far from Uncle Jenk's church) was just sixteen, and because her parents were not happy with Wright's attention they sent her off to Mackinac Island for three long months. He rails against the hypocrisy that would honor Nature while forbidding behavior that is plainly natural. Anna Lloyd Wright objects as well, and her son responds that all her objections accomplish is to make an innocently natural thing seem scandalous. But his greatest disdain is for society itself. In a mood that anticipates the defense he'd make twenty years later regarding his illicit relationship with Mamah Borthwick Cheney, a genuine scandal at the time, he sees a plot to make the couple give up all they love in their relationship and get married instead.

Frank and Catherine do marry, making their home in Oak Park while Anna and her two other children live in an older house next door. Wright's income from Silsbee had grown to a generous eighteen dollars per week, but for his new situation he'd need much more. He'd find it with a larger and more prosperous firm, Adler and Sullivan, architects not of homes but principally skyscrapers and public buildings. Their current project was the huge Auditorium Building on Michigan Avenue. It, together with the occasional commissions for houses the firm felt obliged to accept from important clients, would be enough to keep a talented young man like Wright busy. He would rise quickly to become designer Louis Sullivan's chief assistant and second-in-command (Dankmar Adler's responsibility was engineering), and to be valued so highly that the firm lent him the substantial sum of five thousand dollars to build his own new home. Sullivan also requested a clause in the contract that Wright would not compete by designing houses for others on his own. This clause would soon become more important than the loan itself.

Frank Lloyd Wright's five years with Sullivan are what most scholars and he himself regard as the key to his architectural education. *An Autobiography* supports this fact not just by Wright's testimony but by the context in which this association with Sullivan occurs. Louis Sullivan was the most innovative architect of his day, pioneering the notion that "form follows function" by doing just what Silsbee and other established architects were not doing: working not from an exterior sketch but from the inside of a building, determining first its function and from there deciding its form. His *métier* was the skyscraper, a logical enough affair. By transposing this idea for design to houses Wright would have more to work with in terms of space and movement, even though the physical scope was smaller.

Simply meeting Sullivan takes Wright's breath away, and the author of *An Autobiography* does all he can to replicate that experience for the reader. Having shown the man some of his own drawings, he is invited to see the master's—not from a portfolio, but from his hand in action. As the session continues, Sullivan draws on, lost in himself as the younger man looks on, thinking that as Silsbee's touch was like corn brushed by the wind, Sullivan's was like a passion vine in full bloom. What, Wright wonders, would his own touch be like some day?

Wright develops quickly under Sullivan. They work together, and afterwards talk, often late into the night. The older man at times seems to speak to himself, organizing his own thinking, and in Sullivan's murmuring Wright hears his own newly formed sense of rebellion expressed. For Wright, *radical* means "of the root," and so for him "rebellion" involves not an overthrow of everything but rather a recourse to essential nature, simply discarding what has put itself in the way. In this sense it is as important to learn whose work Sullivan values. Though he has contempt for most current architects, he maintains an imaginative dialogue with the work of Henry Hobson Richardson, as evidenced by the Auditorium Building's façade. He also likes John Wellborn Root— personally. Richardson and Root will be among the few practitioners for whom Wright will have kind words in coming years. But in *An*

Autobiography the young man can see his master's limitations as well. For example, Sullivan had no interest in the machine's impact on architecture, whether theoretical or practical. In larger terms, he cared only for rules that would bear no exceptions, whereas Wright felt exceptions were the key to proving or disproving rules. There is no feeling for the nature of materials that Wright would later champion; but after all, Louis Sullivan is designing skyscrapers and huge public buildings at this time, not Prairie Houses in which the intimate joys of life would be enhanced by art glass and naturally finished wood. One wonders what Wright might think of Sullivan's jewel-box banks in small towns scattered about the Midwest, but these would be from the master's period of decline beginning in the first decade and a half of the next century. At this point in his memoir, the author wants to show Louis Sullivan at the height of his powers and at the peak of his success. Anything less would detract from Wright's own sense of importance.

There is fellowship in Sullivan's office. When George Grant Elmslie joins it, Wright takes him to his side and forms the type of colleague-ship he admits he always needs. George has his limitations, some of them physical. But so did Robie Lamp. As Cecil Corwin had befriended young Wright, so too does Wright befriend the younger Elmslie. In time there will be a gregarious school of young architects at work in downtown Chicago, and soon after that Wright will attract the best of the youngest ones to his own studio in Oak Park. But that is in the future, only anticipated here, although the author's sense of deep foreshadowing is inescapable.

Wright's induction into Sullivan's office happens in the context of specific rediscoveries. The young man is reading Victor Hugo again, taken even more with the writer's theory of how the literary works against the architectural and how the Renaissance was a sunset, not a dawn. He also examines the Lloyd Jones family motto, "Truth against the World," in terms of God's trust placed in humankind to do its best, according to what it thinks is best, and the rest be damned. With five thousand dollars of the firm's money in his pocket, he can survey his future Oak Park neighborhood with a rare reference to thought from the other side of his family. Walking block after block of suburban construction, he tries to understand the builders' thinking but fails to discern anything beyond their empty forms, signs that are as meaningless as the phantasmagoria of streetside advertising he'd encountered when first arriving in Chicago. Oak Park's progression of mimicking styles lacks even the feeble basis in meaning behind the commercial signage downtown. Wright recalls how his father deplored sentimentality in music, and wonders if the same standard might apply here.

The young architect is candid about what brings his association with Sullivan to an end—and candid about how in the bootlegged houses he had begun designing he tried nothing radical and nothing that could be further developed, not because of any secrecy but because his out-of-office time was limited. His side of the argument with Sullivan has merit, for not only were the personal projects done on his own time, but Sullivan himself had asked Wright to work on the Charnley House (1891) after regular hours. That had been acceptable to both, as the firm could satisfy a friend's desire for housing (not a Sullivan specialty) while Wright could experiment with ideas such as the decorative value of a plain surface, something a bit radical and certainly an innovation that could be developed, as it would be in the Winslow House (1894), Wright's first publically recognized independent commission. But Sullivan is incensed at the division of interest; all of his employee's energies, no matter how boundless, should remain within the firm. Because it is the firm's loan of five thousand dollars that has let Wright build his own home (with drafting room) right in the center of all this moonlighting activity, Sullivan feels justified in refusing to release the promissory note, even though Wright has by now repaid it (albeit with bootlegging income). At this Wright quits. Sullivan is wrong, he insists. But so is he himself, probably more so, he admits.

Here a structural link makes its point by juxtaposition rather than causal development, a reminder that the author's manner of thought is more spatial than linear. The technique is effective, as it lets him rest an indictment that logic alone might not achieve. Wright's account moves directly from his breakup with Louis Sullivan to setting up a household with Catherine. "Architecture was my profession," he states firmly. "Motherhood became hers." If this seems a blunt and even cold way to begin his account of his marriage, it is nothing compared to the next sentence, set off as a paragraph: "Fair enough, but it was division" (*CW* II: 177). The term is not a common one for relationships, but is uncomfortably familiar in context—in the section of *An Autobiography* just

concluded Louis Sullivan has used this same term to end his own relationship with Frank Lloyd Wright. "I won't tolerate any division under
any circumstances" (*CW* II: 175), the master has said. Because of Wright's
moonlighting a division exists, and hence his association with the firm
is terminated. Using the same term for his marriage acknowledges that
family life will not work out, the blame laid at Catherine's feet for her
own maternal moonlighting. It can be presumed that *An Autobiography*'s
readers know all about Mamah, sensational as the events eighteen years
before had been; even more notorious were the widely publicized in-
volvements with the two other women that followed. But no one could
appreciate the inside story of Frank's life with his first wife, his first
love, unless he would tell it now. And so he does, with full disclosure of
its reason for dissolution right up front.

Children dominate the story. To Frank, they are an amusing diversion. He delights in their rambunctiousness, and likes telling stories of
client interviews being interrupted and studio business being distracted
by urchins peeking through the door. They can do this because the Frank
Lloyd Wright Home and Studio are ingeniously joined by a passageway
that encompasses a living tree the architect could not bear to cut down.
Intrusions are welcome not just for Wright's sense of the ridiculous but
because he really does want his children to grow up in beautiful, stimu-
lating surroundings. But in time the two responsibilities begin to compete. He cannot escape being an architect, and that job overpowers the
role of being a father, much as he never felt close to his own.

Book One concludes with a confession of self-indulgence, in the
belief that if one concentrated on the luxuries of life the necessities would
take care of themselves. Wright is honest about the price for this, as a
staggering $850 grocery bill is being compounded at 25 percent interest.
He recognizes the expense and vows to do better by the providers who
have trusted him. But this pledge does not last, and once again necessities
fall victim to the luxuries he could not do without.

Although he has jumped ahead of strict chronology to tell of the
playroom (1895) and studio (1898) additions and all six of his children
(the last born in 1903), Wright marks the transition from Book One to
Book Two as 1893. This second book is titled "Work," and 1893 is when
he left Adler and Sullivan to begin practicing on his own. But it is also
the year of the Columbian Exposition, a fateful year (as he would rue it)

when his country's culture surrendered to the falsely classic. It is when the principal architect of this project, Daniel Burnham, offers Wright a free education in Europe followed by a partnership in his firm (made available by the death of John Wellborn Root, himself a leading practitioner). 1893 also marks the early design phase of the Winslow House (1894), a structure that would put Wright on the path toward conceiving the fundamentals of the Prairie House as built in the coming decade. All this he views as a challenge and more, as Burnham's offer puts nothing less than his freedom at risk.

Once again Wright begins a book of his *Autobiography* with an interface of language and graphics. Writing about agricultural fieldwork as a metaphor for his architectural tasks, he draws another page divider to display the structure he has in mind: a flat ziggurat of right-angled turns, tight lines suggesting the plowing pattern of a farmer in his field, continuing as if to fill the page until an obstacle is encountered, diverting the plough's path. This diversion not only departs from the pattern of tight right angles but also cuts across the borders that frame the field; it departs from the design entirely, causing the frame itself to head off toward parts unknown. As with the variations Wright as a boy made on his Uncle John's steady line of progress, these graphics suggest what Wright will be doing now: making not a deviation but an outright departure.

The first departure is from the career track Chicago's powers-that-be have set for him. If Burnham's offer is too good to be true, Wright's polite refusal of it is flabbergasting. His explanation has substance: he can't run away from his country, because he can't run away from himself. The two need each other, especially now, with the pseudo classicism of the Columbian Exposition's White City having set American architecture back fifty years, as Louis Sullivan was complaining. To leave now would break faith with himself and with his country—a reminder that Wright is forever identifying himself with the United States, and vice versa.

That's the first departure, a taking leave of official Chicago for a path of his own toward a uniquely American architecture. The Winslow House is a second departure, one for which he is ridiculed, and also one from which he has to step back a bit to design a superficially more traditional home for neighbor Nathan Moore. A third involves designing the "Romeo and Juliet" windmill (1896) for his aunts' Hillside Home School. His uncles mock the plan, swearing it won't survive the first strong wind. (It did, and stands today.) A fourth departure is mandated when he adds the Studio to his Oak Park Home, ignoring logical construction in order to preserve the wonderful old willow tree that has shaded the house. But Wright's major departure of these early years in private practice is his disgust with the nature of conventional home design and his determination to build the Prairie House.

Because his account of this development has already taken anecdotal form in the fourth of his Kahn lectures, "The Cardboard House," details of its inception and development come easily, as does the inspiration of the prairie's horizontal appeal as first described in his opening lecture to the Art Institute of Chicago in October of 1930. It is interesting to note that Wright's presentation is much the same: for students at Princeton, for a cultural audience in Chicago, and for the mass-market readers of *An Autobiography*. Such is the coherence of his argument and the simple common sense of its underlying principles. Plasticity, continuity, an entire building growing like a plant in nature, free to be itself—it all seems so simple, even obvious. Wright's departure from the practice of the day is "radical" in the way he prefers to use that word, as relating to the root of a thing. Of all his departures, this is the most accessible one, dedicated as it is to human use and comfort.

Will this last departure from the fraudulent excesses of popular design in favor of a comfort-enhancing and spirit-lifting simplicity be successful? It depends upon the readiness of clients to throw off inhibitions and embrace the new. They can expect to encounter trouble at the sawmill for their lumber and at the bank for their financing, as a Prairie House fits none of the norms. For the architect, each project is a new experience, and to emphasize this Wright follows up his explanation of the Prairie House with accounts of his two larger structures from this period, the Larkin Building (1903) and Unity Temple (1904). His task with the former is to design an environment insulated from the pollution-filled train yards surrounding it. The larger design finds power in simplicity, especially that of the straight line and flat plane that put power to purpose, much as does the ocean liner, airplane, and automobile (though the streamlined examples of each are current to 1932, not 1903). Mechanically, the key has been to separate the stairs from the central block, letting them function as ventilation. In the Larkin project, character and beauty become one.

Character and beauty also meld in Unity Temple, though its building material calls for a different way of working out this principle. Built with poured concrete, it relies on four free-standing elements to carry the overhead structure, as the architect puts it. Note his careful choice of words. Not "hold up the roof," for what's above seems to float of its own volition, flooding the room with brightness from its large skylight. Congregants have praised this sense of spiritual uplift, while acknowledging the Unitarian sense of community that's enhanced by seating not just on the floor in front of the pulpit but in the galleries closely ranked on three sides with organist and choir behind. Rather than the traditional church and steeple, Wright has seized upon his own faith's manner of worship that places its trust in humankind on Earth instead of fretting over a heaven about which nothing can really be known. Instead of building a temple to God, he builds one to man, where humankind can study itself for God's sake. A room proportioned to this purpose could be made beautiful in the simple sense of having a naturally built structure for a natural purpose.

The minister is liberal, the congregation is progressive, and so the architect challenges them to use their imagination, allying it with his own—and he is, after all, a member of this church. But he will have nothing to do with competition. As he had warned the young men of architecture listening to him at the Art Institute of Chicago, any such contest simply averages out the averages to set a greater mediocrity. For Unity Temple he does have to deal with a building committee, but he knows that its head is a mechanical engineer and inventor, creative in all pursuits—an image of the typical Wright client, which in fact he was— and that one such bright person in charge is all that's needed to push things past any obstructively dull organization.

Wright takes this opportunity to add thoughts about the suggestive nature of geometric shapes and the positive benefits of brooding over them for long periods before picking up his instruments and getting to work. Unity Temple is a good example for readers to have before them so that these processes can become evident. Before it existed, there was no clear analog in the history of religious structures that could suggest how it would turn out. There was no style to be copied. What did exist was the square or cube, with its suggestion of integrity, as opposed to other shapes in nature such as the circle or sphere (infinity), the straight line of rectitude, and the triangle's aspiration. As shapes, they are the basis of organic design and construction. But first comes thought—lots of it, at all times of day and night, until the plan is fully envisioned. Only then can it be drawn.

Wright is proudest of Unity Temple when it achieves a harmony of the whole, a true challenge to an architect when working with the diverse functions of different masses. From it all emerges the soul of a design, a living motif that conveys a sense of the inside becoming the outside in a way that not only suits the room's purpose but makes a significant architectural statement. It is noteworthy that as many pages in Wright's *Autobiography* have been given to Unity Temple as to the Prairie House—partly because the architect has spoken about the latter in his recent lectures, but mostly because it and the Larkin Building were garnering attention in Europe. For the memoirist, Europe is the next destination in the series of departures that have characterized Book Two.

"The Closed Road" is Wright's heading for the section that follows his description of how visiting professor Kuno Francke has prompted Wright's travel to Europe and preparation of a monograph of his complete work with the German publisher Ernst Wasmuth. In *Frank Lloyd Wright: Europe and Beyond* (1999) Anthony Alofsin has established that Wright's German contact was not Francke but rather Bruno Möhring; in any event, the forty-two-year-old architect has reached a critical point in his life, one he associates with the departure from Wisconsin for Chicago that initiated Book Two. The absorbing initial period of his work has ended, he writes of 1909; weariness has set in. As on the farm during his boyhood, he has been overworked, adding tired to tired. Seeing no way out, he wants simply to get away from his life in the Oak Park Home and Studio. The logical direction for flight is to Germany, where more artistically appealing work on the Wasmuth portfolio awaits him.

Europe may provide the distance from responsibility he craves, and which he has not found in Oak Park. He describes how most days at four o'clock he takes off on his young black saddle horse for spirited rides across the prairies north of Oak Park, with pauses for outdoor readings of Walt Whitman (the poet of unfettered exuberance—and of candid sexuality). Wright recalls his constant hunger, all his life, for such pleasures: riding, swimming, dancing, skating, omnivorous reading, and music. In a curious aside, he mentions how motoring, a new exuberance, had become "a disturbance of all values, subtle or obvious, and it brought the disturbance to me" (*CW* II: 219). Disturbance? He turns at once to "Domesticity," professing love of children and home but having a need for freedom that was greater. He asks for a divorce. Catherine asks him to wait a year. He does, to no avail. And so to clarify his ideal he composes a brief statement with the heading *Sociology: A "Tract,"* in which he specifies three principles for an honest relationship between the sexes: that marriage per se is slavery, that love is not property, and that children don't need legalities of legitimacy.

All because of the automobile? Wright is assuming, correctly, that readers will catch his implication. It is now 1932; the Roaring Twenties had loosened the last restraints of Victorian morality and set young people free, the mobility for which was as common as the homely Ford Model T and as racy as the Stutz Bearcat. As always, Frank Lloyd Wright has been ahead of his time, spending the first decade of the twentieth century tearing up Oak Park with the suburb's first high-powered roadster. And he hasn't been alone. There is no mention of it here, but friends and neighbors had been scandalized not just by his wild driving but by his companionship for these rides: Mamah Borthwick Cheney, the wife of a client. In a temporal and spatial jump worthy of moviemaking, Wright creates a montage by shifting scenes completely, to a little villa perched above romantic Florence in quietly charming Fiesole. He names the place to invoke its history as a shelter from domestic woes, asking how many others have sought refuge here and answering with an exclamation point. For now, he does not name Mamah, but it is her shared presence that's important in this rebellious act. The two are there not for sex, and only by way of love; it is an ideal that has taken them from their families and brought them here.

The departure is one he associates with his earlier move from Wisconsin to Chicago, taken resolutely in the same faith. Now the language and graphics that began Book Two become clear, and demonstrate the spatial dimension of Wright's thinking. The strict right-angled turns that constitute fieldwork have been his previous departures: from Madison to Chicago, from Silsbee to Sullivan, from Sullivan to his own practice, from the bootlegged projects to the Prairie House, and so forth. In sum, they have created an estimable body of work, a brilliant career; albeit one that now frustrates him. Obstacles have been met and overcome, but in comparison to what has just happened they are no more troublesome than turning a team to keep the plowing on track. Now, however, something much greater has been encountered, and the line of development can no longer stay where convention would mandate. Instead, it crosses several framing boundaries until the frame itself is broken, opening to an infinity the architect is eager to explore.

The heavenliness of life in the villa above Florence transitions to Taliesin. "Work, life, and love to be transferred to the beloved Valley" (*CW* II: 222) is how Wright put it, associating his move back across the Atlantic with his grandfather's emigration not just to this same hillside but to the idea of America itself. Wright's move will respect that hillside, his home becoming of it and not on it. There it will combine stone and wood of the region, with walls and chimneys having their rock faces exposed and facing outwards, as if in nature itself. And also like nature, it will never be finished. About Taliesin the memoirist can be rhapsodic, calling it a house of the North that seeks fellowship with its surroundings, as open as a campsite to the breeze. The picture Wright draws of it is a living portrait, employing as many senses as practical to physically involve the reader, just as the author feels the home's presence. Showers would make music on its roofs while broad eaves shelter open windows from the rain. Only at the end of this description, which continues for quite a few pages, does Wright mention the one thing that will break the harmony. "No one feeling the repose of its spirit could believe in the storm of publicity that kept breaking outside," he remarks, "because a kindred spirit—a woman—had taken refuge there for life" (*CW* II: 229).

This is the only mention of Mamah since the "work, life, and love" reference that has begun the section on Taliesin so many pages before. After it, there comes the account of Wright's work in Chicago on Midway Gardens, filled with as many business details as architectural notes. In the midst of it comes another guarded reference to Mamah, who is still unnamed: the phone call with its news of the tragedy at Taliesin. Will he speak frankly of Mamah Borthwick Cheney now? No, not until another two thousand words covering the subsequent history and failure of the Gardens. Is this a jarring digression from chronology, a refusal to face the tragedy, or—at worst—a suggestion that Frank Lloyd Wright's work is more important to him than his partner's life? Not at all. Encouraging a sensitive and sympathetic response, he prompts his readers with inferences within the memoirist's requiem for Midway Gardens:

> What they might have been had the Gardens found in Chicago a true mate and help meet? They would still be more wonderful, covered with the climbing ivy which the scheme craved with a natural hunger. Arching trees massed about the walls, the little significances in the empty places that had longed for them all those years and that would have been like a happy glint in the eyes. The whole solidly built place would now be polished, mellowed, enriched by years of good care, hallowed by pleasant associations—a proud possession for any great city. (*CW* II: 239)

In writing this epitaph for Midway Gardens—opened in 1914, abandoned in the 1920s, and demolished in 1929—Wright is personifying his creation. The building is feminine; in regretting its conversion into a dance hall, he has decried the sight of "a distinguished beautiful woman dragged to the level of a prostitute" (*CW* II: 238). But that is just a parallel. His closing words are much more personal, looking into a future which could not happen, to years that never came with their growth of ivy and maturity of trees. It's a heartbreaking tribute. Only after it is delivered, with respect for a project that in the hands of others went wrong, does Wright return to the subject of his 1914 telephone call with the news that Mamah, her two children, and four others had been murdered and the residential wing of Taliesin burned to the ground.

Wright's description of what he found is moving. His last act is cutting the flowers from his lover's garden to fill her casket, which he, his son John, and two helpers lower into the grave. He then asks them to leave, as "I wanted to fill the grave myself." He leaves it unmarked. "Why mark the spot where desolation ended and began?" A gravestone may not name her, but *An Autobiography* finally does; in this last bit of narrative he utters her first name.

Nature can be merciful as well as cruel, and in time Wright heals. Solace is found in rebuilding Taliesin, but also in looking East—to the Far East, Japan. Again, for the purpose of his book's (if not his life's) coherence, Frank Lloyd Wright simplifies the order of development.

His interest in Japan has predated his flight to Europe, his construction of Taliesin, and his work on Midway Gardens, not to mention the murders and fire. Yet he saves mention of Japanese art and culture until after the events of 15 August 1914. The implication is that these interests are part of his rebuilding, part of his reinvention of himself in the wake of tragedy and destruction. In truth, his interest in Japanese prints had generated several essays in the wake of his 1905 visit. And as for the Imperial Hotel commission, his trip to Tokyo in 1913 with Mamah was to bargain for it. For the artificial history of *An Autobiography*, however, the sequence is this: Mamah is mourned, Taliesin (now called Taliesin II) is rebuilt, and the Wasmuth portfolio makes its impact. After all this comes the call to build the Imperial Hotel and Wright's first discussion of Japanese life. Once again the author's life story is arranged with an eye to deep characterization and strong thematic development — in other words, according to the standards of good fiction.

As with his treatment of the Prairie House, Wright's extensive commentary on Japan over the first three decades of the century allows the informed reader to observe what Wright now considers crucial enough to be included in his memoir. The first point the architect mentions is how the Japanese print succeeds at eliminating the insignificant, a process he notes in his own work with the commencement of independent practice. Hence the prints are not an influence but rather a parallel example of shared ideals. Those same prints have led him to consider Japan as the most artistic country on earth, because its art is indigenous, organic, and one with the nature in which it was produced. This introductory thesis, stated so directly, is a conclusion toward which Wright had worked his way over much time and writing. Here it serves as a helpful guide to the importance of what follows: the Japanese home as a triumph of elimination and simplicity (achieved by standardization), a naturalness and quiet dignity of conduct among the people, and a clean honesty of expression in their religion.

At this point, before his narrative about designing and building the Imperial Hotel, Wright brings up another point of history: his relationship with Miriam Noel. Just as Mamah had been associated with the cruel failure and ultimate destruction of Midway Gardens, Miriam is allied with work on the hotel and with a specific aspect of Japanese culture as well. That aspect is part of another jeremiad against conventional marriage and celebration of the sounder ethics grounded in honesty that an open relationship demands. Its corollary is the ancient Japanese culture of the courtesan. She is not immoral, he argues, only unmoral. Unmoral, but definitely sensual. Surveying a print of courtesans in their glory, Wright observes how those depicted are not dressed in the proper sense but just robed, implying that they can become unrobed as easily as the model for Midway Gardens slipped out of her one-piece garment. Mamah, we know, has been identified with Midway Gardens—including its demolition. Now Miriam is introduced in the narrative company of Japanese courtesans, so appealing in the prints Wright loves and in the culture he admires. Yet for all of Miriam's appeal, there is a hint of the unhappiness to come. Can what is "naturally sordid be made beautiful?" he asks. "Probably not—we shall see" (*CW* II: 256).

The author's troubles with Miriam Noel, who had introduced herself just months after the Taliesin tragedy, develop in Japan (where she has accompanied him as his mistress) and continue for the next decade. Even with this in mind, Wright argues for the key distinction, claiming that for Japanese courtesan culture (and by implication his life with Miriam) as long as the "'moral' element that could make it bestial was lacking" the affection could be pure (*CW* II: 258). Again, thinking like the innovative architect he was, Wright privileges the higher principle of ethics over momentary contrivance, especially that of what he elsewhere calls the mob. With Mamah, the sensationalistic press had introduced the moral element, scandalizing and shaming their love. In the case of Miriam, that moralization would come from her, and she would rally not just the press but also the police, FBI, and immigration authorities to punish Wright for his subsequent relationship with Olgivanna beginning in 1924.

The Imperial Hotel itself is dealt with concisely, with the emphasis on why his design survived both the initial severe earthquake (during construction) and the later catastrophic one on the day of its formal opening. Wright starts with the principle that the quake by nature is a force that cannot be met by anything within human power. But nature has provided a remedy as well, sixty to seventy feet of soft mud lying beneath eight feet of soil. The building, he suggests, can be floated on this mud. Just as Wright's thinking has balanced one natural principle with another, structure itself will combine tension and flexibility by means of a cantilever. In terms of its footprint, the building is divided into parts so that each can move independently if forced. Japanese and Western labor practices are combined. Wright concludes his account proudly, citing the 13 September 1923 telegram following the massive earthquake: "Hotel stands undamaged as monument of your genius." For once, he notes, it is good news that is flashing around the world.

Next comes California, where the story is less rewarding. Wright begins uncharacteristically by making excuses and describing factors working against him. Years of effort in Tokyo have depleted him. Stricken with fever, he was nursed back to health by his eighty-year-old mother who crossed the Pacific to aid him—in the process driving away Miriam Noel and the last of that domestic relationship. Work on the Hollyhock House commission competes with finishing up the Imperial Hotel in Tokyo; when he has been able to return for stateside visits, matters at Taliesin in Wisconsin often command his attention. Heiress and patroness of the arts Aline Barnsdall is herself not only strong-willed and independent, but is given to even more international travel than Wright. Described as a restless spirit compelled to traverse the globe, "she would drop suggestions as a war-plane drops bombs and sails into the blue" (*CW* II: 271). Consequently Wright is forced to build the house by telegraph, as it were, as far as any relationship with the client was concerned. Her people are hard to work with, but it is no easier to delegate authority to his own on-site associates, Rudolf Schindler and Wright's son Lloyd. If the memoirist's account of Japan had ended with a triumph over disaster, his preliminaries about working in California prepare readers to expect the worst.

How sympathetic, then, will the readers be when Wright begins his account of designing Hollyhock House (1917) with a sigh of envy for Bach, Mozart, and the other masters of classical music. Like him, they would concentrate on creation. But with that done, the composers lifted the baton and directed the orchestra to play. What a joy to have so many fingers ready to produce exactly what was intended on instruments fashioned for that purpose. Wright has enjoyed similar support in Tokyo, having the advantage of drawing his design next door to where it would be built, and within a few days seeing that design take objective form—executed by not just a thousand fingers but by almost that many workers.

He won't have that advantage in Los Angeles, but the ideal persists, sustained by a cleverly extended metaphor, the author performing with language as he does with architectural design. As a symphony is an edifice of sound (so his father taught him), Wright feels architecture should be symphonic. He cites the romanza of music, the freedom to make one's own form, governed only by the musician's sense of proportion. There's a mystery to it, a feeling to the work that overpowers any indications of how it was made. Change the aural to the visual and the romanza seems possible for architecture.

Despite all the obstacles to his work, Wright concludes with a feeling of success, just as the reader feels rewarded by following his metaphor this far. In Hollyhock House atop Olive Hill's thirty-six acres set in Hollywood and overlooking much of Los Angeles he has made a house that is site-specific, as natural to California as Taliesin is to Wisconsin. His romanza exploits the fact that architecture employs a mathematical coordination of form, a form that in the Barnsdall home adds to straight line and flat plane an integrity of ornament that creates a rhythm for it all. Weary of duty, he considers work on the house a holiday, and in this sense it has turned out well. His play with the music of poetic form delights the client to the point that she accepts it as a symphony.

Then come the troubles, ones that musical composers never face thanks to the existence of proper orchestras. Here is where the metaphor deliberately breaks down. The contractor should have been a competent concertmaster, but he can read nothing beyond the average score. Wright's associate Rudolf Schindler takes the client's side in most debates, while at the same time claiming to be in charge of Frank Lloyd Wright's office when the man is absent. Wright objects that he himself is his office. To top it off, for reasons the architect professes not to understand, Aline Barnsdall views the finished house and decides to give it all away, keeping just the ancillary residence for the time being and leaving the larger theater complex unbuilt. Yet the designer regrets nothing.

Instead, he is on to another California innovation, the textile-block house. Its basis lies in the plasticity of concrete, a material perfect for showing the imagination at work. Wright's idea is to weave blocks of it together with steel rods, the latter for warp and the former for woof. Recalling how he had used blocks in a textured way for the upper walls of Midway Gardens, he reasons that by eliminating the mortar joint he can make the entire fabric mechanical. In the process, he could do away with skilled labor, something always seen as a cost menace. The medium's lightness and strength prompt a metaphor that typically stretches the distance between tenor and vehicle. Steel is a spider, he suggests, spinning a web anchored in cement. The means are plastic, and thus they insure that the process is organic.

The results would include one of Frank Lloyd Wright's most beautiful residences, La Miniatura, the Alice Millard House (1923) constructed in Pasadena. As opposed to the popular local Mission Style, in La Miniatura Wright seeks something genuinely expressive of southern California. Because his client has only ten thousand dollars for the project, the architect satisfies her desires for spacious living and dining rooms by placing one atop the other. This un-Wrightian verticality becomes an organic factor when another cost-saving factor is introduced, in the form of an otherwise unsaleable lot wedged in a presumably unbuildable ravine. La Miniatura will rise from the gardens of this ravine like the tall eucalyptus trees beside it, Wright envisions. From inside the building balconies look out on nature and terraces would lead down to it. Even the unused front of this lot beautifies the area, providing garden space for the happy neighbors. As with his other homes in the hills above Los Angeles, Wright's classic horizontal line would be inappropriate to the landscape here. But given his solution of vertical stacking, a new kind of artistry becomes possible. Crocheting with masonry, as he sees it, allows a great variety of beauty, so much of it that he forgets that the house belongs to someone else. Whose is it, in terms of art? Palladio, Bramante, Sansovino, and others were sculptors, but here he can be a weaver. That is indeed a more commonplace form of expression, but who knows what may follow from it.

The Storer, Freeman, and Ennis Houses (1923) follow in quick order. In them viewers see the same lyricism with textile blocks and stacked levels, climaxing with the massive home for Charles Ennis set near the top (but not atop) the steep rise of the Los Feliz neighborhood towering over Hollywood and Los Angeles proper. The structure is as noteworthy a feature as the huge sign spelling Hollywood and the dome of the Griffith Observatory. People in the city see it every day, and movie audiences know it as the setting for any number of popular films such as *Blade Runner* and *An Inconvenient Woman*, not to mention such drive-in fare as *The Howling II: Your Sister is a Werewolf.* As such, Wright could consider his attempt to build the characteristic California house a success, as from the romanza of Hollyhock and the lyricism of La Miniatura to the eminence of Ennis his architecture has become an icon for the area, extended by former associates and apprentices such as Richard Neutra and John Lautner. He proudly mentions that the greatest successes of his career have been those when he was at a disadvantage, particularly when time, place, and circumstances intersect with his own faults. But whether it be Alice Millard's ravine or Aline Barnsdall's personality, Wright could be at his best. When challenged, he notes, it is easier to stay alert. But the area can present only a few opportunities like La Miniatura and Hollyhock House. Local practice favors cheap expedience and quick sales. To stay would subject his work to these indignities, as everyone is dedicated just to getting by. And so he gets out, heading back to Taliesin for work on the projects (most of them unbuilt) that would round out the 1920s.

Book Two of *An Autobiography* concludes with a reprise of issues from the Kahn lectures given at Princeton and published the year before as *Modern Architecture.* But as with material from the earlier essays, Wright now weaves it all together in an anecdotal manner that emphasizes his continuing professional growth. The "glass skyscraper" designed in 1924 (but never built) for the National Life Insurance Company in Chicago adapts the cantilever principle of the Imperial Hotel to the towering office building. This new style of skyscraper is described with the same sensuous details as he summoned for his listeners at Princeton. His old master Louis Sullivan admires the plan, giving praise the younger architect loves to repeat: that Sullivan never could have done it by himself, but that Wright could not have done it without Sullivan. Taliesin burns again, and is once again rebuilt (1925). Its priceless art collection has been once more destroyed, but these are objects that live on in him and in the work he does. Louis Sullivan dies, and is remembered in the text. Olgivanna arrives, and he loves her. Taliesin and what remains of Wright's practice are saved by incorporation and the intervention of friends. Miriam uses all aspects of civil and criminal law to pursue and harass him, and eventually she dies. He can mourn only what he could remember of what had once been a remarkable woman who for fifteen years "had been going up in flame, seldom knowing real rest unless by some artificial means" (*CW* II: 322).

As Wright prepares to turn the page of this section called "Work" he pauses to appreciate the scarlet sumac of autumn, and the seeds of the future that lie perfected in hanging fruit. Book Three, titled "Freedom," causes the reader to wonder if, given his age, a wintertime of retirement beckons. Instead, it is freedom *from* something that Wright appreciates; freedom from confusion and turmoil. The trouble and confusion he alludes to concern, most recently, the difficulties in formalizing his relationship with Olgivanna. But one can hardly forget the two decades of wild disruption that began with the flight from his family and period of companionship in Europe with Mamah in 1909. There's an implicit reminder of this when the *Wendingen* volume of 1925 brings back what the architect had taken abroad, together with the architecture now being imported from Europe as the International Style—as though any reduction to style could not be offensive, he notes. Book Three concludes, not that many pages later, with an explicit remembrance of a lonely night in Paris, just three weeks after abandoning his wife and children. And so it is reasonable to consider that Wright sees himself in 1927 (as he dates the start of Book Three) emerging from a substantial period of grief. With all such distraction removed, creativity resurges as new goals can be seen clearly. He has brought it all back home in order to start again. Could Frank Lloyd Wright have foreseen at this point how a second career, even greater than his first, would develop? The energy for it is certainly there.

The third book of Wright's autobiography is brief, about one-third the length of either of the previous parts, as if the writer were eager to get on with the future. Its structure also welcomes the revisions and substantial additions to come in the 1943 edition. There are some topics to introduce, others to review. New on the agenda is Arizona, which the architect and his wife have discovered when helping with the Arizona Biltmore Hotel and Cottages (1927) and planning the San Marcos in the Desert resort (1929, project). Taliesin West (1937) is still in the future, but the Ocatilla Desert Camp (1928) had been built and is already in deterioration as other quarters are used for temporary occupation. The essentials of Wright's desert vision are already in place, including the two principles he would cite frequently in coming years: the saguaro cactus as an example of reinforced construction, and the straight line of the prairie here becoming the dotted line of the desert.

As always, what Wright builds for himself comes closest to realizing his thoughts. Ocatilla Desert Camp, its spelling changed from convention to suit his fancy, is made of cabins grouped like giant butterflies conforming to the outcroppings of rock that define the landscape outside of Chandler, Arizona. A zigzag of boxboard walls connect them. Roofing is of canvas, and can be opened to make the structures look like sailing ships. When stretched overhead, the canvas diffuses the light that makes the thought of anything more opaque depressing. That the Wrights and their forthcoming Fellowship would soon be spending half of each year in the Arizona desert is no surprise.

A section on "The Usonian City" raises expectations of Broadacre City (1934 and afterwards, as a demonstration project). But Broadacre must wait for the Fellowship's labor (and residential example). At this point in the first edition of *An Autobiography* the author simply draws, at length and in detail, on his skyscraper lecture to the students at Princeton. Once again he retells the history of civilization, concluding that what first made the city necessary is now choking it to death. Skyscrapers have been devised only as a way of avoiding the problem, in the process making the exploitative practices of landlords all the worse. But there is hope in sight. Although Broadacre City itself is not yet proposed, certain features of it that were introduced at Princeton are repeated here. Highways will be designed with the care and art of architecture, carrying people from the city's congestion to freedom farther out. Decentralization will be facilitated by an innovative roadside service station that provides for people as well as for automobiles. Chain merchandizing, home entertainment centers, and travel itself not as a matter of commuting but as holiday-making to what he calls automobile objectives — all these elements forecast in the Kahn lectures are repeated here, and reappear as key parts of the Broadacre City plan the Fellowship will help to complete.

New to those who have been following Wright is his manner of presenting the St. Mark's Tower. Earlier descriptions had emphasized the clever way of financing such a project; here the focus is on its promising design with straight lines and flat planes characteristic of the machine age serving as outline instead of mass. Unlike the dark stone caverns of today's cities, Wright's structure will benefit from its principle of design, which opens itself to light. Thanks to its cantilevered construction, the tower can be narrower without sacrificing inside space, which means the building can be set back from the street, allowing a park-like setting. The results are spectacular; Wright pictures it as a spider spinning its web of steel to enmesh clear, translucent, and colored glass. The iridescence of this fabric is set against the blue sky above and greenery below, everything shimmering with light. Like the beautiful presentation drawings Marion Mahony did in the Oak Park Studio thirty years before, Wright's description creates a vivid impression. His words use their sonority—*reflected, refracted*—to mimic the lushness of visual effect. Colors cascade off the page. As in a drawing, the passage itself has a spatial unity, beginning with the structure's park-like setting and returning there after the building has risen in all its splendor.

Book Three moves to its close with a grab-bag of topics. In Chicago, where his work is on exhibit at the Art Institute, a "tall handsome woman came toward me smiling. A moment's hesitation and I recognized Catherine" (*CW* II: 352). Encountered in the gallery amid samples of his work from earlier days, she is a reminder of his youth. Now remarried, unseen by Wright for fifteen years, she is a pleasant sight, looking young and happy. They continue through the exhibit together, recalling the works that emerged from the studio adjacent to their home. Wright is happy to be loyal to his work, and also delights that Catherine remains loyal to one she has loved: him.

A few minor matters follow, as if the author is putting off the conclusion to *An Autobiography*. There's a squabble in Milwaukee about the city's classically inspired courthouse design, and more squabbling in Chicago over how its upcoming world's fair, "A Century of Progress" (1933), should be represented in architecture. Wright advocates for the freedom he finds in the horizontal, repeating familiar arguments that now seem to carry on a bit beyond their effectiveness in earlier essays and lectures (and which had their say again in Book Two). Finally, with an admission that autobiographies are at their truest between the lines, he gets to the point he probably has been considering since describing his recent meeting with Catherine—so many memories that his mind can scarcely contain them, even as they mock his attempts to do so.

The memories involve his distance from the children. One features a lonely night at a café in Paris, just a few weeks after leaving home. He's too miserable to eat or drink, but hopes to find solace listening to the orchestra. But when the cellist begins playing Simonetti's Madrigale Wright cannot help but recall how his son Lloyd performed this piece as a favorite, sometimes in a duet with his father on piano. In anguish, Wright leaves to wander the streets for hours. Another takes place in more settled times, during the first two years at Taliesin. On business trips to Chicago the architect would go to Oak Park after dark to assure himself all was safe and secure. The scene is set in single-sentence paragraphs to enhance its poignancy, one each for the window light and the children's voices, the sounds of the piano, their singing, and their calls. Relieved, Wright would turn away and return to the city. Anguish in Paris, relief in Oak Park—both emotions are enhanced by their nighttime setting with the accompaniment of music, so important in Frank Lloyd Wright's life. A third memory concerns his little daughters. He remembers so much, he admits, that ending his book could be a problem. Therefore he decides to willfully forget what he meant to write. *An Autobiography* thus ends with a closure to the sense of memory and a celebration of the present, which is happening these days at Taliesin. "Taliesin!" Wright exclaims, in a sentence that would subsequently typify his devotion to this house: "When I am away from it, like some rubber band, stretched out but ready to snap back immediately the pull is relaxed or released, I get back to it, happy to come home again" (*CW* II: 377). Suddenly, even abruptly, the past—before it can become cloying—is replaced by the present. Wright as always is careful to make the reader's mood match his own. Once Taliesin West was established in 1937, this contrast would define the dual nature of Wright's regional allegiances. Here in 1932 he is allowing for the fact that as he has travelled widely in the past, the future may well hold similar temptations. Throughout the volume, experiences have called him away at times, but the home place has been the center of his faith since he chose it as such in 1911. No matter that the past might call, such as the memories in these last few pages of family life in Oak Park "when I would have given all that I had lived to be able to live again" (*CW* II: 376). As his story closes, Frank Lloyd Wright is again living in his beloved Taliesin, with Olgivanna and their little daughter, Iovanna, and preparing for the next phase of his career.

An Autobiography appeared in the spring of 1932. By October, its first fruit was being brought to Taliesin in the persons of twenty-three people, one as old as thirty-one but most of college age, who would be the first members of the Taliesin Fellowship. Innovative in form and idealistic in its goals, the Fellowship would in fact be the most practical undertaking of Frank Lloyd Wright's life. For the next twenty-seven years—to the end of his life—it would give him something akin to the supportive structure he so envied musical composers having in their orchestras: hundreds if not thousands of fingers eager to do his work. Initially twenty-three but at times as many as sixty or more apprentices were for Wright what he himself had been for Louis Sullivan, the pencil in his hand. In the best of times, this resource would allow Wright to produce hundreds of designs, sometimes dozens at the same time, well beyond the output of a conventionally organized studio. In the lean years of the Depression that marked its beginnings, the Fellowship would provide the Wrights with income, as each Fellow paid $675 in annual tuition. In addition, their course of study included such supposedly enriching tasks as construction work and agricultural and domestic labor. They would learn by doing and become architects from the bottom up, actually building their drafting studio and living quarters around them and keeping the vast estate running. For much of this, Olgivanna deserves the credit, just as it was her encouragement that had set Wright to work on *An Autobiography* several years before. A prospectus circulated to colleges and universities in the summer of 1932 had got the word out, and several of the apprentices had learned of Wright from newspaper accounts of his work and his earlier publications. But most were drawn by the book itself, either reading it (as did Edgar Tafel) or having its ideas recommended by a parent (as happened with John Lautner, whose mother had read Wright's memoir).

Frank and Olgivanna had seen the need for something like the Fellowship several years before, and had sought the aid of friends and support of other institutions (such as the University of Wisconsin) in setting up some type of school in the old Hillside School quarters. Discussions beginning in 1928 led to a preliminary brochure printed and circulated in 1931, "The Hillside Home School of the Allied Arts." Grander in scope than the Fellowship, the school would include not just architecture but painting, sculpture, pottery, glasswork, metalwork, dance, and drama. History and philosophy would contribute to the students' rounding as well. Reading the brochure today, in light of how the Taliesin Fellowship would be reconceived the following year, illustrates what the Wrights considered essential.

Foremost is the need for a culture "above the matters of behavior, commerce, industry, politics, and an unsure taste for objets d'art." Wright sounds a bit like Sinclair Lewis and H. L. Mencken when he grounds his case with Londoner C. R. Ashbee's comments made while visiting Chicago, that the great Midwestern city was aesthetically ugly. Ashbee is answered by a local "Captain of Industry" to the effect that the visitor may be right, that "Chicago isn't much on Culture now . . . maybe. But when Chicago gets after culture, she'll make Culture hum" (*CW* III: 40, ellipsis in original). Rather than mock this boisterous Americanism, Wright seconds it, albeit in a more thoughtful manner. Culture is in fact bound up with commerce and industry, and for this very reason cannot be made to hum at will when people are finally ready for it. It is there all the time. The issue is whether it is treated well or poorly. At the Hillside Home School of the Allied Arts it will be handled as it should be, as both a foundation for human activity and a superstructure for its refinement. Only then will American culture truly "hum."

Specifics fit the Wright doctrine. American culture needs to be authentic, not borrowed from Europe, and organic, growing naturally from within, rather than being applied from without. There's idealism that the project must help build a nation in which everything contributes not just to its wealth but to its integrity, all in greater service to the human spirit. Even the machine must be used not just productively but for this greater principle. Wright has a sound proposition to make. Architecture will be the center of his proposed school, with the fine arts as divisions of it, but the industrial arts—glass-making, pottery, textiles, and such—will benefit from $150,000 subsidies from the respective industries the school's workshops serve. These companies would in turn be able to purchase designs and offer employment to students as approved by the director. Intellectual property, dedication of talent—these considerations read like terms in a business contract, which is what the document is. As for what the Hillside workshops produce, that can be sold at market, likely to net $50,000 each year. Wright describes them as artistically attractive and useful beyond common standards, as their designs would be not only innovative but based on the informing principle of organic design as executed by machine. As an operation, the school's books will balance, all the way down to the cost of "feeding 124 people for one year at 26¢ a day each" beyond what farm production provides (*CW* III: 47). Farm production? Yes, this bottom-line practicality results from another ideal, that the school be located out in the country, where the quieter rural environment and rigorous outdoor work raise the spirit and morale to be creative when working indoors.

Although the Great Depression would make commercial support impossible, and despite the fact that on his own Wright could not support the activities of seven industrial arts schools (each with a resident master, who would have to be housed and paid), the most important aspects of the Hillside Home School of the Allied Arts are realized in the Taliesin Fellowship. Architecture does of course remain the central interest, and not as an isolated subject—rather it is a philosophy of design that informs all the other arts as apprentices practice them on their own, as hobbies and pastimes rather than industrial disciplines. There won't be resident masters, but apprentices who have brought special talents share them with others. There will not be artifacts for sale, but on Sunday afternoons the public will be invited to the Taliesin Playhouse for a high quality foreign film, discussion led by an informed apprentice, and a cup of coffee at the lobby fireside, all for just fifty cents. The fare was attractive and the price was right: rural neighbors and visitors from Madison made for packed houses. Most importantly, at either Hillside as proposed or the Fellowship as realized, there would be no calendar courses, no examinations, no graduations, and no diplomas. Instead, apprentices learned by watching and doing, with Frank Lloyd Wright's ultimate form of guidance being his example, supplemented by his talks. It was how he had learned from Louis Sullivan, and how his best apprentices would learn now.

But knowing well the history of Wright's relationship with Louis Sullivan, how would the matter of ego fit into the Hillside scheme and, afterwards, the Fellowship's reality? In the Hillside document Wright addresses it directly, and adds an important literary reference. His school would grant ego its natural scope and rights, given that the creative impulse depends on such. Anything inhibiting it only breeds hypocrisy, as Walt Whitman taught.

Note the inhibitors, which are the restrictions by conventional education. And note the liberator, which is not the triumph of one ego over another but rather the ideal Walt Whitman proposed: democracy. For Wright and Whitman both, democracy is dedicated to an individual's growth precisely as an individual, into something of one's very own that no one else can take away. Throughout the architect's literary canon democracy is characterized as not just a freedom for people in general but as guarantee of an individual's right to develop as chosen, according to one's own principles derived from within instead of answering to rules and practices imposed from without. Later in the 1940s a more famous Frank Lloyd Wright will refine Whitman's notion, distinguishing it and his own from a simple leveling that is more properly called "mobocracy." Whitman and Frank Lloyd Wright see democracy as enabling individuals to emulate what is infinite in humankind. That is what "ego" means in this Hillside brochure, and how it will be encouraged in the Fellowship.

The Hillside Home School of the Allied Arts could have been a great operation, but conditions conspired against it. Even in the best of times it would have been difficult to attract (much less remunerate) the level of talent proposed: Erich Mendelsohn and Le Corbusier as regular visitors from Berlin and Paris, Joseph Stella in residence from New York, Pablo Casals, Leopold Stokowsky, and Igor Stravinsky teaching music, Eugene O'Neill and Sherwood Anderson supervising drama and cinema. And these are just a few from the page-long list Wright supplies, announced with the same certitude as his accounting for food, fuel, and electricity. With the Great Depression at hand, such planning was fatuous. Yet for how Frank Lloyd Wright's thinking proceeds, it is absolutely necessary to commit to the material reason.

It is this same economic calamity, after all, that would make the Fellowship a reasonable proposition. Scaled down to what Wright himself and his existing physical plant could provide, it was financially feasible. As for its students, the high expenses of traditional college education and dim prospects for employment made them think that at Taliesin there was nothing to lose. That the country's economic structure was in shambles gave them reason to join the larger movement that was challenging it; "radical" was, after all, one of Frank Lloyd Wright's favorite words, and if he used it in the conservative sense of "root," then his reform would be all the more fundamental. Without the Great Depression, it is unlikely that the Taliesin Fellowship would have attracted such a steady stream of high-quality students; with it, some of the best young minds in America could think of no better place to go.

In the summer of 1932, with *An Autobiography* being reviewed and available in bookstores and with the Great Depression locked in for its frightful duration, Wright issued his reconceived brochure announcing "The Taliesin Fellowship." It drew an initial twenty-three young people to his estate near Spring Green, Wisconsin, where the work described would begin. The brochure is candid about that work, which included not just architectural study but design and construction of buildings to be added to the existing structures of the old Hillside Home School, both of which needed remodeling. "Work" would also take place in the fields, growing food, and in the kitchen and dining room preparing and serving it. As things got underway, the brochure was modified and expanded until it reached satisfactory form in an edition dated December 1933, which Bruce Brooks Pfeiffer combines with a brief retrospective on Wright's aunts added in 1941 to serve as the definitive text in the *Collected Writings*. Later on, parts of it would be incorporated into the 1943 expanded edition of *An Autobiography*, but by then the Fellowship had proved its merit to the world with work on such masterpieces as Fallingwater and the S. C. Johnson Administration Building. It is the 1933 document that captures the Taliesin Fellowship in its first year of operation and demonstrates the nature of Wright's thought about the project.

"TRUTH AGAINST THE WORLD" are the words Frank Lloyd Wright uses to begin his preamble to the Fellowship document. He applies it to his aunts' educational methods as inspired by Francis Parker and John Dewey and underscored by the family's motto, carried out "to the point, some said, where there was no intolerance quite so intolerant as the Lloyd Jones' intolerance of intolerance" (*CW* III: 159). Wright cites this belief as a factor leading to the aunts' economic failure. But their ideals for education live on, in the later years of their lives because Frank borrowed money to rescue the buildings from foreclosure in 1915 (when in truth it had been the scandal and ultimate tragedy at Taliesin that had prompted many parents to withdraw their children from the Hillside Home School), and at their deaths with his pledge to someday found another school in their honor.

That time has come with the inauguration of the Taliesin Fellowship. It, too, begins in the face of economic hardship. But tuition (at first $650, soon raised to $675) could buy material to build with and seed money for crops that would provide food. The farm, as Wright calls it, is of great use even beyond providing sustenance. Working as a community, the Fellowship will learn architecture quite literally from the ground up, harvesting and preparing the land's bounty even as they plan to build on it. Wright's educational aim is the same as was his aunts', which is to fashion a culture for American democracy. Only the specific line of endeavor would be changed.

"Our Cause," as the Fellowship prospectus proclaims it, is to counter current trends in education with more progressive ones, just as Wright's aunts had done. In some senses, those trends have become worse since the Hillside Home School was founded in 1886. Wright's complaint draws less on the educational philosophy of John Dewey and more on the economic thought of Henry George, at least metaphorically in the sense that inflation and overproduction characterize the evils of mass schooling. For the past half-century or more, the architect believes, students have been "over-educated and under-cultured" (*CW* III: 160), thanks to the stress on production over sustainability. His own plan is to offer the appreciation of life that comes from honest work, a quality beyond the grasp of any academic formula. True, he grounds his belief in architecture, but only as that art is dedicated to the harmony of all structure, from which a great culture can emerge. Like his aunts, Wright is proposing not a course of study but a manner of life.

Taliesin is not a back-to-the-land movement, Wright objects, nor is it an art-for-art's-sake endeavor. He implies that each of these have become regressive rather than progressive. Instead, the Fellowship will simply proceed with its feet on the ground, experiencing how an appreciation of art and the culture it expresses can make living a more rewarding affair. Its very being is a commitment to action. Wary of being taken as a foolish idealist, Wright nevertheless believes that integrity of process precedes the merit of any final product, and cites Cervantes to this effect: that the road is always better than the inn. As late as 1933, with the

Fellowship in operation for a year, Wright still has hopes of industrial support (by virtue of supplying free services), and wants to attract six experienced leaders in music, painting, sculpture, drama, motion, and philosophy. In practice, the services provided will be to Wright himself, as within the next few years major commissions arrive that need communal effort to complete with now-veteran apprentices such as Wes Peters, Bob Mosher, and Edgar Tafel working as lieutenants. As for performance, there will be short-term visitors, notably violinists and the occasional string quartet; but here too the idea is to inspire apprentices themselves to develop their talent and share it with colleagues. These practices fit Wright's overall thesis that what he has to convey cannot be taught, it can only be experienced. This style of experientiality is the most obvious quality of the Taliesin Fellowship. Comprehending how the design of the whole is integral thanks in part to an understanding of the nature of materials, Fellowship members will saw trees and quarry stone, making daily life and cultural growth simultaneous.

The Taliesin Fellowship brochure ends with the information that there is no graduation involved or diploma to be awarded. After several years of experience, "should the apprentice desire to leave the Fellowship"—note the conditional verb mood Wright chooses!—"a personal testimonial will be given" (*CW* III: 166). Even at this early date, the master finds it hard to envision that anyone would ever leave. Of course many did after widely varying years of residence, but several stayed for extended periods of a decade or more. John Howe would remain until after Wright's death, and a few, such as Wes Peters and Eugene Masselink, lived out their lives in the Fellowship.

One would leave, Wright presumes, only when prepared for life. And as the best life possible was being perfected right here at Taliesin, why would anyone want to leave? For Frank Lloyd Wright personally, the Taliesin Fellowship at once became the center of his own life, and continued so until he died—at which point it served to keep alive the spirit of his work and promote ideas for architecture and living. After 1932, we can say, Wright's autobiography and the Fellowship are one.

5

Broadacre City and
the 1930s

IN 1932, WITH THE PUBLICATION OF *An Autobiography* and the founding of the Taliesin Fellowship, the nature of Frank Lloyd Wright's writing changes. A lack of commissions in the second half of the 1920s had forced him to write essays and deliver lectures for a living, and the onset of the Great Depression assured little architectural work would be coming along for anyone, much less for an old man whose reputation and personal conduct were matters of controversy. There was no alternative but to write himself back into existence, which is precisely what *An Auto-biography* and the prospectus for the Taliesin Fellowship accomplished.

Broadacre City and the writings that describe it are examples of how the Fellowship's support put him on a new path, not just as a builder but as a thinker. In *Communities of Frank Lloyd Wright* (2009) Myron A. Marty warns that Broadacre City is not a utopian organization, for it was never organized at all—except in Wright's head. It is an idea, Marty argues, and asks that it be considered that way, as advance planning for a suburbia Wright saw coming as early as the 1920s, when his extensive automobile travel across the United States revealed not just the vast spaces available but the practical means of shrinking those distances for a better style of human use. But it was also an idea that needed a model, a physical rendering of what could become reality. In the days before computerized modeling, constructing a wall-sized layout of a four-square-mile project at a scale of seventy-five feet to the inch was more than a labor-intensive project; it was an undertaking of gargantuan proportions, especially when models of every building (comprising many of Wright's built structures and projects to date) were added. Only the hundreds of willing fingers available in the Fellowship could do it. And only a $1,000 check extracted from the wealthy father of apprentice Edgar J. Kaufmann, Jr., could begin to finance it. Then there was the matter of exhibition. Apprentices were charged with transporting it to New York City's Rockefeller Center for its first showing in 1935, and from there to galleries in such diverse locations as Philadelphia; Washington, D. C.; and Madison, Wisconsin. Wright continued to support the idea for the rest of his life, showing the model abroad in the 1950s and publishing his last book on the topic just a year before his death, all of which could only happen with the support of his many apprentices. Not only did it form a part of their education, but it provided an introduction to and experience with major figures in the art world and government. They could work on it outside, during summers in Wisconsin and winters in Arizona, where Wright arranged temporary quarters while scouting locations for Taliesin West.

Just as Broadacre City could not exist without the Taliesin Fellowship, so too did Frank Lloyd Wright's idea for the future provide a project for the Fellowship. Before Fallingwater, there was precious little for the Fellowship to do. During its first years apprentices filled their days with work on the Taliesin buildings and in the fields, the only semblance of architectural experience being the tracing over of old plans from Wright's earlier heyday. Between the Richard Lloyd Jones House (1929) for his cousin in Tulsa and Fallingwater itself (1935), Wright's canon would have but one work, the small proto-Usonian home for Malcolm E. Willey (1933) in Minneapolis. "Hosanna, a client!" Wright is said to have inscribed across the top of Willey's inquiry letter as it was posted on the drafting room's bulletin board.

And just as Broadacre City kept the Fellowship busy, so too did it occupy its creator's mind. *The Disappearing City* was published in 1932, just before the Fellowship begins. Throughout the decade Wright would advance its ideas by means of various essays and speeches, markets for which increased dramatically as news of his success with Fallingwater and the S. C. Johnson Administration Building spread. Written contemporaneously with his planning for the Fellowship, it builds on his views on city living as advanced in the Kahn lectures at Princeton and in the "Usonian City" section of *An Autobiography*. There the emphasis was largely on the past, showing how the reasons that mandated urbanization in the first place now served only to impose unneeded restrictions on human life. This binary opposition sets the tone and structure for Wright's argument as it develops. Centralization has run out of control, and the natural progress of horizontal growth has been stifled. Humankind is condemned to an "unnatural, sterile verticality—upended by its own success" (*CW* III: 71). But instead of the simple history-of-civilization narrative Wright had used at Princeton and in *An Autobiography*, we now have an opposition that in its very structuring implies a way out, a synthesis of the thesis and antithesis so apparent in Wright's thinking. Open fields versus the cave, horizontal as opposed to vertical—the direction of the architect's thinking is obvious. It is the adventurer's instinct to break out that grounds Wright's ideal of freedom.

The next set of oppositions is between the landlord and the individual, between the exploitation of restrictive space and the free enjoyment of it. Rent for land, rent for money, even rent for intellectual property (such as the innovations of the machine) are for Wright the chief contributing causes of poverty. His thinking here is derived from a favorite source, one he has used metaphorically for problems concerning education: Henry George and his economic theory of a Single Tax (which would protect personal ownership while preventing exploitation). George's ideas have come in for complex criticism, based on how they alternately can or cannot function in an open society. To his credit, Wright does not get involved with these arguments, never mentioning the reformer except in passing, and then usually in the company of a broad swath of others: Thomas Jefferson, Abraham Lincoln, William Lloyd Garrison, John Brown, Ralph Waldo Emerson, Henry David Thoreau, Walt Whitman, and Louis Sullivan, all as general proponents of the idea that the best government is the one that governs least, as well as the tenet that human rights precede property rights. Against all restrictive economics Wright poses "the modern conception of God and man as growth—a concept called Democracy" (*CW* III: 75). As Bruce Brooks Pfeiffer points out in his biographical sketch for this volume of the *Collected Writings*, an identity exists between the principles behind Wright's ideas for organic architecture and "in his way of thinking, . . . a true democracy" (*CW* III: 13). Democracy privileges not personalities but individuals, not a collection of libertines (whom Wright would come to call the mob) but instead those people in whose strength of character and enjoyment of genuine culture is reflected the ideal of human perfection.

It is the growth of individualism that Wright sees facilitated by the new freedom generated by technological devices, from the internal combustion engine to electrification and improved communications. Unlike his previous writings, *The Disappearing City* does not at this point start scattering fantastic inventions across the page. Instead he focuses on the individual's needs as expressed in the idea of Broadacre City itself, a concept fully formed and ready for consideration.

That he has a community of his own on the brink of formation surely shapes his thinking, so different is its manner from that previously expressed. The plan he proposes is not a machine miracle of futuristic dreaming, nor is it an ungrounded fantasy. He of course has great hope for the future, but with the proviso that before anything else the growth of individuality will be assured. The spirit of organic architecture recognizes this as the foundation of a civilization's greatness. For a proper spirit, communal forces must support this ideal, and by allowing a minimum of one acre to each family, individuality within the community can be achieved, thanks to the expansiveness of space his Broadacre design allows. The space is horizontal, not vertical, so that one owns what one occupies, and not levels above it to be rented to others. Horizontal versus vertical is a binary opposition, and with this rhetorical structure established Wright pushes on with it, enriching the distinction by using metaphors, a device that puts the oppositions into even closer contrast. Again, rather than parsing out the history of civilization, as he'd done in earlier commentaries on this subject, Wright now turns to the poetic. He contrasts the city at night, a visual delight of artificial illumination, with the daytime reality of rent's "sordid reiteration" and the "overpowering sense of the cell" (*CW* III: 82). Medical metaphors abound, from malignant tumors and occluded tissue to painfully constricted circulation. Contrasting forms of government follow this same opposition: monarchy with its centralization of power, democracy with its integrity won by decentralization.

The key for Wright's success with this plan is the proper use of new materials that make dispersion possible. Electrification, which lets urban congestion look so pretty at night, should be used to spread things out, leaving the difference between short and long distances irrelevant. Automobiles make people portable, just as refrigeration, heating, and lighting are no longer tied to the city. Glass, steel, and concrete allow a building style that opens living space to the environment, expanding one's relationship with the ground. The herd instinct now takes wing, replaced by the dream of individual empowerment.

Architecture's job will be to interpret this ideal of human freedom and seek the spaciousness and light that will break up and disperse the urban blockage. Glass, steel, and electromagnetic science are gifts architects may use to begin a new era. If the architect's imagination is trained to see them for what they are and how they can be harmonious with nature, personal effort will enhance communal good, individual and collective enriching each other. Human values give life, rather than take it, and by providing an acre for each family, architecture will have the scope to serve not the landlord but people themselves as organic exemplars of ownership. This was a key feature in Henry George's economic theory, and Wright's focus on the mechanical specifics for making all this possible reflect directly on the notion of individual freedom, unlike the earlier commentaries in which they seemed to glory in their own invention. A new style of highway system, prescient concerning the postwar interstates, would replace archaic and unpleasant roads with genuinely pleasurable ones—safe, quiet, and pretty. Service stations are no longer eyesores but rather centers of real service, satisfying all needs in an integrated system of distribution and supply. Skyscrapers would have their place in Broadacre City, set in park-like sites as proposed for the St. Mark's project and later realized in the Price Tower in Bartlesville. As it all comes together, residents are granted their God-given right "to live abundantly in the exuberance that is beauty—in the sense that William Blake defined exuberance," Wright emphasizes. Blake did not mean excess, the architect cautions. "He meant according to nature, without stint" (*CW* III: 92). What Blakean exuberance Wright himself expresses may have a mystical touch, but it is applied to hard and fast realities of what is meant to be a very practical city. He can go on at length about highways, but with details of design that make travel both more efficient and more aesthetically pleasing. The open road, safe to travel, is a noble agent of culture, and has a beauty all its own. Wright's arguments establish superhighways and improved hard roads as a new basis for order. Thus does Wright's agile and capacious manner of thought encompass Henry George, William Blake, and the wide-open American highway in the same spirit.

Living and working quarters share this new sense, which is actually an application of principles Wright had developed over the past four decades. Integration is now the key. Old standards of spacing go out the door, thanks to the mobility now possible. Space itself also comes inside, to define the building from within. From the outside, buildings fit in with the landscape. Farms are small, sharing a tractor and supplying food to nearby residents. Service stations fulfill every practical need for both vehicle and passenger, anticipating today's convenience store. Churches as well share space, with compartments for various denominations, though the overall effect will be nonsectarian. Each Broadacre City will have a design center, the description of which follows the Taliesin Fellowship brochure Wright was circulating at this time, right down to its discipline of agricultural fieldwork supplementing an apprenticeship in architecture. Most important, the home is Broadacre City's central factor, the only bit of centrality allowed. Architecturally, it has been made into the house beautiful, Frank Lloyd Wright's aim as expressed in his earliest essays of the 1890s, and living there can be the focus of life's supreme pleasures. But what good was Wright's ability to design and build such a home, if the pressures of the city still drew its occupants away? Now *The Disappearing City* has come up with a manner of thinking about urban needs that takes the conventional metropolis out of the picture. What Wright has proposed re-centralizes the satisfaction of all those needs right in the home itself.

Will this change be superintended by politicians? Wright knows better than to think so. For that statesmen are needed, for they, unlike politicians, are architects of social order. He has already reached to the level beyond this truth by arguing for architecture as the grounding for his whole project—social, moral, aesthetic, economic, as well as building design. It certainly was such in ancient times, he reminds his readers. And for the modern era it must be so again.

Is Frank Lloyd Wright proposing that the chief authority for Broadacre City be the architect? As egomaniacal as this seems, there is a practical aspect to it, and also a demonstration of its efficacy in current life. Architecture in its broadest sense (how Wright always conceived it) is what drives the formation of Broadacre City, because the plan will work only if all its parts are set in place to function in harmonious order. That's the organic nature of the idea, and it is the architect who not only proposes it but will design a structure (again, in the largest sense) by which it can function. In today's world there is just such an authority: city planning. Unregulated growth earlier in the twentieth century mandated that there be some higher order, usually at the county level, so that cities could not continue to sprawl in a chaotic manner. In the Progressive Era of Frank Lloyd Wright's early career, city planning was an ideal in both the United States and Great Britain, and in his own studio two of his brightest associates, Marion Mahony and Walter Burley Griffin, were already at work in this direction. In the years following World War II, explosive demographic growth had to be channeled in productive directions; by then city planning was not an ideal but a necessity. While it is tempting to scoff at Wright's notion of a county architect's supreme authority as a version of Plato's philosopher king in *The Republic*, one must remember that unlike Plato Wright does not banish the poets. Rather, the exuberance of William Blake and the democracy of Walt Whitman are among the essential ingredients of his own ideal world.

The Disappearing City is an original piece of work, but it draws support from the four decades of essays and lectures preceding it, in addition to the example of Wright's architecture itself. It introduces the idea of Broadacre City the same year, 1932, that the Taliesin Fellowship begins. If the book is a coherent expression of all the architect's ideas to date, then the Fellowship serves as an example of life practiced according to the principles conveyed. As a result, Frank Lloyd Wright's other writings of the decade are, compared to the steady march of ideas that leads up to the two great events of 1932, ancillary and topical. They are various in their appearance and many are unpublished. But they are also voluminous, and bear reading for their occasionally fresh angles on familiar yet critically important themes. The architect did not stop thinking when his book appeared and the Fellowship got underway, and at times that thought finds bright new means of expression.

Take the consideration of how much space a plan like Broadacre City would require, especially if developed to the extent of housing all America. Wright's extensive automobile travels of the past several years had taught him how distances were shrinking and suburban sprawl was coming in the not too distant future, but it also made him realize just how much presently unoccupied space this country had to offer. Here is how he dramatizes it for the 1932 Convention of the National Association of Realtors, in a speech published in their *Journal* for July of 1932. "There is a lot of ground in this country," he observes, and not all that many people. He teases his audience that if the entire population of the world were placed on Bermuda, they wouldn't cover it "standing up—I don't know about sitting down" (*CW* III: 125). Even in the United States, civilized as it is, there are more than fifty acres available for each person, children and all. The fact is an amusing one, probably culled from *Ripley's Believe It or Not*, a popular media entertainment of the day. But Wright knows that what will catch his listeners' attention is that spaciousness is characteristic of modern life and that it is natural for democracy to demand more of it. In similar terms he tells the realtors about his new type of gasoline station that will be "the advance agent of decentralization," a specific agency they can picture in order to appreciate Wright's argument for the new "fluidity" and "spontaneity" of modern living (*CW* III: 125). Another piece, this time with medical matters in mind, praises the country doctor (one of whom has just treated him for severe pneumonia and saved his life). Self-reliance, acting on judgment in emergencies—this is what not just the doctors but all the professionals of Broadacre City will have in abundance. As for its location, "this city will be everywhere and nowhere" (*CW* III: 345), because it is an idea and not an institution.

Supplementing the idea of Broadacre City is the design of the Usonian House, announced as "The Two-Zone House—Suited to Country, Suburb, and Town" when published in Wright's own *Taliesin: Journal of the Taliesin Fellowship* (1932). The old-fashioned parlor only existed because of squeamishness over food preparation in the kitchen, he argues. Why not call the kitchen a workspace, acknowledging that work is part of life and should not be sequestered from the living room? Where work takes place is a natural space for getting together, and also for centralizing utilities. One zone of this house can be used for living and working while a second serves as a quieter zone for study. Where does one sleep? In a mezzanine overlooking the first zone, which at bedtime is not being used! By 1939, when delivering the lectures published as *An Organic Architecture* to the Royal Institute of British Architects, Wright's Usonian House has been developed (and built in several variations) in more complete form. The work/living zone is still central, often located where two wings meet at a right angle (as in the first Herbert Jacobs House, 1936) or at an oblique angle (as in the Jean S. and Paul T. Hanna House, "Honeycomb," 1936). But the second zone, originally a quiet area for study, is now a wing that includes bedrooms as well, with the mezzanine idea dropped (for now). Equally dramatic is how garden and building are one, as terracing encompassed by the angled wings flows naturally into a sheltered back yard. Organic design implies that there should be no emphatic division between garden and house; instead, "ground-loving animals" that people are, their homes should "court the ground" as a "birthright" (*CW* III: 309).

Wright's description of the Usonian's fluidity of inside and out could not be better stated, and anticipates Herbert and Katherine Jacobs's account of living in this home, *Building with Frank Lloyd Wright* (1986). To his listeners in London the architect adds that economic necessities spawned by the Great Depression, which he habitually describes as a breakdown rather than a phase, have led him to make his Usonian design part of the movement for affordable yet quality housing. As a newspaper writer with limited income, Herbert Jacobs had approached Wright with a challenge to provide a design that could be built for five thousand dollars in Madison, Wisconsin. Proximity to Taliesin gave the apprentices hands-on experience, and the abundance of brick at the S. C. Johnson Administration Building site in Racine allowed Wright to designate enough culls to keep this part of the Jacobs House within budget, especially as brick was a luxury. All other materials and methods were cost-saving: walls of board and batten with an insulating space within; modular construction on a cement base, with heating coils installed before the floor was poured; clerestory windows on the street side, small, efficient and providing privacy, with openness reserved for the wing-embraced garden.

Usonian homes do not look like low-cost housing. Organic design accounts for this, plus the fact that building them was simple enough that at least part of the work could be done by the owners if so desired. But many ran over budget, no surprise for any Frank Lloyd Wright project. As is, the hundred and more that were built in almost every region of the country between 1936 and 1959 stand as a distinguishing factor in Wright's second career, equaling the brilliance of his earlier Prairie Houses. Economics mandated that he express this brilliance on a smaller scale, but domestic life itself had changed over the half century. With a small but exceptionally functional kitchen overlooking the garden and acting as the fulcrum between living and sleeping wings, a modern homemaker could multi-task at the center of family life with ease and enjoyment. The hearth, still the family center, was just a few inviting steps from the back yard, itself an integral feature of the home as lived in. Usonian Houses are the ultimate proof that when form and function are one, beauty as well as economy results. Granted, Frank Lloyd Wright's Great Depression turned out to be less than personally catastrophic, thanks to the great commissions of Fallingwater and the S. C. Johnson Administration Building at the heart of it, completed with the help of the newly established Fellowship. Conditions in the next decade, the 1940s, would have a more disruptive effect on his thinking, because as a pacifist opposing American participation in World War II he found it difficult to write about anything but politics, using his *Taliesin Square-Papers* as a convenient if self-serving vehicle. In the 1930s, however, the politics of economic policy are for him small potatoes. A quick citation of Henry George and his argument for the Single Tax, an idea already fifty years old, was enough thinking about economics for Wright—which was really no thinking at all. His mind was still set on the organic means to comfort and beauty; that these means could now save money as well was just further proof that organic is most natural and therefore the best answer for anything.

If it sounds like a truism, the kind for which Frank Lloyd Wright would be taken to task all his life, the proof of its validity is in the designs he derived from it. The first Jacobs home, whether viewed in person or in the gorgeous color photographs of it that are a feature of any illustrated volume of Wright's work, counters the objection that the architect's ideas are fatuous. And in reading his essays and addresses of the 1930s, as varied a body of work as he would produce at any time in his career, one finds two points of consistency in his intellectual concerns: the problem of eclecticism in design, and the solution to it with organic architecture.

At the decade's beginning, in an address of 21 February 1931 to the Michigan Society of Architects in Grand Rapids, Wright introduces the topic. In these times art has become more a matter of taste than of substance, its forms being the panderings to eclecticism. Taste is no substitute for creative impulse, he avers. Criticizing his friend Raymond Hood (in an unpublished book review of 1931), Wright's charge is even more brutal. A person eclectic by habit cannot be a true architect, he charges, as eclectics are capable of nothing more than exploitation of something else. What has angered Wright is Hood's manner as displayed in Chicago's Tribune Tower building; there is also cause for envy of Hood's success at landing the Rockefeller Center's Radio City commission. But as the architect complains to the *New York Evening Post* and *New York Tribune* in 1932, there is reason for his ire. Hood's Radio City is haphazard because it relies on a nineteenth-century sense of composition that current practice has discarded. Moreover, its masonry mass falsifies materials and the nature of construction, which is in fact tall steel frames contributed by the project's engineers. By itself steel framing could be beautiful, but as presented the result is pure fraud.

Being excluded from the 1933 World's Fair in Chicago, the "Century of Progress" exhibition, prompts Wright to compare it to the 1893 version with its classically inspired White City. It is nothing more than the old fair scrubbed up and presented as new, Wright tells the Michigan Society of Architects, an example of "an outrageous senility" posing as the modern (*CW* III: 55). He introduces a metaphor for this practice in "Caravel or Motorship" for *The Architectural Forum* in August of 1932. In terms of shipping and sailing, the caravel is "picturesque but not practical," he points out, knowing that his readers will agree that the motorship, once invented, is more practical. The same reasoning applies to design and building, Wright insists. For whatever era, an architect works creatively with the tools it supplies, and today that means making best use of the machine. As for the International Style, it may look up-to-date, but it is in fact tailor-made for eclectics to seize upon, having been reduced to a formula that gives no thought to moment or milieu, as Wright objects in the February 1932 issue of *T-Square*. Historic eclecticism tacks on styles, while the International Style's reliance on formula in fact kills the architect before anything valid can be created.

At bottom, eclecticism in this field is a consequence of architects having no talent. Asked in the November 1933 issue of *The Architectural Record* to comment on eight new designs by prominent Americans in the profession, Wright tries to list particular objections but in the end gives up. "Dear boys—your senior speaking," he says to them directly. "Why not go back to eclecticism and, safely, stay there?" These juniors are incapable of organic architecture, he insists; were they, it would undo their present success. "With it," he mocks, "you never could have made the New York Skyline what it is today" (*CW* III: 148). In unpublished comments intended for *Izvestia* during his 1937 visit to the Soviet Union, Wright is similarly ungenerous when considering his European colleagues; some of these architects are just painters playing with pictures. Sculpting is another detracting metaphor. In *Architecture and Modern Life* (1937) he notes that as architects of later eras developed their art from the style of ancient times they worked with their buildings like a sculptor modeling clay, molding and enriching the mass with a preferred style. The result? Shaping the exterior dictates the concept of what lies within. Contemporary California buildings are no better. Where siting could be a great advantage (in terms of collage and effect), local developers misunderstand the entire process, with unfortunate results. Wright coins names for them—"realtoristocrats," "hill-toppers"—and bemoans their practice of pushing everything up over the hills until the hills themselves are destroyed. From Los Angeles, he turns east to Williamsburg, Virginia, where his comments at William and Mary College drew some ire. Responding in an unpublished essay (November 1938), Wright clarifies that his objections are not to Williamsburg as an historical display but to how such examples inspire an eclectic style of applied architecture. This cultural lag may well persist for another generation unless such pretty, sentimental allusions can be abandoned in favor of something more life-enhancing.

Those are Wright's objections, delivered over the decade but consistent in their expression of what's wrong with current architecture. What could be right with it is the other half of the binary rhetoric that characterizes his thought in the 1930s. Because positive references outweigh the negatives by two-to-one, the direction for a synthesis is clear. Organic architecture views a building in terms of its enclosing interior space, which is itself the structure's reality. Walls no longer exist as instruments of segmentation; the room itself must emerge through all aspects of design. This principle, familiar in Wright's thinking since the start of the century, is now allied with his ideal of the "house beautiful" from the 1890s. As he emphasizes for the Michigan Society of Architects, this handling of space from within speaks for a better life experience there. For these same listeners he concludes with an old reference, the art and culture of Japan, explaining how it is the manner of growth within a thing that makes it what it is—not its existence, but its becoming. This distinction from the Platonic idealism of static signs is important, because it is art as well that comes from the inside. Architecture is part of nature's life, Wright concludes in his "Architecture of Individualism" essay from *Trend* (March-April 1934). It is such insight into the process of growth from within that makes such designs as the Brooklyn Bridge and the Cord automobile organic architecture.

Wright's vision of an organically principled future prompts him to wax poetic. From Taliesin he can write for *Liberty* magazine (10 February 1932) that the beauty of architecture is shown best in the countryside, freed from the city to flow across the land and alongside the hills, like "streaks of light enmeshed in metal strands, as music is made of notes" (*CW* III: 171). There is a way of architectural thinking as organic that the ancients did not know, he seeks to tell the readers of *Izvestia*; it is the idea that a vase is not the clay shaped on the potter's wheel but the space that is created inside it. The vase can be identical in Etruscan and modern American times, even made precisely the same way. But in Wright's view they are different. This is far from Platonic idealism. Instead, Wright uses a term for it introduced into thinking about physics just three decades before, "the thought that not any fixed points but what lies between them in space established by the relation of each to each and each to all—relativity—is reality" (*CW* III: 214-15). Yet Wright is no Einstein, nor does he wish to be. Instead his ambitions are allied with idealism, but of a different order than Plato's. Structure is what the mind seeks to know in things. Because Wright describes the process as musical, readers of *Architecture and Modern Life* might wonder if the author is a romantic. To his credit, he gives them a direct answer: "Architecture is this aura (or 'oversoul' as Emerson might say) of structure. It is a true expression of the life of the human and social world" (*CW* III: 219).

Primed on Emerson, Frank Lloyd Wright's romanticism comes on strong with the one he sees as the philosopher-poet's popularizer, Walt Whitman. Truths purported to be "modern" are in fact eternal, especially the truth of the organic. "Walt Whitman sensed it," Wright advises, allowing only that architecture employing it has been rare (*CW* III: 221). Even when he tries to speak anthropologically, Wright soon begins sounding like the nineteenth-century poet he admires. "Man, the animal, has always sought safety first," he intones. "As a man, he continually seeks permanence." For successive lines Wright repeats the phrase, almost as a mantra: *as a man*, each time linking these words to an ascending order of qualities ending with the immortal. Once there, he associates eternal life with architecture "as man's most obvious realization of this persistent dream he calls immortality" (*CW* III: 226).

From anthropology through romantic poetry to architecture: in five short sentences Wright not only makes the transitions but builds his argument. Once established, in this case for the readers of *Architecture and Modern Life*, his rhetoric soars. An inspired structure is convincingly creative, he suggests, once its sense of finality emerges "from the within outward." When form and function are one, we have found "the center line of architecture, organic," which "places us in line with nature and enables us sensibly to go to work." The results are impressive and, remembering how Wright uses the term, inspiring. With form and function as one, the building's pattern and purpose become one as well. Such integrity is a reliable guide, the formulation of which is poetic: "Out of the ground into the light," accomplished with the identity of form and function and expressed in the nature of the building materials themselves (*CW* III: 239). What Nature was for Ralph Waldo Emerson and what Democracy could be in the work of Walt Whitman, so too is Architecture for Frank Lloyd Wright: not just a task and a process, but an idea.

As an idea, Architecture serves a high purpose. Every design for a building should be a design for better living, Wright tells an assembly of six hundred architects ("Speech to the A. F. A.," *The Federal Architect*, June 1939); homes should make life richer and more pleasant, and that's unlikely to happen in a relic from times pleasing only to one's grandmother. In London, he has a similar message for the Royal Institute of British Architects. As published in *An Organic Architecture: The Architecture of Democracy* (1939), his remarks emphasize how a building can be poetic when it does the proper work of serving reality while making daily life worth living. More expansively, he insists that "the *interpretation* of life is the true function of the architect because we know that buildings are made for life, to be lived in and to be lived in happily, designed to contribute to that living, joy and living beauty" (*CW* III: 304). And most expansively of all, Wright can warn his listeners that "we cannot have an organic architecture unless we can achieve an organic society!" (*CW* III: 305).

Though far removed in time and space from the University Guild of Evanston, Illinois, in 1894, Frank Lloyd Wright's message as delivered to the Royal Institute in London has remained in essence the same. Along the way he would improve it, expand it, and dress it in the trappings of poetry. Over the decades more and more structures would be designed, built, and happily lived in as proof of his message's point. But the idea of an organic architecture and the example of what it can provide motivates him not just to design and build but to write and speak. His message is simply that organic architecture is not a fashion or cult but is instead a dedication to the integrity of all human life, uniting religion and science in the same way that form and function are one. Such are the workings of a true democracy.

Frank Lloyd Wright's 1930s end with the architect established as a major figure in American culture. For some, he *is* American culture, given his span of years dating back almost to the age of Lincoln, and still being influential seventy years later. *An Organic Architecture* stands as an appropriate tribute to both his accomplishments and what he sees for the future. The successes of Fallingwater and the S. C. Johnson Administration Building have brought media attention back to him, but five decades of publication have kept his ideas in circulation even when there were no stunning architectural achievements to show off. This combination of factors leads to a signal event in Wright's career, an entire issue of *The Architectural Forum* (January 1938) given over to his work, the editing of which would be placed under his own control. Producing an entire magazine—a big, complex one at that—is a gargantuan task, handled customarily by a large staff. In the Taliesin Fellowship Wright had just that. With the apprentices gathering 117 illustrations of his work, the architect is free to sprinkle quotes from Whitman and Thoreau throughout the issue, and to write a narrative that includes commentaries on his most distinctive work.

The jewel of his architectural canon is Taliesin. After beginning with a quick list of seven organic principles (ground, shelter, materials, space, proportion, order, and technique), he writes at length of his home and studio in the unspoiled Wisconsin countryside. As his principles mandate, it emerges from the ground in a timeless manner and offers shelter that is physically restful and aesthetically pleasing. Even the large drafting room built for his Fellowship is natural, what he calls an abstract forest, with sap dripping from the freshly cut logs even as they are shaped into beams and supports. From Taliesin and the school's drafting room Wright moves to that room's first completed project, the Malcolm Willey House (1933) in Minneapolis. Here is his introduction of the Usonian home, not fully realized in this early example but having several key ingredients of the type, including privacy from the street and neighbors, a sequestered garden, and an open plan set atop a concrete mat. Its sense of space, Wright says, is modern "without getting at all 'modernistic,'" a caution that Usonian is not part of the International Style. Instead, it regards vista as generating a feeling for space both inside and out, with the balance of interpenetration yielding the sense of shelter that, when combined with senses of space and materials, is "the purpose of the whole structure of the dwelling" (*CW* III: 279). Every aspect here fits Wright's initial seven principles; none of them correspond to what strictly modernist architects were doing, except in occasional straightness of line. No privileging of edge (Gropius); no preeminence or purity of idea (Mies); and no obsessiveness with theory (Le Corbusier). Then comes another project completed with Fellowship support, Fallingwater (1935). Here attention to new materials comes first: reinforced concrete for the cantilever system of horizontal extension, steel sash for the dramatic vertical rise, both of which combine to let the house clutch big boulders to project over and rise above the stream. The result demonstrates how Wright's sense of shelter has no limitations of form except for materials and how they are used, always having "the methods of construction come through them." He can be emphatically conclusive about his achievement. "That is all," Wright judges. "The effects you see in this house are not superficial effects" (*CW* III: 280). *What you see is what there is*, his thinking suggests, much as the art and literature of a coming age would insist.

One design, as yet unbuilt, is discussed: a skyscraper standing by itself in a park-like setting, free of city congestion, and therefore fit to be occupied. The project is the St. Mark's Tower. At present the only built versions of it are models in the Broadacre City display, but that alone is proof that Wright will stay with the idea for the rest of his life— and eventually build the Price Tower in Bartlesville during the 1950s. For readers of *The Architectural Forum* he describes it in loving and in- spired detail, its steel in tension making it akin to modern achievements in shipbuilding. A concrete core does the same work as a ship's keel, providing a shaft for construction that the tower, being vertical, uses to support its cantilevered floors. Each floor is slightly bigger than the one below it, enabling an outer enclosure of glass and copper to be hung from the floor above. A quadruple plan isolates each of four apartments on a level from each other. As would be shown in Bartlesville, the building is a beautiful work of art and an enjoyable place to live and work.

"Wingspread" (1937), the home designed and built for Herbert F. Johnson, is introduced as a Prairie House (Wright would declare it his last), meriting the term because of its articulation of separate areas for various family purposes in the manner of the 1907 Coonley House. What distinguishes Wingspread is its integrity with the prairie landscape and its huge living room standing at the center of the home's four zones, a tall chimney stack with five fireplaces on two levels anchoring both the house itself and its varied activities. Details are furnished for the bricks and finish work, all of which delights the architect's sense for quality. Wright is careful to show how every aspect of design and construction fits the Great Lakes landscape and climate, just as the very different conditions of the Arizona desert led to the concrete-block construction of the Arizona Biltmore Hotel and the proposals for the San Marcos resort that acknowledges how "the dotted line is outline in all desert creations" (*CW* III: 283). His work cannot be offered for display, it seems, without corresponding points of instruction. In northern Cali- fornia, the hexagonal shape of the honeycomb provides a basis for the Hanna House, offering more possibilities for flexibility and flow than does the square. If moderate cost is the goal, then the basic Usonian House is the ticket. As designed for Herbert Jacobs in Madison, Wis- consin, simplification permits the building to be completed "in one operation as it goes along, inside and outside" (*CW* III: 286). As built, the residence is both beautiful and functional, with its big living room off the garden and cooking and dining spaces adjacent, if not part of it.

Wright sees "a cultured American housewife" looking well in it, as will the "now inevitable car" in its carport, each space designed with its occupant in mind. "Where does the garden leave off and the house begin?" he asks, riddling in return that it is where the garden begins and the house leaves off. "Withall, it seems a thing loving the ground with a new sense of space—light—and freedom to which our U.S.A. is entitled," he concludes (*CW* III: 287), as always uniting function with principle.

Wright's last example is the S. C. Johnson Administration Building (1936). Here is the perfect structure to make his case that modern architecture should be able to produce as inspiring a place to work as any great cathedral. Its slender dendriform columns keep the room's effect as light and as plastic as possible—much more so than the viewer can believe. Having this impressive structure in mind makes it easier for the magazine's readers to sympathize with Wright's concluding comments: "Neither realism nor realistic is the stuff of which the universal is made." Instead, "the universal is made of intense and lively personal matter asking only that the matter have individuality" (*CW* III: 289). The way to the universal is by working with the principle that form and function are one. Hence structure itself is the ultimate reality, what Wright (in conversation with Baker Brownell at the end of *Architecture and Modern Life*) claims "Plato meant by 'Eternal Idea'—the essential framework of reality" (*CW* III: 336). To understand Wright's thinking, one must note the distinction: not "ideal," but *idea*. It is a manner of thought that lies at the heart of Frank Lloyd Wright's work.

The 1930s close for the architect with "A Dinner Talk at Hull House: November Eighth, 1939." It had been his 1901 lecture on "The Art and Craft of the Machine" in this same location that had introduced his thought to a highly influential audience. At the time, they had not agreed with much that he had to say. As he told the Princeton students attending his Kahn lectures in 1930, Hull House was still enthralled with the Arts and Crafts movement, reacting against the machine rather than considering how it could improve things. At the time, Wright had little but his vision to support him—no books, no international travel, not even the Prairie House as an innovation. In 1901 he was still a very young architect indeed. How different is the situation in 1939! The Arts and Crafts movement has become a quaint reminder of an era eclipsed by more change than in all of previous history, while Frank Lloyd Wright stands not only as one of the prime agents of architectural change but as a still-fresh contemporary.

Greeting his audience, he is a picture of ease and self-confidence, yet in a self-deprecating way. Joking about his age and the welcome prospect of sitting down, he notes that forty years ago his thoughts provoked a rowdy fight with those who wanted a local Arts and Crafts Society. Despite expecting to speak informally today, to just a group at tableside, he continues for another six thousand words—an hour's talk, at least—in brilliantly organized fashion. Of course he has history on his side, and a lifetime of experience with the topic. But his rhetoric is in excellent shape as well. Everyone present would surely know what he believes in and stands for, but sharing an hour with him in person provides the opportunity of learning how he thinks. And the man is surely thinking on his feet (or while he sits, as it were), reviewing not only the conditions of his lecture four decades before but what has developed in the meantime.

Wright's memories of the old days are quick to fix upon an enemy: not John Ruskin and William Morris themselves, but the "Ruskin and Morris reactionaries." The distinction is an important one, because forces of reaction are reductive of the better parts of an idea into something preposterous, and thereby an easier target for attack. Their ambition had been "to make things by hand, pound their fingers and do all sorts of unbecoming handicraft—good in its way but entirely beside the mark in our Chicago day's work." True, the machine they detested was "out of hand" and things were becoming "hideous" because of that (*CW* IV: 20), but this was why Wright felt technology had to be addressed in a way that made it humankind's servant and not its master. In 1901, his Hull House audience wouldn't listen to such an idea. Today, the architect does not blame them, but notes how the machine has fallen into the hands of those least willing or capable to use it for proper effect. So as far as his original topic, he lets it rest in balance: handiwork did not save us, but neither did the machine.

With this old disagreement out of the way, Wright moves to a larger foe, the enemy of American architecture itself, which he sees as the "Colonial—bastard of Classical tradition washed up on our Eastern shore" (*CW* IV: 21). Although the term would not be in use for another half-century, the speaker proceeds with an argument that is persuasively postcolonial. Because he wants a broad basis for reference, he selects the U.S. Government and state governments as a constant on which he hangs responsibility for much of what he sees as wrong. Government underwrites lending policies that support only derivative architecture, and of that only the blandest kind. No faith whatsoever is invested in "the radical ideas which are the natural basis of all creative endeavor" (*CW* IV: 22). Instead, governments insist on the traditional model, which because of the country's youth is colonial in nature. For patrons at Hull House, the tragedy of this policy is in public housing, which is little more than a skyscraper laid on its side with the poor put in it to stay. Thus architecture is used to institutionalize poverty, as Wright underscores in his rhetoric—another anticipation of social thinking more common to the postwar era. There is no room for creativity in this process, no room for art—which, in an allied argument, is why Wright feels government and education should leave both to take care of themselves. When institutions do intervene, it is only to squelch what should be imaginative, leading to the "average of an average" that the architect has long decried as the result of any endowed competition. To answer any doubts about this, Wright points to what governments do with their own architecture. In the nation's capital, federal designs suffer from a debilitating self-righteousness. False tradition is everywhere, honoring Abraham Lincoln with something from Greece and remembering Thomas Jefferson, a leading radical of his era, with a style from Rome. State governments are even worse. Their choices are driven by fear of looking provincial—which is just what makes them look that way. Consequently, the best America can do is to come off like "a little One-Horse England" (*CW* IV: 23).

Following the customary plan of thinking so evident in his writing and speaking of the 1930s, Wright turns from the problem to a proposed solution. As is his habit, that solution is grounded in the nature of the problem itself. Government is by definition centralized, and so if government is what has been inhibiting the growth and development of an intrinsic American architecture, then decentralization might well be the solution. Anyone in the least bit familiar with Frank Lloyd Wright's causes will know that this has been his answer for any number of problems, be they in housing, urbanization, education, or the arts. Therefore when he presents his answer at Hull House, it is couched in the nature of his profession and career. His study of structure having been devoted to overcoming "this deadly cultural lag," he can urge his listeners to decentralize "all along the line!" The opposite of this is to exaggerate, and "Time was when it was one of the wonders of the world with us. It is now our curse" (*CW* IV: 24).

Is this a lead-in to Broadacre City? Most definitely yes, although Wright gets there by a cleverly engaging route. Nearly forty years ago he had championed the intelligent use of the machine to an audience at Hull House, and they hadn't listened. But he has listened to them, and taken their own mission to heart. He compares this episode to what his uncle, the Reverend Jenkin Lloyd Jones, was doing on Chicago's South Side—where, in parallel fashion, the nephew's ideas for how his Lincoln Center should be designed and built were also rejected. What impressed Wright at the time was that as Hull House did settlement work for the poor, Lincoln Center would do settlement work for the rich in terms of providing a community culture supportive of a better quality of life, a quality apart from and beyond economic concerns. With Hull House credited and his uncle's church allied to the cause, Wright brings himself into the mix, getting to his favorite topic of the day: Broadacre City. Uncle Jenk's example corresponds with his nephew's own first concern, which the architect admits is with the rich, because their territory is "the real slums of our great country—the upper income brackets of the gold coasts, peacock alleys and penthouses of our cities." His listeners may laugh, but Wright feels the plight of these benighted rich is tragic. "I well know the real poverty-stricken America today," he insists, thinking of lives bereft of true beauty and lacking the simple pleasure of a comfortable, inspiring house, "is our ultra-successful rich citizenry" (*CW* IV: 24). Forty-five years after preaching a sermon that amplified Reverend Gannett's *The House Beautiful*, Wright continues with his contrarian notions of wealth versus poverty, and where true impoverishment resides.

As the speaker's mind jumps from one economic level to another, first conflating the differences in favor of cultural improvement and then coming to rest with the assumption that those wealthiest in money are the poorest in architecture (and hence true happiness), his listeners are prepared for the next apparent contradiction: that Broadacre City is not a communal idea or other form of utopia but is in fact a genuine test of what capitalism can most successfully be. Wright's basis lies in testing this system of economics in an honestly democratic fashion. There, with a respect for the nature of materials and an understanding that life is essentially structure, his architecture will let the American economic system fulfill its promise and provide the makings for a life well lived and socially productive.

As a postscript to his talk, following his listeners' applause and comments by a Hull House official, Wright adds three thoughts that organize his thinking of this decade just about to conclude. The first is to make all possible use of modern advantages in pursuit of beauty—a reminder of his topic from 1901. The second is to identify the great task of the day as elimination—cutting out the insignificant and correlating what remains. The last and most important is to recognize how creative minds must be trained in structure by those who have mastered the integral. Who will do this training? The crowned subject of Frank Lloyd Wright's thought number three is the architect, who is master of all—master of Broadacre City, of the Taliesin Fellowship, and ultimately of his own vision for America.

Conclusion
A Second Career

NEARLY ONE-THIRD OF FRANK LLOYD WRIGHT'S drafted
thoughts date from the 1940s and 1950s, just as do an even greater proportion of his built designs. This volume of output speaks for his genuine
second career, beginning in the mid-1930s with his success of Fallingwater, the S. C. Johnson Administration Building, and the introduction
of the Usonian home. For the next twenty years he would feast on
publicity and turn out an astounding number of homes, several churches,
a skyscraper, a civic center, and the Guggenheim Museum. And he would
write.

Like other creative figures "rediscovered" late in life, Wright had a
substantial literary canon to draw on, and during these latter decades
much in his writing is recycled. He had published books, essays, and
lectures totaling almost one million words, evidence of his well-developed
thinking and a worthy basis for continued comment. He also had the
support of his Taliesin Fellowship, several score of eager helpers ready
to assist with matters architectural and editorial. The 1938 issue of *The
Architectural Forum* could not have been assembled without them. Nor
could Fallingwater and the S. C. Johnson structure have been built save
for their help.

Writing in 1939 to the Royal Institute of British Architects, which
had hosted his lectures several months before, Wright notes that "today
my building is as far in advance of my building, 1893–1911, as my building
of that period was in advance of that around about it at the same time"
(*CW* IV: 28). His achievements of the mid-1930s bear this out. Can the

same be said for any structure of the 1940s and 1950s? The Price Tower, after all, is almost identical with the St. Mark's Tower project of 1929, and draws essentials of its construction from the 1924 design for the projected National Life Insurance Building. Another structure of the mid-1950s, the Beth Sholom Synagogue in Elkins Park, Pennsylvania, reflects a design Wright had proposed in the 1920s for a massive Steel Cathedral. Works that do stand apart, such as the Annunciation Greek Orthodox Church (1956) in Wauwatosa, Wisconsin, and the massive Marin County Civic Center (1957), are just that: remarkable structures that are done as one-offs, impossible to account for within a canon of design. As for the Guggenheim Museum, its form finalized in 1956 and construction completed in 1959, its originality dates to Wright's first plans drawn at the time of commission, 1943. It would be the most difficult work of his life, taking an inordinate amount of time and effort for sixteen years—years during which the Fellowship had to take responsibility for realizing Wright's designs for a staggering number of homes, most of them different but all developed from the principles of the Usonian House introduced in 1936.

Frank Lloyd Wright's published and unpublished writings of these years rely to an even greater extent on ideas that had emerged and taken form during his first career, a career with long periods of unemployment when there was not only time for authorship but a need for it to support himself and his family. Now even his manner of publication was retrospective. The 1940s began with a new publisher—Duell, Sloan and Pearce—who suggested a three-volume format capitalizing on Wright's repurchase of fame. The first, *On Architecture* (1941), had Frederick Gutheim collecting and introducing essays Wright had written beginning in 1894. *In the Nature of Materials* (1942) put Henry-Russell Hitchcock to the task of cataloguing the architect's work with photographs and drawings, its commentary written under Wright's supervision. Only with a revised and expanded edition of *An Autobiography* (1943) would Wright hold the pen himself, presumably to offer an update of his life since 1932. But as the first edition had already presented visions of such 1930s business as Broadacre City and the Taliesin Fellowship, there would be little original material to add. Comments on such achievements as Fallingwater and the commissions from Herbert Johnson are recycled from the 1938 *Architectural Forum* special issue, and descriptions of life at Taliesin itself are more lushly lyrical than substantive. In terms of thinking, Wright's Wisconsin home and studio were substances of his first career. Now the success of a second would make that life all the more enjoyable. This satisfaction, however, is with things as they are, not how they will be.

Much of the architect's concern for the future during the early 1940s is based on his displeasure with present reality, notably America's participation in World War II. As an isolationist, Wright's thinking is original only to the extent that he allies the rights of personal freedom (against military conscription) with his notion of democracy as developed from an understanding of the organic. For the most part, his opposition to the war is based on two very personal facts about England: that as a descendant of Welsh nonconformists he detests English politics, and as an American architect he decries the colonial influence that inhibits innovation. His larger thinking on the war's import is sound, and actually prescient, especially on the points of how Britain will come out of the conflict as a social welfare state and how American dominance will diminish her ally's world stature and economic health.

Wright begins the 1950s with another new publisher, Horizon Press, and between 1953 and 1959 sees no less than one book per year issued. All, however, draw heavily on previous material. The two most coherent volumes, *The Natural House* (1954) and *The Living City* (1958), would be good introductions for readers who hadn't read (respectively) either *An Autobiography* or *The Disappearing City* as published in 1932. In similar manner, the many essays of this period serve as occasions for Wright to propound principles long established in his thinking. Indeed, it is because his architecture has become so noteworthy that journals are eager to learn about the thought behind it. These are also the years when Wright becomes a television personality, one of the era's best for a scintillating interview (as with Mike Wallace) or an entertaining engagement (most notoriously on the quiz show *What's My Line?*).

The 1940s and 1950s, then, are a time for reaching conclusions about Frank Lloyd Wright's manner of thought, and as usual he does his best to facilitate the reader's understanding. With the Great Depression scarcely past and World War II already being fought in Europe, he is quick to relate his ideas to social reality. In the October 1940 issue of *Taliesin* magazine, he introduces the topic of Broadacre City this way:

by exercising the rights of humanity to decentralize and reapportion its work, Wright's plan for an ideal community can take shape in the real world. Whereas earlier arguments had begun by decrying the evils of big cities, now the value of Broadacre City is based on a positive, which is a good way for the concept to take its place within the canon of ideas. There are three inherent rights supporting it: a simple and fair medium of exchange, a right to land as undeniable as right to air and light, and a right to the ideas by which people live, denying private patents for anything pertinent to the common welfare. Here at last is the economic thinking of Henry George not so much brought up to date as shown to be emerging freshly and naturally from the conditions of Broadacre City itself. With these points made, Wright can proceed with the physical specifics confident that his readers will not dismiss the concept as a primitive back-to-the-land movement but instead a "breaking down of the artificial divisions set up between urban and rural life" (*CW* IV: 66). Nor is it communal in an economic sense, and certainly not socialistic. Rather it is "a capitalist society broadly and firmly based on the ground" instead of, as presently true, "in the air" (*CW* IV: 49–50). It is indeed "'capitalism' carried to a humane conclusion" (*CW* IV: 64).

Before making his argument, Wright seeks agreement on common ground. Yes, the times are ones of economic chaos. But as an architect he knows that true forms owe their truth to inner struggle. With this in mind, he takes the proposals he had made in the first of his careers and reshapes them as conclusions for the second. The concept of democracy has underwritten much of his thinking, and now he can reconcile it with his own style of behavior, which at times has been criticized as being above and beyond the norm. America's national ideal must be something more than "quantity and the police," he argues in "The New Direction," an unpublished essay from 1953. "Quality and Faith" are much better, because "Democracy is the highest form of Aristocracy the world has ever seen," Wright insists. "Aristocracy intrinsic: in the nature of man. Not handed down" (*CW* IV: 118). Here is Frank Lloyd Wright's organic thinking, first discerned in the nature of materials and now expressed in the nature of humankind.

Wright's "democracy" is far apart from (and well above) the concept of leveling. For that he coins the term "mobocracy," and uses it to distinguish the contributions of Louis Sullivan from negative trends. *Genius and the Mobocracy* (1949) turns on the notion of the nature of a building material being "in its honor," just as a man's individuality "is his honor!" Sullivan is thus contrasted with what lies beneath him. "No imitator knows honor," we are reminded. Our country's dishonor is its "mobocracy," supported by imitation. Mobocracy swarms and swamps democracy, making "our commonplace a battlefield for divided interests" (*CW* IV: 339). In architecture mobocracy copies superficial effects, neglecting fundamentals. Wright counters all this with a metaphor that is applicable to Sullivan's work but even more one treasured for his own. "Why not the edifice symphonic throughout from footing to coping of the *structure* itself," he asks, "a harmony like music?" His father, he reminds readers, taught him that a symphony was an edifice of sound. As an architect, Wright wants to see "a building continuously plastic from inside to outside," with no interruption whatsoever of principle. As for Sullivan himself, "Assertion of pure form as *integral* rhythmic movement was what made him a lyric poet" (*CW* IV: 362).

The book added to the 1943 edition of *An Autobiography*, "Form," extends this sense of plasticity to all aspects of life. True form is always organic in character, Wright insists. Because form is a matter of structure, it is pertinent for government as well as for architecture, and beyond that frames society and defines its level of civilization. Because it is a memoir being written, the author forgoes his customary arguments about society and state in favor of demonstrating just how life is lived according to these beliefs in form, structure, and plasticity. Descriptions are exquisitely appealing, and are borne out in subsequent memoirs by the apprentices themselves, many of whom remember Taliesin as a paradise on earth. Sociopolitical rhetoric is saved for what Wright intended to be a concluding book of *An Autobiography*, "Broadacre City." Because his publisher felt the topic had already been covered in other volumes, Wright issued this version privately. In a concise ten thousand words he shows how the concept grows from his larger views of democracy, politics, and economic concerns, drawing on Henry George "for the ground" and Silvio Gesell "for the money" (*CW* IV: 247). If there is any difference to these comments on Broadacre City, it is Wright's more mellowed tone, befitting the statement's autobiographical character. As a builder, he has known how true form is organic, not only prophesying it but seeing the principle realized in both better homes and better lives within them. An "architect of social order," Wright's manner of describing a statesman "could in one lifetime lay down outlines on which we could build the Democratic State for which I would be happy to build organic buildings," he acknowledges. They should be built as normal, not revolutionary. "The life of a revolutionist is not easy to sustain" (*CW* IV: 246).

This proposed conclusion to *An Autobiography* is best read as Wright intended it; he did hurry to have the Broadacre City pages printed and bound and ready for private distribution when the 1943 edition as his publisher wanted it appeared, and in his *Collected Writings* it follows the other book as he had hoped. The full volume's conclusiveness is evident in other ways as well. He can write of the joyful life at Taliesin and its sensuous beauty when at rest, including lyrical passages on its sights and smells, rhythms and seasons. He can visit the family burial ground at Unity Chapel and remark on the scope of tradition, one to which he has already made his own tragic addition: the unmarked grave of Mamah Borthwick Cheney. Scattered among the personal narratives are seemingly random comments on his major buildings. In capsule, these descriptions have much in common with what has been said in the January 1938 issue of *The Architectural Forum*, but in sequence here the effect is quite different: that of a memoirist looking back at some highlights of a career. Thus the S. C. Johnson Administration Building is seen in the special light of the Larkin Building three decades before, and Wingspread identified with the Coonley House yet contrasted in terms of its bold directness in form and treatment. He notes that it is the last of his Prairie Houses, but adds that he doesn't know why. There's a sense of history as well to his description of his latest work for himself, the Fellowship's new outpost in Arizona. "That desert camp belonged to the desert as though it had stood there for centuries," he opines. "And also built into Taliesin West is the best in the strong young lives" of the apprentices over the past seven years (*CW* IV: 170). The eternal desert, seven years of a young person's life: it is Frank Lloyd Wright's sense of autobiography that holds this range together, conveying the sense of who he is. That identity rests, as it were, with not just a lifetime's achievement of buildings but the establishment of two Taliesins, their natures complementing his own rich complexity of character.

Had Wright been able to execute his design for the Guggenheim Museum in time, it could have figured as a climax to the architectural highpoints of his career as ticked off in his autobiography's revision. Its writing, however, took place in 1942, a product of wartime restrictions putting a halt to much architectural work. It would be June of 1943 before Hilla Rebay, curator of Solomon R. Guggenheim's peripatetic collection of nonobjective art, contacted Wright about designing a permanent home for this work. Because the architect fancied a location in the country while Rebay and Guggenheim insisted on siting the museum in the heart of New York City, specifics had to wait until December 1944, with presentation drawings ready only in early 1945. Once the location was purchased, working drawings were prepared, taking another year. On 7 September 1945 an agreement was signed and a model built. Wishing to publicize the museum's innovative spiral form, the architect had photographs taken for *The Architectural Forum* and an accompanying text added to the packet for *Magazine of Art*. With the two articles appearing in January 1946, Wright might well have felt conclusive about this latest success. Little did he know that construction delays, objections by city authorities, Rebay's dismissal, and problems with the Guggenheim heirs (after the collector's death in 1949) would push back the final design date to 1956 and delay its opening until 1959, six months after its architect's death.

Nevertheless, "The Modern Gallery" reads with the same sense of confidence evident when Wright describes his other major achievements in *An Autobiography*. "For the first time in the history of architecture a true logarithmic spiral has been worked out as a complete plastic building" (*CW* IV: 281), he announces, glorying in the ultimate expression of this manner of design emerging as proof of the organic. Not one floor atop another but a single ramp, grand and slow, widening as it ascends but intended for the museum goers' leisurely descent (after taking an elevator to the top): the structure is so physically natural that Wright fancies it would bounce if tossed up from the ground. But beyond all its features that privilege the patrons' experience in viewing art is the way the building reflects on the people themselves instead of being scaled to grand proportions. Without stating it, Wright is able to imply why he wanted to build out in the countryside instead of on New York's busy Fifth Avenue. Conceding to his patrons' wish for accessibility, the architect manages to design an enclave where citizens of the pig-piled metropolis, as he had called it in so many treatises about the city, could recover a sense of themselves. In the Usonian House design, this was accomplished by turning the back of the house toward the street, allowing the exuberance of simple existence to flow uninhibited through welcoming spaces out into the sheltered garden. In the S. C. Johnson Administration Building, light-filled space created by the delicate dendriform columns provided an ideal, uplifting place to work, just as the architect's church designs, dating back to Unity Temple, offered perfect places for fellowship and worship. Now with the Guggenheim Museum Wright could present a facility that brings out the best in human beings as they invest some time, comfortably and rewardingly, in one of life's best undertakings, the appreciation of truly great art.

Similarly, Wright's conclusive feel for the nature of democracy could not be expressed in the 1943 revision and expansion of *An Autobiography*, but would have to wait until World War II (a terrible disruption of his ideals) ended. That conclusion comes in "Building a Democracy" as published in *Taliesin Square-Paper Number 10* (October 1946). Having seen the last half-century evolve, he can state with great authority that "Democracy and architecture, if both are organic, cannot be two separate things." The recently concluded war had frustrated this, of course, quite personally for Wright, who not only had his practice put on hold and his Fellowship depleted by the draft but was humiliated by having his country go to war in support of an allegiance that went against his ancestral nonconformism and professional postcolonialism. Now, with all that in the past, he can make his major point, based on the type of distinction that catalyzes the rhetorical success of his best arguments. "Democracy is not so much a form—even were we to find it—or a policy—even were we to make it—as it is abiding faith in man's indivisible right to himself as himself." Here is what everyone should have learned from the war: "Man-made codes come in to obstruct, expropriate or punish only when we lose sight of the way to live naturally, as we build, and build naturally as we live." And what is that way? Architecture and democracy: "Both must come from within, spontaneously" (*CW* IV: 300).

His argument made, the author can wax poetic, praising organic structure as growing like humankind itself in all its nobility. In a reference new to his writing at this time, but more common in his last decade of work, Wright argues that the architecture of democracy "will be the externalizing of this inner seeing of the man as Jesus saw him, from within—not as an animal or a robot, but a living soul." Such loftiness is contrasted with "this cinder strip here in the East" that imitates England. The Soviet Union is no better, slavishly imitating buildings of the culture it overthrew. All in all, "The democratic code must be designed to *complete*, not to *prevent* the man" (*CW* IV: 301). If that involves alluding to Marx and Jesus in the same short essay, so be it. The age Frank Lloyd Wright was living in these last years was about to eclipse the modernism that had kept these two figures separate.

In his last decade the architect's written work reprises his important themes of half a century before, but with a conclusive emphasis on their importance for life as lived in this realm of thought. For readers of *The Architectural Record* in May 1952, Wright's "Organic Architecture Looks at Modern Architecture" presents a familiar argument with a newly underscored moral. After detailing the features of what he would soon be calling his natural house, Wright sums up its major advantage, which is a sense of space scaled not just to human size but to human need. "The interior space to be lived in became *the reality of the whole performance*" (*CW* V: 48), he clarifies, combining thoughts from *The House Beautiful* of the 1890s with the Usonian home as conceived in the mid-1930s and still ahead of its times as he writes. Yet Wright would argue that success for organic architecture was a matter of discernment and not fashionability. Above all, because it was individual in nature, organic architecture did not do well among journalists, especially in a country enthralled by communications media. Wright himself had tried to report on his work, but even at its best such representations are by nature second hand. His *Taliesin Tract* of December 1953, "Man," makes the point that while literature tells, architecture shows. For true impact, he believes, his structures would have to be lived in to be understood.

The Natural House (1954) is probably Wright's most accessible book. As a paperback in the decades following his death it popularized his concepts in a culture becoming increasingly postmodern—which is to say, a culture that increasingly questioned the authority of any text even as it recognized how experience itself is intertextual in nature. In a concise forty thousand words Wright's volume distills the essence of many others, including both editions of his autobiography and numerous essays and addresses on the subject. This short work would allow readers to bypass the specifics of Wright's life story and personal politics, by now familiar to all from his wide exposure as a media personality, in favor of getting right inside the house itself. There is no need to lecture about the evils of urbanization; a quick image says it all in terms of human effect, which is the "mean tendency to tip everything in the way of human occupation or habitation up edgewise instead of letting it lie comfortably flatwise with the ground where spaciousness was a virtue" (*CW* V: 79). Against this condition stands the natural house, taking advantage of the horizontal as the line of repose, the "earth line of human life" (*CW* V: 80). Built using brick as brick and wood as wood, with newer materials such as concrete, glass, and steel each being themselves as well, it follows the correlations and integrations of life itself. With the proper thought behind it, the machine can be of great help in this regard.

Specifics of the natural house are the ones Wright has been describing since the first Jacobs residence of nearly twenty years before. But now he has a broader sense of their importance. Walls, ceilings, and floors work together so well in the Usonian House because they are components of each other. Surfaces flow together in a continuity of the whole, all constructed features eliminated, much like how Louis Sullivan had discarded background in his ornamentation so that there might be a sounder sense of the whole. Thus a point from *Genius and the Mobocracy* is combined with another from Wright's various statements about the Usonian dwelling not just for mutual support but to suggest a point of resolution (if not closure) in the author's thinking. This is especially appropriate given *The Natural House*'s larger thesis, that "there can be no separation between our architecture and our culture. Nor any separation of either from our happiness. Nor any separation from our work" (*CW* V: 94).

Two decades of Usonian Houses give Wright evidence for his conclusion that because of the freedom experienced when living in a house wherein everything is genuine and harmonious one enjoys a better life, as opposed to the traditional structure where habitation is contained in a series of boxes. Residents may recognize this for what it is or simply benefit from the more pleasing atmosphere. Clients have written Wright to this effect, which doesn't surprise him: like plants in rich soil, they have flourished, but because they are human beings they can take pride in the purpose they feel as individuals and as a family.

Superintending it all is Wright himself as master of a consistent grammar. This consistency is why his clients so enjoy their homes, but it is not their duty to know why. "Grammar is no property for the usual owner or the occupant of the house," he allows. "But the man who designs the house must, inevitably, speak a consistent thought-language in his design" (*CW* V: 121). Note the coinage: *thought-language*. A Usonian home, the true natural house, is not an assemblage of rooms but a manner of thought. "I doubt that this affair can be taught to anyone," Wright warns, which is why his Taliesin Fellowship enrolls apprentices and not students. Nor is it a philosophy derived from other sources, not even the understanding of space expressed by Lao Tse. Yes, there are parallels, Wright admits, but only ones he became aware of "after I had found and built it for myself" (*CW* V: 126). Democracy's celebration of the individual informs this organic principle that privileges the habitation of space over any outward feature. Lao Tse may have thought it, Wright reminds readers, but neither he nor anyone else in history "had consciously *built* it." Anyone other than Frank Lloyd Wright, that is, whose history now stands as example. "When I thought of that, naturally enough I thought, 'Well, then, everything is all right, we can still go along with head up,'" he concludes. "I have been going along—head up—ever since" (*CW* V: 127).

The Story of the Tower appears in 1956, celebrating the opening of the H. C. Price Tower in Bartlesville, Oklahoma. This commission dates from 1952, but realizes the design proposed for the St. Mark's Tower in New York in 1929 and employs the cantilever and sheathing features of the National Life Insurance Building project of 1924. With his building finally in existence, Wright can be conclusive about its effect: what for a third of a century beforehand was just thought has become material reality. Frank Lloyd Wright the visionary can now enjoy talking in practical terms, describing the cantilever and rating its efficiency, noting the added living space gained from this saving of weight, and boasting of the light gained from the abundance of glass made possible by this design— "ten per cent more glass area as 'exposure' than you may see in the average commercial building such as Gordon Strong's Republic Building down on State Street, corner of Adams, in Chicago" (*CW* V: 150), a comically specific reference to a developer who had considered giving Wright exceptionally daring commissions in the 1920s, including a mountain-like drive-through planetarium, and then backed out. Eminently practical, the Tower is physically beautiful, drawing on the aesthetic of the sleek ocean liner, streamlined airplane, and striking automobile. Lyrically, it suggests a spider spinning its web to capture slivers of glass. Iridescent colors rise from the cityscape that is the Tower's park, and the metal shafts themselves take on attractive coloration—all images used decades before to describe the St. Mark's project. This beautiful and efficient wonder, Wright can now prove, has been delivered at "half the cost of the stuffy caverns it replaces" (*CW* V: 153). With the reality of his building before him, its beauty evident and its cost-effectiveness proven, the architect cannot help but become visionary again. Eventually all buildings will be like this, he rhapsodizes. No reality is ever enough to bring rest to his manner of thought.

The publication of *A Testament* occurs in 1957; this is a book given almost entirely to the refinement of the author's ideas. It starts with the notion of beauty itself, described by William Blake as the consequence of utter fullness of nature in expression: expression intrinsic. Exuberance and not excess is what both Wright and his model poet value. Excess is vulgar, exuberance is sublime. In similar manner, there is a world of difference between the physicality of form following function and the spirituality of form and function being one. Intellect itself faces the same challenge: should it be degraded by education or uplifted by the principles of one's own being?

Should William Blake be too exuberant for readers' tastes, there is "the master-poet of our world" to heed, one who preached that "The Kingdom of God is within *you*." The "only visible evidence of this in modern art," Wright adds, "is organic architecture," the subject of his own preaching (*CW* V: 170). Before it had been Marx and Jesus, and in a few more pages it will be Lao Tse and Jesus. For now, it is Jesus and Frank Lloyd Wright. The architect feels comfortable in such company because of his lifelong understanding, dating from his training with the Froebel blocks, that there is an "innate sense of origin" that works as the "activating cause of all visible effects" (*CW* V: 189). When applied to social life, this belief informs democracy with a faith in humankind as individual, "a new kind of aristocracy—as I have said—*of* the man, not *on* him" (*CW* V: 205). Organic architecture is the way to realize this, Wright concludes; through its art a culture will develop that enriches society, empowering individuals by letting them consider their lives as their own. This idea of organic architecture is one that Wright has come up with by himself, with no outside influence This is his testament as published two years before his death.

Yet even at age ninety-one Frank Lloyd Wright could not let go of the idea of Broadacre City. *The Disappearing City* had appeared in 1932, *When Democracy Builds* in 1945, and other descriptions of his plan for a decentralized democracy had been made in his lectures, essays, and private publications. But there would still be room in his canon for one last, conclusive statement on the topic: *The Living City*, published in 1958. At eighty thousand words, it ranks as his most exhaustive treatment of the Broadacre idea. Before, he has written as a social critic. Now he speaks as a philosopher, looking at the world as it is today and remarking that "*space* values have entirely changed to *time* values" in terms of mobility (*CW* V: 284). Space, we know from Wright's other works, is determined by the interior. But as far as exterior spacing, it is the time taken to cover the distance that is the determining factor, newly introduced by telecommunications and the automobile. Because of these new conceptions of time and space, humankind is closer to nature, both in terms of travel and in the nature of housing that erases the "hard and fast lines between outside and inside." As a philosopher, the ultimate status for any lifetime thinker whose ideas not only coalesce but have some worldly proof, Wright can measure human progress. "Continuity, plasticity, and all these imply," he notes, "are fast coming home to him— a miraculous new release in life as well as architecture" (*CW* V: 305).

Had Wright lived to see the Guggenheim Museum completed and opened, he could have written about it, as he did for the Price Tower, as an idea long held and finally realized. He did manage to push that idea along, in the 1950s establishing "Taliesin East" in a suite at the Plaza Hotel in New York so that he could be close for negotiations with city authorities and contractors and ultimately for the construction itself. As the structure rose with its distinctive spiral form, Wright climbed the ramp, pointing with his cane as if willing the museum into existence— photographs of him doing just this filled magazine pages in 1958 and early 1959. In 1958 the building was close enough to completion that he felt comfortable writing a short essay on the subject. Had he lived, it would have been published to celebrate the Guggenheim's opening later in 1959; as it happened, the piece appeared in a volume on the museum issued by the Horizon Press in 1960.

What Wright says to readers from the grave is simply what he could see in 1958: that the building's walls and spaces, both inside and out, "are one in substance and effect." That is the reality. Behind it stands an idea, that of a unity present among the paintings, their viewers, and the building that hosts both. Here Wright looks forward to how the art-works would be viewed. Famous painters, including such leading abstract expressionists as Willem de Kooning and Franz Kline, had complained that the slanted walls and ramps would make proper display of their work impossible, but for them Wright has an answer. "The character of the building itself as architecture amounts to 'framing,'" he suggests. Detached from the wall, the picture "is presented to view much as a jewel set in a signet ring. Precious—as itself" (*CW* V: 245). As in any Wright design, everything works together for the proper notion of interior space, whether for people in their homes or in a gallery to view works of art. The walls curving outwards make for a sense of repose in the spiral's upward sweep, with the paintings "freely floated in an atmo-sphere of architecture instead of framed," he remarks. The artists should be happy, he implies, because in his design their works will be presented "as features in themselves—not as if painted on or subservient to the wall behind them." Indeed, the architect accords them the highest privilege he can grant: "They are now seen as master of their own allotted space" (*CW* V: 248).

Frank Lloyd Wright's last two essays speak to the future. In the first, written for the forward-looking readers of *The Progressive* (January 1959), he celebrates "A Culture of Our Own," as his title has it. What is indigenous to American culture is the nature of things, of and for the thing's nature, he writes, adding that it is "only by way of a nature study intimate, persistent, relentless, that young men or women can inform themselves of what constitutes reality in this life" (*CW* V: 347). "Nature" in this sentence does not mean flora and fauna, but rather the ultimate reality of things, as described before. Wright would agree with Ralph Waldo Emerson and the other Transcendentalists that nature's physical creations are imprints of an ideal Nature, but simply as a basis for going much farther with the idea, going into "the nature of things" themselves as a principle for his own organic design. For Wright, architecture is "the basic endeavor of mankind, the mother art," the art that "*presents man*" instead of simply talking about him (as does literature) or picturing him (as does painting). To *experience* him, "go into his buildings. That is where you will find him *as he is*" (*CW* V: 346).

In the very last of his writings, "Preamble to *The Wonderful World of Architecture*," Wright speaks to young readers. Not published until 1962, the piece was found on his desk the morning he died, as Bruce Brooks Pfeiffer notes when using it to close the *Collected Writings*. "Man's greatest gift lies in his vision," Wright emphasizes, cautioning that an over-reliance on science usually prevents this vision from focusing on "the beauty of himself: man's own spiritual haven." When vision does focus, however, beauty becomes an experience of greater importance. And at the most important level stands "man's creative architecture: the greatest proof of his immortal soul" (*CW* V: 349).

It is hard to imagine any other architect, certainly of modern times, being able to make such a statement. Just picturing their work, however admirable, severely limits the notion. But with Frank Lloyd Wright's achievements in mind—Fallingwater, the S. C. Johnson Administration Building, the Guggenheim Museum, and countless Prairie Houses and Usonian homes—the sentiment soars. Very few can state, as he does in 1958, that "I have lived to see things happen few men see." Who else can add that "Ideas fought for when I was young and dark-haired have been accepted." And who better than Frank Lloyd Wright to say that "I know the price of success—unremitting devotion, hard work, and an inextinguishable love for the things you want to happen." For over seventy years he had designed and written. Now nearly all of that had come into realized form, with the world so much different, so much better for it. "You can't achieve this much," he concludes, "without this deep-seated feeling for all life that we call love" (*CW* V: 232).

Appendix

Divorce Papers of
William C. and Anna L. Wright

The following public document is housed in the University Archives, Steenbock Library, Room 425, University of Wisconsin, Madison, Wisconsin. It is kept in a brown manila envelope labeled "Frank Lloyd Wright File from: Gaylord L. Moser, 754 E. So. St., Richland Center, Wis. miscellaneous information re: William C. Wright." Words crossed out in the original are indicated as such and spelling and punctuation idiosyncrasies have been retained.

Dane County Circuit Court
William C. Wright
vs.
Anna L. Wright
Drawer No. 734 [224 superimposed]
Tax pd. Fees pd
Action for Divorce
J. H. Carpenter Plaintiff's Attorney.
Ct Record, Vol. 10, Page 24
04/24/5

Folio 1
State of Wisconsin.
Circuit Court Dane County.
William C. Wright Plaintiff
vs
Anna L. Wright Defendant

The complaint of the above named plaintiff appearing by J. H. Carpenter his attorney respectfully shows to this court that on the 17th day of August

A.D. 1866 the plaintiff and defendant intermarried:-that the plaintiff and defendant are both residents of Dane County, Wisconsin and have both resided in said county and state for six years last past.

The plaintiff further shows that he has always hitherto treated the defendant with kindness and forbearance and in all respects been to her a true, kind and faithful husband, and kept and performed his marriage vows, but the defendant disregarding her duties as a wife did, on or about February 25, 1883, willfully unjustly and without cause or provocation desert this plaintiff and has ever since and still continues such willful and unjust desertion.

The plaintiff further shows that the parties hereto have three children, the fruit of their marriage, whose names and ages are as follows: Frank L. Wright, 17 years old, June 8, 1884. Mary Jane Wright, 15 years old April 26, 1884. Margaret Ellen Wright 7 years old, June 19, 1884.

Wherefore the plaintiff demands judgment that the bonds of matrimony between the plaintiff and defendant be absolutely dissolved, and that the custody of said children be awarded as to the Court shall seem just and proper and that such other relief be granted the plaintiff as shall be just.

J. H. Carpenter Plaintiff's Attorney
State of Wisconsin
Dane County s.s.

William C. Wright ~~the plaintiff above named~~ being duly sworn says that he is the plaintiff above named & that he has read the foregoing complaint, and is fully informed as to the contents thereof, and he further says that the foregoing complaint is true to his own knowledge, except as to those matters therein stated on information and belief, and as to those matters he believes it to be true. Wm. C. Wright

Subscribed and sworn to before me this 13th day of December A.D. 1884
J. H. Carpenter
Notary Public Dane County Wisconsin

Filed Dec. 27, 1884
S. H. Butler Clerk

State of Wisconsin
Circuit Court Dane County

William C. Wright Plaintiff
agst
Anna L. Wright Defendant
Dane County s.s.

J. H. Carpenter being first duly sworn says he is the attorney for the plaintiff above named-that on the sixteenth day of December A.D. 1884 he personally served the summons and complaint in the above entitled action upon the above named defendant Anna L. Wright who is personally known to the deponent to be the defendant mentioned as such in said summons and complaint, by delivering to and leaving with her true copies of said summons and complaint, at Madison in said Dane County, and at the same time explaining to her the contents thereof. The said summons and complaint are hereto attached.

J. H. Carpenter
State of Wisconsin
Dane County s.s.

Subscribed and sworn to before me this seventeenth day of December A.D. 1884
C. F. Lamb Notary Public Dane County Wisconsin Filed Dec. 27, 1884. S. H.
    Butler Clerk

Circuit Court, Dane County.
William C. Wright Plaintiff
vs.
Anna L. Wright Defendant
Summons and Complaint
J. H. Carpenter Plaintiff's Attorneys
Filed Dec. 27, 1884. S. H. Butler Clerk [illegible notation]

Dane County, s.s.
I, [blank space], Sheriff of the County of Dane do hereby certify that I have served the within summons and complaint on the within named Defendant Anna L. Wright personally, by delivering to and leaving with [blank] a true copy of said summons and complaint, on the [blank] day of [blank] A.D. 188[-], at the [blank] of [blank], in said [blank] County. Fees:-Travel [blank] m., $ [blank] Service, [blank], Copies, [blank], fol., [blank] [blank] Sheriff.

State of Wisconsin,
Circuit Court, Dane County.
William C. Wright Plaintiff
against
Anna L. Wright Defendant

The State of Wisconsin to the Said Defendant:
You are hereby summoned to appear within twenty days after service of this summons, exclusive of the day of service, and defend the above entitled action in the Court aforesaid: and in case of your failure so to do, judgment will be rendered against you according to the demand of the complaint; of which a copy is herewith served upon you. J. H. Carpenter Plaintiff's Attorney. P.O. Address, Box 254 Madison, Dane County, Wis.

Wm. C. Wright
vs.
Anna L. Wright
Affidavit of No Answer
Filed Apr. 13, 1885, S. H. Butler Clerk

Dane County, Circuit Court
Wm. C. Wright Plaintiff
vs.
Anna L. Wright, Def'd't
Dane County S. S.:

J. H. Carpenter being duly sworn says he is the plaintiff's attorney in the above entitled action that the summons and complaint therein were personally served on the defendant at Madison, Wisconsin, December 16, 1884, and that no answer or demurrer to said plaintiff's complaint in said action has been served upon or received by the deponent or the plaintiff and no notice of appearance on the part of the defendant has been served upon or reveived by the deponent or plaintiff but the defendant is now in default. J. H. Carpenter

Sworn to and Subcribed before me this 24th day of January A.D. 1885.
C. F. Lamb Notary Public Dane Co. Wis.

Wm. C. Wright
vs.
Anna L. Wright
Order of Reference
Filed & entered in Order Book "K." page 557 Apr. 13, 1885, S. H. Butler Clerk

State of Wisconsin,
Circuit Court, Dane County
Wm. C. Wright Plaintiff
vs.
Anna L. Wright Defendant

It appearing to the undersigned by due proof that the summons and complaint in this action, now on file in the office of the Clerk of this Court were duly and personally served on the above named defendant at Madison, Wisconsin on the 16th day of December, A.D. 1884 and that the time for answering said complaint has expired and that no answer or demurrer to said complaint has been served upon the plaintiff or his attorney, and that no notice of appearance of said defendant has been received by the plaintiff or his attorney or either of them and the plaintiff wishing to apply to the Court for the relief demanded in said complaint.

Now on motion of J. H. Carpenter, attorney for the plaintiff it is hereby ordered that it be referred to C. F. Lamb, Esq. to ~~the~~ take proof of the facts and circumstances stated in the complaint and report all the same to this Court with all convenient speed. Dated this 26th day of January 1885 A.D. Alva Stewart Judge

Circuit Court
Dane County.
William C. Wright Plff
vs.
Anna L. Wright Defdt
Referee's Oath
Filed Apr. 13, 1885. S. H. Butler Clerk

Circuit Court
Dane County.

William C. Wright Plaintiff
vs.
Anna L. Wright Defendant

I, C. F. Lamb, of Madison, Wisconsin having by the above court been appointed referee to take proof of the facts and circumstances stated in the complaint, do solemnly swear to support the Constitution of the United States, and the Constitution of the State of Wisconsin, and to perform the duties of referee in this case according to law, and to the best of my knowledge and ability, so help me God. C. F. Lamb

Sworn to and subscribed before me this 6th day of April, 1885 F. J. Lamb Notary Public Dane Co., Wis.

William C. Wright, plaintiff duly sworn and testifies as follows. I am the plaintiff in this action. The defendant is my wife. We were married in August 1866. I had previously been married and my first wife died in 1863. I have three children still living by my first wife. I reside in Madison and have resided here for six years last past. The defendant resides in Madison and has for ~~several~~ six years.

Since my marriage to my second wife I have treated her kindly and so far as I know have performed my marriage vows. I have provided for her as well as my means would permit, during the last two or three years she has had the handling of the largest share of my income.

About ~~two or~~ three years ago in February last she refused to occupy the same bed with me. I have since then repetedly solicited her to occupy the same room and bed with me since she left me as stated she has not occupied ~~[illegible] bed or~~ a bed with me and for the two years last past she has not occupied the same room with me at night.

I have repetedly since she left my bed solicited her to occupy the same bed with me but she her refused to do so. She sometimes said she did not love me and somtimes she said she hated me she told me on 4 March 1883 I hate the very ground you tread on. If you will give me the place you may go when you please. I don't care what becomes of you. She has twice said she would never live with me as a wife and for two years has protested against and refused me intercourse as between husband & wife.

Her language during the last three years has not been kind and I do not know of any ~~thing~~ kind word or expression that she has used towards me during the last three years. ~~In~~ Her conduct and temper toward me ~~she~~ is ungovernable.

I have made special effort during the last two years to have her reconciled to me and become so that ~~she~~ we could live ~~with me~~ togeather peacibly & happily ~~and~~. I made such an effort in August 1883, she was then visiting among her friends. I went to see her. I trid to have a pleasant visit with her and went for that purpose. I went intending to overlook every thing. I treated her kindly pleasently and courteously. She ~~treated me~~ said I had blackend her to her people and been the cause of all her unhappyness.

During this inteview there was no reconsailiation nor any apparent desire on her part for a reconciliation-She has never since shewn any desire for a reconciliation. I have sought both by interview and letters a reconciliation. I have written letters three different times seeking reconciliation ~~In these interviews~~ neither in my interview nor in response to my letters has she shewn any desire for reconcilation. I have felt and still feel there is no hope of our ever being able to live togeather.

I have never intentionally blackened her character. I had once confidentially inquired of one of her relations if there had been insanity in the family. I did not suppose this was ever to be spoken of. It was communicated to her and she complained of it. The idea of any insanity in the family was promptly denied. I have three children by my present wife. I have no real estate anywhere except my homestead here in the city. I have no personal property except household furnitur at my house library, a little office furnitur, some musical instruments ~~in my office~~. I am a teacher of music.

~~It was~~ It is now several months since I have lived in the same house with her. For more than two years the last that I trid to live with her, I was compelled to go upstairs and sleep alone. During all that time she shewed no signs of relenting and living with me as my wife but was constantly grewing worse. The reason I inquired if there had been any insanity in the family was on account of her violent conduct towards me. Her expression about me giving her the place and going when I had a mind to was not a solitery one, it has been often repeated. In May 1883, thinking that a change for a few days might benefit her, and give a more pleasent turn to her feelings, I gave her money to go on a visit to Chicago, and presented it in a new purse that I bought. She took the money about the 15th of May and exclaimed about the purse what a clumsey thing. She went away and I supposed she was to be gone about a week, but she went also to Milwaukee Watertown, and did not return for about 3 weeks. In the mean time she did not write to me but wrote to my daughter Jennie. When she got back I received her cordially, but she was very cold and repellant to me at two other times she came to me for money ostensibly for nessaries but used it in going to visit her relatins without notifying me that she intended to go. At last her brothers came to me and spoke about the necessity of peace in the family. I said there was nothing I wanted more, that I had been outrageously abused and she had no just ground of complaint. They suggested we seperate. I asked how or on what terms. They said give her the place and they would see that her children were cared for. After deliberation I told them I had suffered a good manny years that I was entitled to a divorce for cruelty, personal violence, and refusal of my marital rights, that if a seperation was to take place it ought to be by law. That I was willing to give up almost anything in way of property to her and the children. Many times before I had thought on the subject of a divorce but had made up my mind that for the sake of our children, and her friends ~~on~~ with whom I supposed I was on good terms, I would never bring the case into court if I could live without, but when after suffering violence indignity and abuse for years I was represented as being prime offender I could endure it no longer willing however to cause as little scandel and as little pain to all parties as possible at the request of her friends I had the suit brought for desertion only believing it could be maintained on that ground. There was other neglect and abandonment of her duties as a wife on her part. Very many times I had to make my own bed. Though I paid a kind girl at the time. She became during the last year or two neglectful of my wishes and comfort in respect to food, a larger part of my mending I did myself or carried away because when I requested her to do anything it was often neglected, never ~~chearfully~~ cheerfully done, and when it was done, often threwn in my face or on to the floor.

The room that I slept in was the coldest room in the house she slept in the bedroom warmed from the sitting room, was unwilling I should go in there for any purpose even in the day time, and often would drive me out. This was for the two years last past. I left at last because comfert and peace were out of the question and I did not deem it safe to stay.

Our married life had been unhappy from the start. She was jealous of the three children by my first wife. I had to ~~have~~ send them away as soon as possible. I sent the daughter away when she was 11 or 12. She wanted more money than I could furnish and constantly blamed me for not having more, tortered me with doing nothing for my family when I did all I knew how or was able to do. She ran me in debt, contrary to express understanding, after giving her the largest monthly allowance I could besides a large extra sum for putting new things in the house, she would be violenty angry if I remonstrated against her course, would resent any suggestions about economy. Between 2 & 3 years ago, when I had received some money from my fathers life insurance, and paid it out to clear off the debt on the place besides making some improvments I had about $50 left she wanted that at her disposal. I told her it must be saved for an emergency for I had nothing else to fall back on. She has said several times since that that the time when all the love went out of her heart for me was when I withheld that $50 from her. But I had not been able to see the love for ~~a long time~~ years before that one night. Wm. C. Wright

Taken Subscribed & Sworn before me this 6th April 1885
C. F. Lamb Referee

Filed Apr. 13, 1885, S. H. Butler Clerk

William C. Wright Plff.
vs.
Anna L. Wright Deft
In Circuit Court Dane County Wis.

Testimony taken before C. F. Lamb a referee duly appointed in the above entitled action commencing on the 6th day of April A.D. 1885.

Present. J. H. Carpenter plaintiffs attorney. No appearance of defendant.

J. H. Carpenter sworn as witness on the part of the plaintiff. I am the plaintiffs attorney in this action. I know both the plaintiff and defendant, have known the plaintiff twenty years or more and the defendant from five to eight years or more. They have both resided in Dane County more than five years last past and both still reside in Dane County.

Prior to the commencement of this action at my request the defendant with two of her brothers met the plaintiff at my office in the city of Madison, the first object of the interview being to see if there could be a reconciliation, at this interview the defendant stated to me in the presence of the other persons named that she had not lived with the plaintiff as his wife since February 1883 and that she never would again live with him as his wife she gave as her principal reason for refusing to live with him as his wife, that there was no affection on her part for him and none on his part for her as she believed and under such circumstances she did not consider ~~him~~ it proper to live with him as his wife. This inteview was in November or early in December 1884.

From February 1883 to the time of said interview they had for the most part lived in the same house, but during all that time had never occupied the same bed nor had any intercourse as husband and wife as she stated. In this inteview she also stated that she should not oppose the plaintiffs getting a divorce. In this same inteview the plaintiff insisted that he should commence proceedings for a divorce and it was agreed between the parties the brothers the defendant concurring, that the brothers would see that provision ~~she~~ was made for the children of the parties to this suit if the plaintiff would deed or cause to be deeded to the defendant his interest in the homestead in Madison and leave for the use of the defendant and family in such a way that the same should belong to the defendant the household furniture and house keeping goods and a part of the library, reserving only some few items of house keeping goods that belonged to the first wife of the plaintiff.

The plaintiff has children living by his first wife and three children by his present wife the names and ages of the children by his present wife are given in the complaint. The plaintiff was also ~~the~~ to furnish some supplies for the use of the family during the winter of 1884–1885.

In persuance of this arrangment, a deed has been made and executed, conveying to the defendant the plaintiffs right in their homestead and it is in my possession to be delivered to the defendant as soon as a decree divorcing the parties to this action is rendered by the court.

There are generally other matters of difference between these parties which with the difficulty already stated satisfies me beyond a question that they can never live togeather a knowledge of these other matters comes to me from both parties. They relate purely to their personal intercourse.

In this opinion that the parties will never live togeather and never be reconciled to each other the brothers of defendant before refered to concur. The supplies that the plaintiff was to furnish during the pendency [?] of this action to defendant and family have been furnished and I hold the defendants receipts therefor. J. H. Carpenter

Taken Subscribed & Sworn to before me this 8 April 1885. C. F. Lamb Referee

Filed Apr. 13, 1885, S. H. Butler, Clerk

Dane Circuit Court
William C. Wright Plff.
agt
Anna L. Wright Deft
Report of Referee

Judgment
Filed Apr. 13, 1885, S. H. Butler Clerk

In Circuit Court Dane County Wisconsin
William C. Wright Plff
vs.
Anna L. Wright Deft

To the said Court.
I C. F. Lamb referee in the above entitled action duly appointed to take proof
of the facts and circumstances stated in the complaint and report the same to
the court, would respectfully report

That I was attended by J. H. Carpenter Esqr. Plaintiffs attorney herein and
that there was no appearence on the part of the defendant That I have examined
under oath the plaintiff and J. H. Carpenter as witness for the plaintiff and
have reduced their testimony to writing which ~~was~~ is hereto annexed and made
a part of this report That the testimony was taken to be used in the above entitled action wherein William C. Wright is plaintiff and Anna L. Wright is
defendant—That is was taken in persuance of the annexed order of reference.

That said witnesses before examination were by me sworn to testify the
truth, the whole truth and nothing but the truth relative to said cause and their
depositions were severally read to the ~~deponents~~ witnesses and then subscribed
by them. All which is respectfully submitted. Dated April 10, 1885, C. F. Lamb
Referee

Dane Circuit Court
Wm. C. Wright Pltff
vs.
Anna L. Wright Defdt
Finding for Judgement

Filed & entered in Judgment Book "2" page 427 April 24, 1885. S. H. Butler
Clerk

Circuit Court, Dane County
Wm. C. Wright Plt'ff
vs.
Anna L. Wright Defd't

The above entitled cause coming on in its order for hearing (and the defendant not appearing) testimony having been taken on the part of the plaintiff and the Court being now sufficiently advised finds the following facts and conclusions of law.

As facts the Court find that the plaintiff and defendant intermarried on the 17th day of August 1866, that they are both residents of Dane County, Wisconsin and have both resided in said County and State for more than six years last past.

That the plaintiff has always hitherto performed his full duty to the defendant as her husband and kept and performed his marriage vows.

That the defendant in February 1883 wilfully deserted the plaintiff without cause or provocation and has ever since continued said willful desertion.

That the defendant and plaintiff have three children the fruit of their marriage as stated in the Complaint.

That the defendant is a suitable person to have the care and custody of the persons and education of said children and that all the allegations of the complaint are true. As conclusions of law the Court finds: The plaintiff entitled to the decree of divorce for which he prays and judgment is hereby ordered accordingly, the custody, care, maintenance and education of said children to be by said Judgment given to the defendant during the pleasure of the Court Dated this 24th day of April 1885

By the Court Alva Stewart Judge

Dane Circuit Court
William C. Wright Pl'tff.
vs
Anna L. Wright Def'd't.
Judgment

Filed and entered in Judgment Book "2" page 428 April 24, 1885. S. H. Butler
Clerk

State of Wisconsin
Circuit Court, Dane County
Wm. C. Wright Pl'tff
vs
Anna L. Wright Defd't

This action coming on in its order for hearing on the 13th day of April A.D. 1885 and at the April Term of said Court for 1885 and the Court now being sufficiently advised and having made and filed its finding of facts and conclusions of law wherein the Court finds that the defendant deserted the plaintiff as alleged in the Complaint all the allegations of the Complaint fully proved and true and the testimony having been by order of Court taken by a Referee and reported to the Court and as a conclusion of law that the plaintiff is entitled to the divorce for which he prays and awarded the custody, education and maintenance of the children named in the complaint to the defendant.

Therefore on motion of J. H. Carpenter attorney for the plaintiff it is hereby adjudged that the bonds of matrimony existing between the plaintiff and defendant be and the same are hereby dissolved and each of said parties is freed from all the obligations thereof and at liberty to marry again

It is further adjudged that the plaintiff deed to the defendant all his interest in Lot one Block one hundred thirty nine in the City of Madison, Dane County, Wisconsin and leave to the defendant the house keeping goods now in said house on said lot not including books and that the same shall be in full for all suit money and alimony both temporary and permanent and shall be received by said defendant as her full share of said plaintiff's estate and in full for all claims and demands of every kind against said plaintiff or his estate, and that all further claim on the part of the defendant against plaintiff or his estate for suit money, alimony or right to support shall be hereafter forever and the same are hereby forever barred and the plaintiff is hereby ordered to deed or cause to be deeded his interest in said lot to the defendant on or before May 1st 1885.

It is further hereby adjudged that the defendant have the care, custody, maintenance, and support of the children named in the Complaint until the further order of the Court. Dated this 24th day of April 1885

By the Court Alva Stewart Judge

State of Wisconsin.
Circuit Court for Dane County.
April 25 1885
Wm. C. Wright
vs.
Anna L. Wright

Clerk's Fees.
Entering cause of record, 50 cents
Indexing cause, direct and inverse 10 cents
Entering cause on trial calendar 3 times, 10 cents each 30 cents
Entering 3 motions, 15 cents each 45 cents
Entering 3 orders, 15 cents each 45 cents
Making 1 certificates, 25 cents each 25 cents
Filing 12 papers, 10 cents each 1.20
Recording papers or other matter 14 folios, 10 cents each 1.40
Copies of papers or records 6 folios, 10 cents each 60 cents
Making judgment roll 50 cents
$5.75

Bibliography of Works Consulted

Aguar, Charles E., and Berdeana Aguar. *Wrightscapes: Frank Lloyd Wright's Landscape Designs*. New York: McGraw-Hill, 2002.

Alofsin, Anthony. *Frank Lloyd Wright, Art Collector: Secessionist Prints from the Turn of the Century*. Austin: University of Texas Press, 2012.

———. *Frank Lloyd Wright: The Lost Years, 1910–1922*. Chicago: University of Chicago Press, 1993.

———, ed. *Frank Lloyd Wright: Europe and Beyond*. Berkeley: University of California Press, 1999.

———, ed. *Prairie Skyscraper: Frank Lloyd Wright's Price Tower*. New York: Rizzoli, 2005.

Amin, Kamal. *Reflections from the Shining Brow*. Santa Barbara: Fithian, 2004.

Ballon, Hilary, et al. *The Guggenheim: Frank Lloyd Wright and the Making of the Modern Museum*. New York: Guggenheim Museum, 2009.

Barney, Maginel Wright. *The Valley of the God-Almighty Joneses*. New York: Appleton-Century, 1965.

Bercovitch, Sacvan. *The American Jeremiad*. Madison: University of Wisconsin Press, 1978.

Besinger, Curtis. *Working with Mr. Wright: What It Was Like*. Cambridge, England, and New York: Cambridge University Press, 1995.

Birk, Melanie. *Frank Lloyd Wright's Fifty Views of Japan*. San Francisco: Pomegranate, 1996.

Bixler, Kim. *Growing Up in a Frank Lloyd Wright House*. Privately published, 2012.

Boyd, Virginia Terry, and Bruce Brooks Pfeiffer. *Frank Lloyd Wright and the House Beautiful*. Washington, D.C.: International Arts and Artists, 2005.

Boyle, Bernard Michael. *Wright in Arizona: The Early Work of Pedro E. Guerrero*. Tempe, AZ: Herberger Center for Design Excellence, 1995.

Brierly, Cornelia. *Tales of Taliesin*. San Francisco: Pomegranate, 2000.

Brooks, H. Allen. *Frank Lloyd Wright and the Prairie School*. New York: Braziller / Cooper-Hewitt Museum, 1984.

———. "Frank Lloyd Wright and the Wasmuth Drawings." *The Art Bulletin* 48 (June 1960): 193–202.

———. *The Prairie School: Frank Lloyd Wright and His Midwest Contemporaries.* New York: Norton, 2006 [1972].

———, ed. *Writings on Wright.* Cambridge, MA: MIT Press, 1981.

Brownell, Baker. *The Human Community.* New York: Harper, 1950.

Brownell, Baker, and Frank Lloyd Wright. *Architecture and Modern Life.* New York: Harper, 1937.

Cahan, Richard, and Michael Williams. *Richard Nickel's Chicago: Photographs of a Lost City.* Chicago: Cityfiles Press, 2006.

Cannon, Patrick F. *Hometown Architect.* San Francisco: Pomegranate, 2006.

Casey, Dennis. *Stained Glass Window Designs of Frank Lloyd Wright.* New York: Dover, 1997.

Cheek, Lawrence W. *Frank Lloyd Wright in Arizona.* Tucson, AZ: Rio Nuevo, 2006.

Chusid, Jeffrey M. *Saving Wright: The Freeman House and the Preservation of Meaning, Materials, and Modernity.* New York: Norton, 2011.

Cleary, Richard L. *Merchant Prince and Master Builder: Edgar J. Kaufmann and Frank Lloyd Wright.* Seattle: University of Washington Press, 1999.

———, et al. *Frank Lloyd Wright: From Within Outward.* New York: Skira Rizzoli / Guggenheim Museum, 2009.

Connors, Joseph. *The Robie House of Frank Lloyd Wright.* Chicago: University of Chicago Press, 1984.

Danzker, Jo-Anne Birnie. *Art of Tomorrow: Hilla Rebay and Solomon R. Guggenheim.* New York: Guggenheim Museum, 2005.

Daugherty, Tracy. *Hiding Man: A Biography of Donald Barthelme.* New York: St. Martin's Press, 2009.

De Long, David G. *Auldbrass: Frank Lloyd Wright's Southern Plantation.* New York: Rizzoli, 2003.

———. *Frank Lloyd Wright: Designs for an American Landscape.* New York: Abrams, 1996.

———, ed. *Frank Lloyd Wright and the Living City.* Milan, Italy: Skira / Vitra Design, 1998.

DesBarres, Michael. *Fieldnotes: A Multi-Generational Ethnography of Apprenticeship: Frank Lloyd Wright's Taliesin Fellowship.* Spring Green, WI: Frank Lloyd Wright School of Architecture, 2007.

Drennan, William R. *Death in a Prairie House: Frank Lloyd Wright and the Taliesin Murders.* Madison: University of Wisconsin Press, 2007.

Dunlop, Beth, ed. *Frank Lloyd Wright: Architecture 3* [includes Robert McCarter on Unity Temple, James Steele on the Barnsdall House, and Brian Carter on the Johnson Wax Administration Building]. London: Phaidon, 1999.

Eaton, Leonard K. *Two Chicago Architects and Their Clients: Frank Lloyd Wright and Howard Van Doren Shaw.* Cambridge, MA: MIT Press, 1969.

Eifler, John, and Kristin Visser. *Frank Lloyd Wright's Seth Peterson Cottage.* Madison, WI: Prairie Oak Press, 1999 [1997].

Fell, Derek. *The Gardens of Frank Lloyd Wright.* London: Frances Lincoln, Ltd., 2009.

Fields, Jeanette S. *A Guidebook to the Architecture of River Forest.* 2nd ed. River Forest, IL: River Forest Community Center, 1990.

Filler, Martin. *Makers of Modern Architecture.* New York: New York Review of Books, 2007.

Fishman, Robert. *Urban Utopias in the Twentieth Century: Ebenezer Howard, Frank Lloyd Wright, Le Corbusier.* Cambridge, MA: MIT Press, 1982 [1977].

Forrer, Matthi. *Hiroshige: Prints and Drawings.* Munich, Germany: Prestel, 2007.

Fowler, Penny. *Frank Lloyd Wright, Graphic Artist.* San Francisco: Pomegranate, 2002.

Frampton, Kenneth. *The Evolution of Twentieth Century Architecture: A Synoptic Account.* Vienna, Austria, and Beijing, China: Springer / China Architecture and Building Press, 2007.

Friedland, Roger, and Harold Zellman. *The Fellowship.* New York: Regan / HarperCollins, 2006.

Friedman, Alice T. "Frank Lloyd Wright and Feminism: Mamah Borthwick's Letters to Ellen Key." *Journal of the Society of Architectural Historians* 61 (June 2002): 140–51.

Futagawa, Yukio, and Bruce Brooks Pfeiffer. *Frank Lloyd Wright GA Traveler Series 001 (Taliesin West), 002 (Taliesin), 003 (Fallingwater), 004 (Prairie Houses), 005 (Usonian Houses), 006 (Elegant Houses), 007 (Architecture).* Tokyo: A. D. A. EDITA, 2002–2003.

Gannet[t], William C. *The House Beautiful.* San Francisco: Pomegranate, 2006 [1896–1898].

Gass, William H. *Fiction and the Figures of Life.* New York: Knopf, 1970.

Gay, Peter. *Modernism: The Lure of Heresy.* New York: Norton, 2008.

Gebhard, David. *Purcell & Elmslie: Prairie Progressive Architects.* Salt Lake City: Gibbs Smith, 2006.

Gill, Brendan. *Many Masks: A Life of Frank Lloyd Wright.* New York: Putnam's, 1987.

Gottlieb, Lois Davidson. *A Way of Life: An Apprenticeship with Frank Lloyd Wright.* Mulgrave, Victoria, Australia: Images, 2001.

Griffin, Marion Mahony. *Drawing the Form of Nature*. Evanston, IL: Block Museum of Art / Northwestern University Press, 2005.

———. *The Magic of America*, online edition. Chicago: Art Institute of Chicago, 2007 [ca. 1940s].

Griffin, Walter Burley. *The Writings of Walter Burley Griffin*. Edited by Dustin Griffin. Cambridge, England, and New York: Cambridge University Press, 2008.

Guerrero, Pedro E. *Picturing Wright*. San Francisco: Pomegranate, 1994.

Guggenheimer, Tobias S. *A Taliesin Legacy: The Architecture of Frank Lloyd Wright's Apprentices*. New York: Van Nostrand Reinhold, 1995.

Gurda, John. *New World Odyssey: Annunciation Greek Orthodox Church and Frank Lloyd Wright*. Milwaukee, WI: The Milwaukee Hellenic Community, 1986.

Gyure, Dale Allen. *Frank Lloyd Wright's Florida Southern College*. Gainesville: University Press of Florida, 2010.

Hagan, Bernardine. *Kentuck Knob: Frank Lloyd Wright's House for I. N. and Bernardine Hagan*. Pittsburgh, PA: Local History Co., 2005.

Hanna, Paul R., and Jean S. Hanna. *Frank Lloyd Wright's Hanna House: The Clients' Report*. New York and Cambridge, MA: Architectural History Foundation / MIT Press, 1981.

Harrington, Elaine. *Frank Lloyd Wright Home and Studio, Oak Park*. Stuttgart, Germany: Edition Axel Menges, 1996.

Heinz, Thomas A. *Frank Lloyd Wright Field Guide*. Evanston, IL: Northwestern University Press, 2005.

———. *The Vision of Frank Lloyd Wright*. New York: Chartwell, 2002 [2000].

Henken, Priscilla J. *Taliesin Diary: A Year with Frank Lloyd Wright*. New York: Norton, 2012.

Henning, Randolph C., ed. *"At Taliesin": Newspaper Columns*. Carbondale: Southern Illinois University Press, 1992.

Hertz, David Michael. *Frank Lloyd Wright in Word and Form*. New York: G. K. Hall, 1995.

Hertzberg, Mark. *Frank Lloyd Wright's Hardy House*. San Francisco: Pomegranate, 2006.

———. *Frank Lloyd Wright's S. C. Johnson Research Tower*. San Francisco: Pomegranate, 2010.

———. *Wright in Racine*. San Francisco: Pomegranate, 2004.

Hession, Jane King, and Debra Pickrel. *Frank Lloyd Wright in New York: The Plaza Years, 1954–1959*. Salt Lake City, UT: Gibbs Smith, 2007.

Hildebrand, Grant. *Frank Lloyd Wright's Palmer House*. Seattle: University of Washington Press, 2007.

———. The *Wright Space: Pattern and Meaning in Frank Lloyd Wright's Houses.* Seattle: University of Washington Press, 1991.

Hitchcock, Henry-Russell. *In the Nature of Materials: The Buildings of Frank Lloyd Wright, 1887-1941.* New York: Da Capo Press, 1975 [1942].

Hoffman, Donald. *Frank Lloyd Wright: Architecture and Nature.* New York: Dover, 1986.

———. *Frank Lloyd Wright, Louis Sullivan, and the Skyscraper.* New York: Dover, 1998.

———. *Frank Lloyd Wright's Dana House.* New York: Dover, 1996.

———. *Frank Lloyd Wright's Fallingwater: The House and Its History.* New York: Dover, 1993 [revised from Western Pennsylvania Conservancy edition of 1978].

———. *Frank Lloyd Wright's House on Kentuck Knob.* Pittsburgh, PA: University of Pittsburgh Press, 2000.

———. *Frank Lloyd Wright's Robie House: The Illustrated Story of an Architectural Masterpiece.* New York: Dover, 1984.

———. *Understanding Frank Lloyd Wright's Architecture.* New York: Dover, 1995.

Hokanson, Margo O'Brien. *Monona Terrace: Frank Lloyd Wright's Vision on the Lake.* Madison, WI: Madison Newspapers, 1997.

Hoppen, Donald W. *The Seven Ages of Frank Lloyd Wright.* New York: Dover, 1998 [revised and expanded from Capra Press edition of 1993].

Howard, Hugh. *Wright for Wright.* New York: Rizzoli, 2001.

Hunt, Sara, ed. *The Wright Experience: A Master Architect's Vision.* New York: Metro Books, 2008.

Huxtable, Ada Louise. *Frank Lloyd Wright.* New York: Lipper / Viking, 2004.

Jacobs, Herbert. *Frank Lloyd Wright: America's Greatest Architect.* New York: Harcourt, Brace & World, 1965.

Jacobs, Herbert, and Katherine Jacobs. *Building with Frank Lloyd Wright.* Carbondale: Southern Illinois University Press, 1986 [1978].

Jencks, Charles. *Kings of Infinite Space: Frank Lloyd Wright and Michael Graves.* London and New York: Academy / St. Martin's, 1985 [1983].

Johannesson, Lena. "Ellen Key, Mamah Bouton Borthwick, and Frank Lloyd Wright: Notes on the Historiography of Non-Existing History." *NORA: Nordic Journal of Women's Studies* 2 (1995): 126-36.

Johnson, Donald Leslie. *The Fountainheads: Wright, Rand, the FBI, and Hollywood.* Jefferson, NC: McFarland, 2005.

———. *Frank Lloyd Wright versus America: The 1930s.* Cambridge, MA: MIT Press, 1990.

Johonnot, Rodney F. *The New Edifice of Unity Church.* Oak Park, IL: Unity Church, 1906.

Jones, Chester Lloyd. *Youngest Son*. Madison, WI: privately printed, 1938.

Jones, Richard (Jix) Lloyd, et al. *A Lloyd Jones Retrospective*. Spring Green, WI: Unity Chapel, 1986.

Kaufmann, Edgar Jr. *Fallingwater: A Frank Lloyd Wright Country House*. New York: Abbeville Press, 1986.

Key, Ellen. *The Woman Movement*. Translated by Mamah Bouton Borthwick. New York: Putnam's 1912.

King, Rebecca. *Frank Lloyd Wright Revealed*. London: Compendium, 2007.

Kingsbury, Pamela D. *Frank Lloyd Wright and Wichita: The First Usonian Design*. Wichita, KS: Wichita-Sedgwick County Historical Museum, 1992.

Kleinman, Kent, and Eric Jackson-Forsberg, eds. *On Wright: Frank Lloyd Wright's Darwin D. Martin House Visitor's Center Competition*. Buffalo, NY: School of Architecture and Planning / University at Buffalo, 2005.

Klinkowitz, Jerome. *Rosenberg / Barthes / Hassan: The Postmodern Habit of Thought*. Athens: University of Georgia Press, 1988.

Knight, Carolyn. *Essential Frank Lloyd Wright*. Bath, England: Parragon, 2001.

Kruty, Paul. *Frank Lloyd Wright and Midway Gardens*. Urbana: University of Illinois Press, 1998.

———. *Prelude to the Prairie Style: Eight Models of Unbuilt Houses by Frank Lloyd Wright*. Urbana: School of Architecture / University of Illinois, 2005.

Kruty, Paul, and Paul E. Sprague. *Marion Mahony and Millikin Place: Creating a Prairie School Masterpiece*. St. Louis, MO: Walter Burley Griffin Society, 2007.

Langmead, Donald. *Frank Lloyd Wright: A Bio-Bibliography*. Westport, CT: Praeger, 2003.

Larkin, David, and Bruce Brooks Pfeiffer. *Frank Lloyd Wright: Master Builder*. New York: Universe / Rizzoli, 1997.

Legler, Dixie, and Christian Korab. *At Home on the Prairie: The Houses of Purcell & Elmslie*. San Francisco: Archetype Press / Chronicle Books, 2006.

———. *Prairie Style*. New York: Stewart, Tabori & Chang, 1999.

Levine, Neil. *The Architecture of Frank Lloyd Wright*. Princeton, NJ: Princeton University Press, 1996.

Levine, Neil, et al. *Frank Lloyd Wright's Zimmerman House: A Work of Art for Kindred Spirits*. Manchester, NH: Currier Museum of Art, 2004.

Lind, Carla. *Lost Wright*. San Francisco: Pomegranate, 2008 [revised and updated from Archetype / Simon & Schuster edition of 1996].

———. *The Wright Style*. New York: Simon & Schuster, 1992.

Lipman, Jonathan. *Frank Lloyd Wright and the Johnson Wax Buildings*. New York: Rizzoli, 1986.

Lipman, Jonathan, and Neil Levine. *The Wright State: Frank Lloyd Wright in Wisconsin.* Milwaukee, WI: Milwaukee Art Museum, 1992.

Longstreth, Richard, ed. *The Charnley House.* Chicago: University of Chicago Press, 2004.

Lucas, Suzette A. *In the Realm of Ideas: An Interpretive Guide to Taliesen West.* Scottsdale, AZ: Frank Lloyd Wright Foundation, 1993.

Maddex, Diane. *Frank Lloyd Wright's House Beautiful.* New York: Hearst, 2000.

———. *Wright-Sized Houses.* New York: Abrams, 2003.

Mahoney, Patrick J. *Frank Lloyd Wright's Walter V. Davidson House: An Examination of a Buffalo Home and Its Cousins from Coast to Coast.* Buffalo: State University of New York College at Buffalo, 2011.

Maldre, Mati, and Paul Kruty. *Walter Burley Griffin in America.* Urbana: University of Illinois Press, 1996.

Maloney, Cathy Jean. *The Gardener's Cottage in Riverside, Illinois.* Chicago: Center for American Places, 2009.

Manson, Grant Carpenter. *Frank Lloyd Wright to 1910: The First Golden Age.* New York: Van Nostrand Reinhold, 1958.

Marty, Myron A. *Communities of Frank Lloyd Wright: Taliesin and Beyond.* DeKalb: Northern Illinois University Press, 2009.

Marty, Myron A., and Shirley A. Marty. *Frank Lloyd Wright's Taliesin Fellowship.* Kirksville, MO: Truman State University Press, 1999.

McArthur, Shirley DuFresne. *Frank Lloyd Wright: American System-Built Homes in Milwaukee.* Milwaukee, WI: North Point Historical Society, 1985.

McCarter, Robert. *Frank Lloyd Wright.* London: Reaktion, 2006 [biography].

———. *Frank Lloyd Wright.* London: Phaidon, 1997 [critical study].

———, ed. *On and By Frank Lloyd Wright: A Primer of Architectural Principles.* London: Phaidon, 2005.

———. *Unity Temple: Frank Lloyd Wright.* London: Phaidon, 1997.

McCoy, Robert. "Rock Crest / Rock Glen: Prairie Planning in Iowa." *Prairie School Review* 5, no. 3 (1968): 5–39.

McCrea, Ron. *Building Taliesin: Frank Lloyd Wright's Home of Love and Loss.* Madison: Wisconsin Historical Society Press, 2012.

McGregor, Alasdair. *Grand Obsessions: The Life and Work of Walter Burley Griffin and Marion Mahony Griffin.* Camberwell, Victoria, Australia: Lantern / Penguin, 2009.

Meech, Julia. *Frank Lloyd Wright and the Art of Japan: The Architect's Other Passion.* New York: Japan Society and Harry N. Abrams, 2001.

Meehan, Patrick J., ed. *Frank Lloyd Wright Remembered.* Washington, D.C.: Preservation Press, 1991.

————, ed. *The Master Architect: Conversations with Frank Lloyd Wright*. New York: John Wiley, 1984.

Menocal, Narciso G., ed. *Fallingwater and Pittsburgh: Wright Studies, Volume Two*. Carbondale: Southern Illinois University Press, 2000.

————. *Taliesin 1911–1914: Wright Studies, Volume One*. Carbondale: Southern Illinois University Press, 1992.

Moe, Doug, and Alice D'Alessio. *Uncommon Sense: The Life of Marshall Erdman*. Black Earth, WI: Trails, 2003.

Mollenhoff, David V., and Mary Jane Hamilton. *Frank Lloyd Wright's Monona Terrace: The Enduring Power of a Civic Vision*. Madison: University of Wisconsin Press, 1999.

Moran, Maya. *Down to Earth: An Insider's View of Frank Lloyd Wright's Tomek House*. Carbondale: Southern Illinois University Press, 1995.

Morton, Terry B., ed. *The Pope-Leighey House*. Washington, D.C.: National Trust for Historic Preservation, 1974 [reprint of *Historic Preservation* 21 (April–September 1969)].

Mumford, Lewis. *The Brown Decades*. New York: Dover, 1955 [1931].

————. *Sticks and Stones*. New York: Dover, 1955 [1924].

Muschamp, Herbert. *Man About Town: Frank Lloyd Wright in New York City*. Cambridge, MA: MIT Press, 1983.

Nemtin, Frances. *Frank Lloyd Wright and Taliesin*. San Francisco: Pomegranate, 2000.

————. *Life in the Taliesin Fellowship*. Privately published, 2007. [comprises *Life on Midway Farm, Children at Taliesin, Zrazi Anyone, Music at Taliesin, Work at Taliesin, Taliesin Migrations, Taliesin at Play, 2002; Web of Life, 2001*].

Neufeld, Lesley. *Frank Lloyd Wright's Martin House Complex*. Buffalo, NY: Martin House Restoration Corporation, 2004.

Nisbet, Earl. *Taliesin Reflections*. Petaluma, CA: Meridian, 2006.

Oldsberg, Nicholas, ed. *Between Heaven and Earth: The Architecture of John Lautner*. New York: Rizzoli, 2008.

Pfeiffer, Bruce Brooks. *Frank Lloyd Wright*. Cologne, Germany: Taschen, 1991.

————. *Frank Lloyd Wright: The Heroic Years, 1920–1932*. New York: Rizzoli, 2009.

————. *Frank Lloyd Wright, 1885–1916: The Complete Works*. Cologne, Germany: Taschen, 2011.

————. *Frank Lloyd Wright, 1917–1942: The Complete Works*. Cologne, Germany: Taschen, 2010.

————. *Frank Lloyd Wright, 1943–1959: The Complete Works*. Cologne, Germany: Taschen, 2009.

———. *Frank Lloyd Wright Designs: The Sketches, Plans and Drawings.* New York: Rizzoli, 2011.

———. *Treasures of Taliesin: Seventy-Seven Unbuilt Designs.* San Francisco: Pomegranate, 1999 [1985].

Pfeiffer, Bruce Brooks, and David Larkin. *Frank Lloyd Wright: The Masterworks.* New York: Rizzoli, 1993.

Pfeiffer, Bruce Brooks, and Gerald Nordlund. *Frank Lloyd Wright: In the Realm of Ideas.* Carbondale: Southern Illinois University Press, 1988.

Pfeiffer, Bruce Brooks, and Robert Wojtowicz. *Frank Lloyd Wright and Lewis Mumford.* New York: Princeton Architectural Press, 2001.

Pleisch, Mark L. *The Chicago School of Architecture.* New York: Random House, 1964.

Pridmore, Jay. *The Rookery.* San Francisco: Pomegranate, 2003.

Quinan, Jack. *Frank Lloyd Wright: Windows of the Darwin D. Martin House.* Buffalo, NY: Burchfield-Penney Art Center, 1999.

———. *Frank Lloyd Wright's Buffalo Venture: From the Larkin Building to Broadacre City.* San Francisco: Pomegranate, 2012.

———. *Frank Lloyd Wright's Larkin Building: Myth and Fact.* Chicago: University of Chicago Press, 1987.

———. *Frank Lloyd Wright's Martin House: Architecture as Portraiture.* New York: Princeton Architectural Press, 2004.

Rattenbury, John. *A House for Life.* Toronto: Warwick, 2006.

———. *A Living Architecture.* San Francisco: Pomegranate, 2000.

Reed, Peter, and William Kaizen. *The Show to End All Shows: Frank Lloyd Wright and the Museum of Modern Art.* New York: Museum of Modern Art, 2004.

Reilly, Donna Grant. *An American Proceeding: Building the Grant House with Frank Lloyd Wright.* Hanover, NH: Meadowside Press, 2010.

Reisley, Roland. *Usonia, New York: Building a Community with Frank Lloyd Wright.* New York: Princeton Architectural Press, 2001.

Riley, Terence. *Frank Lloyd Wright: Architect.* New York: Abrams / Museum of Modern Art, 1994.

Robertson, Cheryl. *The Domestic Scene (1897–1927): George M. Niedecken, Interior Architect.* 2nd ed. Milwaukee, WI: Milwaukee Art Museum, 2008 [revised and expanded from Milwaukee Art Museum edition of 1981].

———. *Frank Lloyd Wright and George Mann Niedecken: Prairie School Collaborators.* Milwaukee, WI: Milwaukee Art Museum, 1999.

Rogers, Wallace J. *Frank Lloyd Wright's Samara.* West Lafayette, IN: John E. Christian Family Memorial Trust, 2001.

Rosenbaum, Alvin. *Usonia: Frank Lloyd Wright's Design for America.* Washington, D.C.: Preservation Press, 1993.

Rosenberg, Harold. *The Anxious Object*. New York: Horizon Press, 1964.

———. *The Tradition of the New*. New York: Horizon Press, 1959.

Rubin, Jeanne Spielman. *Intimate Triangle: Architecture of Crystals, Frank Lloyd Wright, and the Froebel Kindergarten*. Huntsville, AL: Polycrystal Book Service / New Century Pharmaceuticals, 2002.

Sanderson, Arlene. *Wright Sites*. New York: Princeton Architectural Press, 2001 [revisited and revised from 1995 edition].

Scott, Margaret Helen. *Frank Lloyd Wright's Warehouse in Richland Center, Wisconsin*. Richland Center, WI: Richland County Publishers, 1984.

Scully, Vincent, Jr. *Frank Lloyd Wright*. New York: Braziller, 1960.

———. *Modern Architecture*. New York: Braziller, 1961.

Secrest, Meryle. *Frank Lloyd Wright: A Biography*. New York: Knopf, 1992.

Sergeant, John. *Frank Lloyd Wright's Usonian Houses*. New York: Whitney, 1984 [1976].

Simo, Melanie. *Barnsdall Park: A New Master Plan for Frank Lloyd Wright's California Romanza*. Washington, D.C.: Spacemaker Press, 1997.

Siry, Joseph M. *Unity Temple: Frank Lloyd Wright and Architecture for Liberal Religion*. Cambridge, England: Cambridge University Press, 1996.

Slotkin, Richard. *The Fatal Environment: The Myth of the Frontier in the Age of Industrialization, 1800–1890*. Norman: University of Oklahoma Press, 1998.

———. *Regeneration through Violence: The Mythology of the American Frontier, 1600–1860*. Norman: University of Oklahoma Press, 2000.

Smith, Kathryn. *Frank Lloyd Wright: America's Master Architect*. New York: Abbeville Press, 1998.

———. *Frank Lloyd Wright: Hollyhock House and Olive Hill*. New York: Rizzoli, 1992.

———. *Frank Lloyd Wright's Taliesin and Taliesin West*. New York: Abrams, 1997.

Smith, Norris Kelly. *Frank Lloyd Wright: A Study in Architectural Content*. Englewood Cliffs, New Jersey: Prentice-Hall, 1966.

Sokol, David M. *The Noble Room: The Inspired Conception and Tumultuous Creation of Frank Lloyd Wright's Unity Temple*. Oak Park, IL: Top Five Books, 2008.

Spencer, Robert C., Jr. "The Work of Frank Lloyd Wright." *The Architectural Review* 71 (June 1900): 61–72 [reprinted in H. Allen Brooks, ed., *Writings on Wright* (Cambridge, MA: MIT Press, 1981), 105–10].

Sprague, Paul E., ed. *Frank Lloyd Wright and Madison: Eight Decades of Artistic and Social Interaction*. Madison, WI: Elvehjem Museum of Art, 1990.

Steele, James. *Barnsdall House: Frank Lloyd Wright*. London: Phaidon, 1992.

Stodola, Barbara. *Frank Lloyd Wright and Colleagues: Indiana Works.* Michigan City, IN: John C. Blank Center for the Arts, 1999.

Storrer, William Allin. *The Architecture of Frank Lloyd Wright: A Complete Catalogue.* 3rd ed. Chicago: University of Chicago Press, 2002 [1974, 1978].

———. *The Frank Lloyd Wright Companion.* Rev. ed. Chicago: University of Chicago Press, 2006 [1993].

Sukenick, Ronald. *In Form: Digressions on the Act of Fiction.* Carbondale: Southern Illinois University Press, 1985.

Sullivan, Louis *The Autobiography of an Idea.* New York: Dover, 1956 [1924].

———. *Kindergarten Chats and Other Writings.* New York: Dover, 1979 [1918].

Sweeney, Robert L. *Wright in Hollywood.* New York and Cambridge, MA: Architectural History Foundation / MIT Press, 1994.

Tafel, Edgar. *Frank Lloyd Wright: Recollections by Those Who Knew Him.* New York: Dover, 2001 [reprint of *About Wright* (New York: John Wiley, 1993)].

———. *Years with Frank Lloyd Wright: Apprentice to Genius.* New York: Dover, 1985 [reprint of *Apprentice to Genius: Years with Frank Lloyd Wright* (New York: McGraw-Hill, 1979)].

Toker, Franklin. *Fallingwater Rising.* New York: Knopf, 2003.

Treiber, Daniel. *Frank Lloyd Wright.* 2nd ed. Basel, Switzerland: Birkhäuser, 2008 [1995].

Twombly, Robert C. *Frank Lloyd Wright: His Life and His Architecture.* New York: John Wiley, 1979.

Van Zanten, David, ed. *Marion Mahony Reconsidered.* Chicago: University of Chicago Press, 2011.

Visser, Kristin. *Frank Lloyd Wright and the Prairie School in Wisconsin.* 2nd ed. Madison, WI: Prairie Oak Press, 1998 [1992].

Von Holst, Hermann Valentin. *Country and Suburban Homes of the Prairie School Period.* New York: Dover, 1982 [reprint of *Modern American Homes* (Chicago: American Technical Society, 1913)].

Waggoner, Lynda S. *Fallingwater: Frank Lloyd Wright's Romance with Nature.* New York: Universe / Rizzoli, for Fallingwater, 1996.

———, ed. *Fallingwater.* New York: Rizzoli, 2011.

Watterson, Kathryn. *Building a Dream: The Sara Smith Story.* Santa Barbara, CA: Smith Publishing, 1999.

Weil, Zarine. *Building a Legacy: The Restoration of Frank Lloyd Wright's Oak Park Home and Studio.* San Francisco: Pomegranate, 2001.

Weil, Zarine, Paul Goldberger, Cheryl Bachand, and Brian Reis. *Frank Lloyd Wright's Robie House.* Oak Park, IL, and Seattle, WA: Frank Lloyd Wright Preservation Trust / Marquand Books, 2010.

Weintraub, Alan, and Alan Hess. *The Architecture of John Lautner*. New York: Rizzoli, 1999.

——. *Frank Lloyd Wright: The Buildings*. New York: Rizzoli, 2008.

——. *Frank Lloyd Wright: The Houses*. New York: Rizzoli, 2005.

——. *Frank Lloyd Wright: Mid-Century Modern*. New York: Rizzoli, 2007.

——. *Frank Lloyd Wright: Natural Design, Organic Architecture*. New York: Rizzoli, 2012.

——. *Organic Architecture: The Other Modernists*. Salt Lake City, UT: Gibbs Smith, 2006.

Weintraub, Alan, and Kathryn Smith. *Frank Lloyd Wright: American Master*. New York: Rizzoli, 2009.

Weston, Richard. *Twentieth-Century Residential Architecture*. New York: Abbeville Press, 2002.

Whiting, Henry II. *At Nature's Edge: Frank Lloyd Wright's Artist Studio*. Salt Lake City: University of Utah Press, 2007.

Wickes, Molly. *A Guide to Frank Lloyd Wright and the Prairie School Historic District*. Oak Park, IL: Oak Park Historic Preservation Commission, 1999.

Wilson, Richard Guy, and Sidney K. Robinson. *The Prairie School in Iowa*. Ames: Iowa State University Press, 1977.

Woodin, Larry A. *The Gordon House: A Moving Experience*. Hillsboro, OR: Beyond Words, 2002.

Wright, Frank Lloyd. *An American Architecture*. Edited by Edgar Kaufmann, Jr. New York: Horizon Press, 1955.

——. *An Autobiography*. San Francisco: Pomegranate, 2005 [reprinted from second edition (New York: Duell, Sloan & Pearce, 1943); first edition of 1932 is reprinted, with additional sections from 1943, in *Collected Writings*, which is the source cited in this study].

——. *An Autobiography*. 3rd ed. New York: Horizon Press, 1977.

——. *Collected Writings*. Edited by Bruce Brooks Pfeiffer. 5 vols. New York: Rizzoli, 1992–1995.

——. *Drawings and Plans of Frank Lloyd Wright: The Early Period (1893–1909)*. New York: Dover, 1983 [reprint of *Ausgeführte Bauten und Entwürfe von Frank Lloyd Wright* (Berlin, Germany: Wasmuth, 1910)].

——. *The Early Work of Frank Lloyd Wright: The "Ausgeführte Bauten" of 1911*. New York: Dover, 1982.

——. *The Essential Frank Lloyd Wright: Critical Writings on Architecture*. Edited by Bruce Brooks Pfeiffer. Princeton, NJ: Princeton University Press, 2008.

——. *Facsimile of the 1933 Taliesin Fellowship Brochure*. Scottsdale, AZ: Frank Lloyd Wright Foundation, 2003.

——. *Frank Lloyd Wright: His Living Voice.* Edited by Bruce Brooks Pfeiffer. Fresno: California State University Press, 1987.

——. *Frank Lloyd Wright: The Complete 1925 "Wendingen" Series.* New York: Dover, 1992 [1925].

——. *Frank Lloyd Wright: Essential Texts.* Edited by Robert Twombly. New York: Norton, 2009.

——. *The Future of Architecture.* New York: Horizon Press, 1953.

——. *Genius and the Mobocracy.* New York: Duell, Sloan & Pearce, 1949.

——. *The Guggenheim Correspondence.* Edited by Bruce Brooks Pfeiffer. Carbondale: Southern Illinois University Press, 1986.

——. *Letters to Apprentices.* Edited by Bruce Brooks Pfeiffer. Fresno: California State University Press, 1982.

——. *Letters to Architects.* Edited by Bruce Brooks Pfeiffer. Fresno: California State University Press, 1984.

——. *Letters to Clients.* Edited by Bruce Brooks Pfeiffer. Fresno: California State University Press, 1986.

——. *The Living City.* New York: Horizon Press, 1958.

——. *Modern Architecture: Being the Kahn Lectures for 1930.* Princeton: Princeton University Press, 2008 [facsimile of 1931 edition, with a new introduction by Neil Levine].

——. *The Natural House.* New York: Horizon Press, 1954.

——. *The Story of the Tower.* New York: Horizon Press, 1956.

——. *Studies and Executed Buildings.* New York: Rizzoli, 1998 [facsimile of Wasmuth edition of 1919 (first edition in 1910), with a new preface by Anthony Alofsin].

——. *A Testament.* New York: Horizon Press, 1957.

——. *Truth against the World.* Edited by Patrick J. Meehan. New York: John Wiley, 1987.

——. *The Usonian House: Souvenir of the Exhibition: "60 Years of Living Architecture."* New York: Guggenheim Museum, 1953.

Wright, John Lloyd. *My Father Who Is on Earth.* Carbondale: Southern Illinois University Press, 1994 [reprint of 1946 Putnam's edition, plus comments by Frank Lloyd Wright].

Wright, Olgivanna Lloyd. *Frank Lloyd Wright: His Life, His Works, His Words.* New York: Horizon Press, 1966.

——. *Our House.* New York: Horizon Press, 1959.

——. *The Shining Brow: Frank Lloyd Wright.* New York: Horizon Press, 1960.

——. *The Struggle Within.* New York: Horizon Press, 1955.

Index